> Revolution Until Victory?
The Politics and History of the PLO

Other books by Barry Rubin

>> Revolution Until Victory?

The Politics and History of the PLO

BARRY RUBIN

HARVARD UNIVERSITY PRESS
Cambridge, Massachusetts
London, England
1994

This book is printed on acid-free paper, and its binding materials have been chosen for strength and durability

Library of Congress Cataloging in Publication Data

Rubin, Barry M.
    Revolution until victory? : the politics and history of the PLO/
Barry Rubin.
      p. cm.
    Includes bibliographical references (p.) and index.
    ISBN 0-674-76803-5
    1. Munaẓẓamat al-Taḥrīr al-Filasṭīnīyah. 2. Palestinian Arabs—
Politics and government. 3. Jewish-Arab relations—1949-
4. Israel-Arab conflicts. I. Title.
DS119.7.R754 1994
322.4'2'095694—dc20   93-31651
                CIP

> *To my beloved Judy*

> Contents

> Preface

Yasir Arafat's moment of victory and moment of surrender were one and the same as he shook hands with Israeli Prime Minister Yitzhak Rabin on September 13, 1993. Standing on the White House lawn in Washington, D.C., the PLO leader accepted peace with Israel almost forty years after his organization began its struggle to destroy that state.

Arafat exchanged his historic claim on all of the land between the Jordan river and the Mediterranean sea for authority over the West Bank and Gaza in a process which he averred would lead to a Palestinian state on that territory. The PLO now had to transform itself from revolutionary movement to governing authority, and Arafat recognized as well "the tremendous difficulties which are still standing in the way of reaching a final and comprehensive settlement."

That sentiment was reflected in Jordan and Lebanon, where some Palestinians demonstrated against Arafat. Even in Gaza, the day began with a strike called by Islamic fundamentalist opponents of Arafat to mourn the event. But precisely at 3 PM, Arafat's supporters pulled down the fundamentalists' black flags and poured, cheering, into the streets from every direction. There were even more joyous celebrations by Palestinians in the West Bank and East Jerusalem. Palestinian flags—hitherto banned by the Israeli authorities but largely manufactured for the occasion at an Israeli factory—appeared in profusion.

There was much talk that day of miracles, hope, and history. "To every thing there is a season, a time to every purpose under heaven," said Rabin in his Washington speech. "A time of war and a time of peace . . . The time for peace has come." That was an apt allusion. Only at the end of a long process of struggle could the PLO—and still not all of it—be reconciled to such an outcome. Even then, only after having exhausted every alternative and facing isolation and bankruptcy was Arafat able to make the tough deci-

sion needed to bring months of secret talks in Norway to a breakthrough.

"An awful lot of taboos are being broken in the last few days,"
said Secretary of State Warren Christopher. "We're all blinking our
eyes at how much is new." Arab states were talking with Israel; in
Washington, Arab ambassadors greeted Rabin. When Arafat arrived
at Washington's Andrews Air Force base, he was received warmly,
though not as a head of state. He met with Palestinian–American
supporters, Jewish–American leaders, and powerful members of
Congress. Arafat looked on approvingly as PLO Executive Committee member Mahmud Abbas and Israeli Foreign Minister Shimon
Peres signed the agreement on the same table used for the 1979
Camp David accord between Israel and Egypt, a peace settlement
he had condemned and tried fervently to destroy.

A few days later, Rabin and Peres visited Morocco, Israeli corre-
spondents broadcast from Jordan and Tunis, Israel and Jordan
signed a framework for their own peace agreement in Washington.
Two weeks after the Israel–PLO ceremony, President Bill Clinton
hosted an international conference in Washington, where over $2
billion was pledged—mainly by Europe, the United States, and Japan (barely five percent came from Arab countries)—to aid Palestinian self-rule in the West Bank and Gaza.

And so it was not altogether surprising that Arafat smiled so
broadly that day on the White House lawn. The kafiyya headscarf
he wore expressed his persona as one of the common people, while
his khaki uniform—worn despite a U.S. request that he wear civilian clothes—connoted his role as a fighter. His costume implied
that, in compromising, he was neither altered nor bowed.

Yet, like everything connected with the PLO, the story was not
so simple. On December 15, 1988, Arafat had indeed spoken words
no PLO leader had ever dared utter in the nearly quarter-century
since that organization's founding. At a dramatic press conference
in Geneva, Switzerland, following a year of Palestinian revolt, secret diplomacy, and open debate in the PLO, Arafat said he recognized Israel's right to "exist in peace and security" and pledged "totally and categorically [to] reject all forms of terrorism." "Our desire
for peace is strategic and not a temporary tactic," he proclaimed.
"We are committed to peace, and we want to live in our Palestinian
state and let others live."

A few hours later, Secretary of State George Shultz announced the opening of a U.S.–PLO dialogue. The achievement of a Palestinian state and an end to the long, bloody Arab–Israeli conflict appeared to be within reach. Yet eighteen months later, these hopes were in ruins. On May 30, 1990, the PLO's smallest member group sent a terrorist force by sea under orders to kill families vacationing on Israel's beaches and attack other targets. Israeli forces killed or captured the attackers. When Arafat, breaking his promise, refused to condemn the attack or punish those responsible, the United States suspended the dialogue in June 1990.

Two months later, when Iraqi leader Saddam Husayn seized Kuwait, Arafat was one of the few regional leaders who enthusiastically backed him. The Arab newspaper *al-Hayat* said on August 21 that Arafat's action simultaneously antagonized the Arab oil-producing states, "his major source of money"; Egypt, "his link with the world"; the Soviet Union, his international sponsor; the United States, "which he had tried so hard to engage in a dialogue"; and Israelis, whom he was trying to convince of his moderation. While Arafat spoke of an Arab solution to the crisis, anti-Saddam Arabs castigated him as being an ally of Iraq and cut off aid.

These events illustrated the PLO's propensity to approach some success and then fail through bad judgment and intransigence, a pattern frequently repeated in a history marked by startlingly dramatic reversals of fortune. This deficiency was as remarkable as the PLO's ability to survive and maintain the support of most Palestinians. The Israeli statesman Abba Eban once characterized the PLO as having never missing a chance to miss an opportunity. Military defeats, political splits, and diplomatic setbacks battered but never destroyed the PLO. No matter how often the spotlight deserted it and observers predicted its demise, the PLO sprang back to center-stage.

By 1993 this pattern was becoming hard to sustain. After twenty-five years of strife that had included massive financial, political, and military help from the USSR and the Arab states, the PLO was nowhere close to achieving through struggle its expressed goals of destroying Israel, creating a Palestinian state, recasting Arab politics, or eradicating U.S. influence in the region. Only by transforming its own politics and ideology could the PLO accomplish the more moderate aim of a negotiated settlement and establishment of a

Palestinian state in the West Bank and Gaza Strip. This was the alternative Arafat chose in making the peace accord with Israel signed on September 13, 1993.

As a case study, the PLO's history—from its founding in 1964 to its transformation in 1993—poses a series of fascinating theoretical, political, diplomatic, and military problems. This is also the multi-leveled context in which the controversy about defining the PLO must be placed. Was it an abhorrent terrorist or a heroic liberation movement? In fact, the PLO had been both. It was bravely persistent against overwhelming odds, rebuilding a shattered people's confidence and identity. Yet it was also responsible for a great deal of criminal brutality and murder, inflicting much suffering on its own people as well as on foes or bystanders. PLO leaders advocated the deliberate massacre of men, women, and children; its members pioneered the most successfully bloody techniques of modern terrorism, including hijacking and placing bombs on airliners.

The organization's ideas and actions were shaped in an environment characterized by internal divisions, a complex friendship/enmity relationship with Arab states, ideologies which ignited enthusiasm but conflicted with reality, misleading preconceptions about enemies, and contradictions between goals and achievable results. Its structure and situation made the PLO give preference to maintaining its own unity, Palestinian popular support, and help from Arab states. As a result, for a very long time the PLO was unable to control members, revise its doctrine, or make the compromises needed for peace. In the end, the PLO's own leaders had to break this impasse by consummating a long process of internal evolution toward moderation and by bowing to external pressures pushing in that same direction.

The PLO's thirty years as a force in Middle East politics make it a significant subject for examination and investigation; the organization's role in a complex Israeli–Palestinian peacemaking process and as ruler over some form of Palestinian state makes it an important factor for the region's future.

I thank Judy Colp Rubin and Dr. Avraham Sela for carefully reading the manuscript, as well as Yohai Sella and Shai Franklin for research assistance, and Ofra Bengio for suggestions on transliteration. I am especially grateful for the generous support of this research provided by the Henry Guggenheim Foundation, the U.S. Institute of Peace, and the Ford and Bradley foundations.

The book employs a simple transliteration system geared for the general reader's maximum understanding. The symbol ' represents the Arabic letter *ayn*. The spelling system is sometimes modified in leaving the names of people or newspapers as they appear in the English translation of texts cited in the footnotes. In a few cases— Fouad Ajami, Hourani, and Joumblatt, for example—the version appearing in that person's own English-language writing is employed to avoid inconsistency.

This book is not meant to be an exhaustive narrative of the PLO's extraordinarily complex story, a social history of the Palestinians, or an account of the conflict's pre-1964 past. Nor is it a record of U.S. or Israeli policy or the Arab–Israeli conflict and peace process as a whole. *Revolution Until Victory?* is intended to be an analytical political history of the PLO, investigating and interpreting its political circumstances, strategies, and doctrines.

Hodja fell off while riding his donkey. The children ridiculed him, "Oh, Hodja, why did you fall?"
Trying to hide his embarrassment, he replied, "Why are you laughing? I was going to get off anyway."

—Middle East folktale

"I can see in the dark!" boasted Hodja.
"If that is true why do you carry a light at night?"
"I only use a light to keep others from bumping into me."

—Middle East folktale

Glendower: "I can call spirits from the vasty deep!"
Hotspur: "Why, so can I; or so can any man: But will they come, when you do call for them?"

—William Shakespeare, *Henry IV,* Part One

"As the proverb says: 'How do you know it's a lie? Because he's talking so big.'"

—Abu Iyad, January 9, 1971

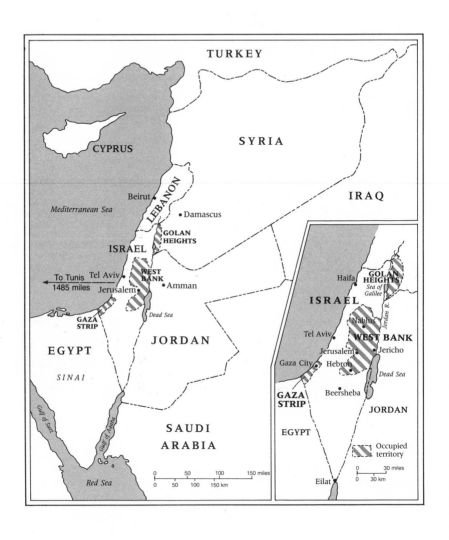

TURKEY

CYPRUS

SYRIA

IRAQ

Mediterranean Sea

Beirut

LEBANON

• Damascus

GOLAN
HEIGHTS

ISRAEL

To Tunis   Tel Aviv•   WEST
1485 miles   BANK
           Jerusalem• • Amman

Dead Sea

GAZA
STRIP

EGYPT

JORDAN

SINAI

Gulf of Suez

Gulf of Aqaba

SAUDI
ARABIA

Red Sea

| 0 | 50 | 100 | 150 miles |
| 0 | 50 | 100 | 150 km |

Haifa•   GOLAN
              HEIGHTS
          Sea of
          Galilee

ISRAEL

Jordan R.

Nablus•

Tel Aviv•   WEST BANK

Jerusalem•   •Jericho

Gaza City•   •Hebron

Dead Sea

GAZA
STRIP

•Beersheba

JORDAN

EGYPT

Occupied
territory

| 0 | 30 miles |
| 0 | 30 km |

Eilat•

1 >> Chameleon in the Labyrinth, 1964 –1968

In May 1964 four hundred Palestinian delegates converged at the Intercontinental Hotel, on the east side of divided Jerusalem outside the Old City's high stone walls, to found the Palestine Liberation Organization. Their purpose was to destroy the Jewish state of Israel and replace it with an Arab state called Palestine.

This site was carefully chosen. In those days, a border guarded by heavily armed troops went through the center of the split town. During the 1948 war, when Israel defeated the invading Arab states and won its independence, the fiercest fighting had been over the city. When the shooting ended, Israel made the western sector of Jerusalem its capital; Jordan controlled the eastern part. The Palestinians' trauma from that defeat and the effort to reverse it would be the central issue shaping the PLO.

From the hotel's windows, those attending the PLO's initial conference could glance a short distance across Jerusalem's dusty valleys into Israel. Many of them had fled homes there in 1948. For sixteen years they had bitterly plotted revenge but had made little effort to obtain it. Now, they hoped that this new organization, supported by the Arab states and their armies, would reverse the Arab defeat in the 1948 war and erase Israel from the map.

The Palestinians wanted to hold their meeting in Jerusalem because of that city's great historic and religious importance. But they needed permission from the government of Jordan, which had captured the West Bank in the 1948 war and annexed it in 1950. Since about two thirds of Jordan's citizens were Palestinians, King Husayn, Jordan's ruler, knew that a PLO successful in winning Palestinian loyalties would directly threaten his power and survival.

So when Ahmad Shuqayri, the meeting's convener, asked if it could be held in East Jerusalem, King Husayn suggested the desolate Dead Sea area instead. The name of that lifeless body of water seemed to symbolize the king's preference that Shuqayri's group be stillborn. As a compromise, the Palestinians were allowed into East Jerusalem, but only as close as the suburban Intercontinental Hotel. Jordanian intelligence carefully monitored their deliberations. The Palestinians could talk as much as they pleased about wiping out Israel, but the delegates did not dare speak about the West Bank and its Palestinian residents.

King Husayn's restrictions were not the only constraint faced by those meeting at the Intercontinental Hotel. The impetus for this gathering had come especially from Egypt's President Gamal Abdel Nasir, who wanted to manipulate the Palestinian cause for his own interests. As Palestinian leader, Nasir handpicked the 57-year-old Shuqayri, who came from a wealthy Palestinian family but was a professional civil servant of Arab regimes. Until 1963, he had been a Saudi diplomat but was dismissed for taking Egypt's side against Saudi Arabia in the Yemen war. From then on, he was Nasir's client.

The PLO's founding meeting was effectively stage-managed to create symbols suited to Egypt's needs. The PLO would have a parliament—the Palestine National Council (PNC)—as well as its own army and treasury. The PLO Charter was adopted as its constitution. But these institutions were show-pieces designed to promote the Palestine issue through propaganda. Real power resided with Shuqayri and his handpicked PLO Executive Committee. The PLO created in 1964 was incapable of either disputing the policies of Arab states or fulfilling the Palestinians' desire to destroy Israel and throw out its Jewish population.

A few younger Palestinians were skeptical about this new PLO. One of those invited to the meeting at the Intercontinental Hotel was a 34-year-old activist named Yasir Arafat, who was living in Kuwait. But he was busy building his own group, named Fatah, and did not even bother to show up. These critics complained that the new PLO was poorly led, too subservient to Arab states, and preoccupied with radical rhetoric rather than effective action.

These criticisms explained the historical failings that had led the

Palestinian elite to be sitting as guests in Jordanian East Jerusalem rather than governing that city as the capital of Palestine. It had lost the competition with the Jewish nationalist movement, Zionism, which had also laid claim to the land between the Jordan river and the Mediterranean.

The British government promised in its 1917 Balfour Declaration to make in Palestine "a national home for the Jewish people" while doing nothing to "prejudice the civil and religious rights of existing non-Jewish communities." That same year, British forces fighting against the Ottoman Empire in World War I captured that land. When the war ended and the Ottoman Empire was broken up, Britain continued to rule there under a 1922 League of Nations mandate which incorporated the Balfour Declaration.

The contradiction between the rights and goals of Arabs and those of Jews plagued British policy throughout the 1920s and 1930s. The Zionist movement wanted Jewish immigration and the creation of a Jewish state; the Arabs of Palestine, who were the majority, mostly advocated a Pan-Arab solution in which Palestine would be part of a larger, united Arab entity. Through alternating periods of peace and conflict the two communities' objectives seemed irreconcilable. Although a British proposal offered to give the Palestinian Arabs most of the territory in 1937, the nationalist leadership rejected the proposal and began an armed revolt. By 1939 the armed groups were defeated, and the movement's main leaders had fled or were in prison.[1]

Worried that the Arab world would side with Germany and Italy in the growing conflict among European powers, the British government sought throughout the late 1930s to find some solution to the Palestine question satisfactory to the Arabs. Such concessions, British policymakers argued, would guarantee Arab allegiance. As ruler of Palestine, Britain tried to block the escape of Europe's Jews to Palestine in response to both Arab demands and Palestinian Arab violence at the very time when Hitler's regime and other European governments were intensifying antisemitic persecution. Still, the Arabs of Palestine mistrusted the British, rejected diplomatic compromise as a cowardly policy, and clung to the hope of a total victory won with the help of Arab and German allies. The leaders of the Palestinian Arab nationalist movement bet on Nazi Germany to defeat Britain.[2]

The Allies' victory in World War II left the Arabs of Palestine in a weaker position. The Palestinian Arab leaders' support for the Nazis, coupled with the Germans' murder of six million Jews in Europe, increased international support for the creation of Israel. Britain continued to seek a solution in Palestine satisfactory to the Arabs, but Arab leaders did not take advantage of this potential opening. Their governments, wrote the historian Albert Hourani, "made no preparation, either for peace with its concessions or war with its sacrifices."[3]

Refusing to accept a November 1947 United Nations' plan to partition the land into Jewish and Arab states, the Arabs of Palestine fought a guerrilla war, aided after May 1948 by an invasion of Israel from four regular Arab armies (Jordan, Iraq, Syria, and Egypt, with some help from the Lebanese and Saudi armed forces). The Palestinians hoped that their guerrilla forces would block partition and destroy Israel. Instead, these local forces, along with the corrupt and militarily incompetent Arab states, each seeking to grab Palestine for itself, suffered a humiliating defeat.[4]

An Arab scholar later contrasted the confident expectations of Arab and Palestinian rulers with the dismal outcome: "Seven Arab states declare war on Zionism in Palestine, stop impotent before it and turn on their heels. The representatives of the Arabs deliver fiery speeches in the highest international forums, warning what the Arab states and peoples will do if this or that decision be enacted. Declarations fall like bombs from the mouths of officials at the meetings of the Arab League, but when action becomes necessary, the fire is still and quiet, and steel and iron are rusted and twisted, quick to bend and disintegrate."[5]

The 1948 war ended with the defeat of the Arab armies and the flight, or in some cases expulsion, of between 630,000 and 730,000 Palestinian refugees. An estimated 450 abandoned Palestinian Arab villages within Israel's borders had disappeared; urban neighborhoods were now inhabited by Jews. Of the two parts of Palestine still held by Arab forces, Jordan ruled the West Bank—annexing it in 1950—and Egypt administered the Gaza Strip.

This debacle—called in Arabic *al-nakba*, the catastrophe—created enormous anger and bitterness in the Arab world. Palestinians felt that foreigners with no right to be there had invaded and seized their land. They had suffered by losing their society, livelihood, homes, and possessions. To make matters worse, other Arabs ridiculed them for having been defeated.

In the aftermath of the 1948 war, the United Nations provided relief for the Palestinian Arab refugees and sought a negotiated settlement. It passed Resolution 194 in December 1948 proposing that refugees "wishing to return to their homes and live at peace with their neighbors should be permitted to do so at the earliest practical date" or receive compensation for their property. Since such a solution was impossible given the lack of a diplomatic settlement, the United Nations urged that the refugees be resettled in Arab countries.

The United Nations Relief and Works Agency (UNRWA) provided aid, but Arab states refused to resettle the Palestinian refugees permanently. The UNRWA representative in Jordan commented in 1952, "The Arab nations do not want to solve the refugee problem. They want to keep it as an open sore, as an affront against the United Nations, and as a weapon against Israel." The Palestinians themselves were profoundly demoralized as well as physically uprooted. Peasants without land, workers without jobs, and notables without honor, they were deprived of self-respect, hope for the future, and the security of citizenship. They developed what a 1954 UNRWA report called a "typical refugee mentality, and passive expectation of continued benefits."[6]

The 1948 disaster also backfired against the Arab regimes which had failed to avert it. Ideological ferment and political unrest contributed to coups in Egypt, Syria, and Iraq during the 1950s. If the war was a catalyst, however, the turmoil mainly resulted from ongoing domestic political, economic, and social developments. These trends sparked debates over how to achieve unity; power struggles in each state among communities, classes, and ideologies; rivalry among regimes for regional leadership; controversies on the best path toward economic development; and strife over eliminating remaining Western influence.

During the 1950s, while some Palestinians in the refugee camps were being slowly consumed by apathy, dependence, and stagnation, a number of young men just coming to adulthood were less traumatized and better able to adjust. UNRWA's school system helped produce that new generation, eager to continue the battle with new methods. They were stirred and inspired by the ideological and political ferment in the Arab world.

Although these young men did not all agree among themselves, they were generally enthusiastic supporters of Pan-Arab nationalism, many of them followers of Egypt's charismatic President Nasir. The Arab states, led by Egypt, they believed, would unite and then reconquer Palestine. Thus, in the mid-1950s, when Egypt recruited Palestinians to launch terrorist attacks on Israel, among the volunteers for training was a trio who had become friends in their student days at the University of Cairo: Yasir Arafat, Salah Khalaf (Abu Iyad), and Khalil al-Wazir (Abu Jihad).

Arafat was always the leader. He was born on October 27, 1929, probably in Jerusalem. While he was related to the powerful al-Husayni family, it was only distantly, through a minor branch. Arafat's father was a merchant, and the family lived in Egypt many years before returning to Palestine around 1940. Arafat grew up in Gaza. Soon after his mother died, Arafat's father remarried and sent him to live in Jerusalem. In later years, Arafat rarely mentioned his father.[7]

After the 1948 war Arafat returned to Gaza. Although he belonged to a Palestinian student group in his teens, his real political involvement seems to have started in Cairo in 1951, when he began his university studies in engineering. He was elected president of the Palestine Students' Federation in 1952.

Arafat and his friends had eclectic political views. They were pious Muslims, with links to Egypt's Muslim Brotherhood, but they were also interested in Marxism. His decision to become known by the name Arafat—the important holy mountain near Mecca—and by the code name Abu Ammar—after Ammar ben Yasir, a helper of the prophet Muhammad—indicated his Islamic orientation. But Arafat's other political influences were shown by the fact that he left the Arab world for the first time in 1952 to attend a Communist-sponsored international student conference in Czechoslovakia.

In 1956, after finishing school, Arafat underwent military training as an explosives expert with the Egyptian army and then served briefly as a reserve officer clearing minefields. But he was harassed by the Egyptian regime because of his sympathy with the Muslim Brotherhood and his involvement in local politics. Thereafter, along with tens of thousands of other Palestinians, Arafat went to Kuwait to seek his fortune in the oil boom. He began by working for the Kuwaiti government. Arafat later claimed that he ran a successful construction business there, but he actually devoted most of his time to politics.

By 1958 Arafat and two college friends also working in Kuwait— Abu Iyad and Faruq Qaddumi—were organizing Palestinians there. The next year they began a newspaper, *Filastinuna* (Our Palestine), in Beirut; and in October 1959, along with Abu Jihad, they founded their own Palestinian nationalist group, Fatah, in Kuwait. In Arabic its name was the Harakat al-Tahrir al-Filastiniyya (Palestinian Liberation Movement), whose acronym, when reversed, spells "Fatah," meaning conquest.[8]

Now a full-time revolutionary, Arafat recruited members and international support by traveling widely. A visit to Algeria in 1962 convinced him of the effectiveness of guerrilla warfare in that country's struggle for independence. Thus, Fatah set up military training bases in Jordan and Syria during 1963 and 1964 to prepare for a military struggle and began armed operations in January 1965.[9]

Whatever their own criticisms and periodic disagreements, Arafat's five most important co-founders of Fatah—Qaddumi, Abu Iyad, Abu Jihad, and the brothers Khalid and Hani al-Hasan— would stick with him for well over three decades. These long, stable personal relations were one of the secrets of Fatah's survival.

But while the embryonic Fatah group was starting to organize, Arab regimes played the principal role in reviving the Palestine question as part of their interstate competition. Nasir was always talking of the need to fight Israel while also invariably adding that the time was not yet right. Meanwhile, Egypt ruled the Gaza Strip with a strong hand, while Jordan ran the West Bank as an integral part of that country. Their rival, Iraqi dictator Abd al-Karim Qassim, sought to exploit the situation, too. In a December 1959 speech, while laying the cornerstone of the Qassim city housing project for Iraqi army officers, Qassim proclaimed that the Palestinians were victims of Jordan and Egypt, as well as of Israel. He urged that the Palestinians struggle to regain their own territory from these "three thieves."[10]

At the January 1964 Arab summit meeting, Iraq tried to embarrass its rivals further. If Jordan and Egypt were really Arab patriots,

Iraq suggested, they would support a Palestinian government over the Jordan-ruled West Bank and Egypt-ruled Gaza. Egypt's Nasir countered by raising the ante. The Arab states would show even more dedication to the cause, he replied, by establishing a Palestine Liberation Organization and a Palestinian army, to recover the rest of Palestine from the Israelis. This event led directly to the PLO's creation at the Intercontinental Hotel a few months later. Ironically, then, although the PLO would eventually struggle with Arab regimes and come to favor a West Bank/Gaza Palestinian state, it was set up precisely to oppose any such state and to be a puppet for those regimes.

In contrast to Shuqayri's PLO, which already saw itself as representing the Palestinians, Arafat's Fatah thought it could win that mandate through political and military action.[11] But to do this, these young Palestinians had to provide an explanation for the overwhelming defeat their people had suffered in 1948. They did so by combining traditional ideas and rhetoric with some very modern political concepts.

On the one hand, they argued that Israel's existence was analogous to the Christian Crusades, a temporary conquest of Palestine that was doomed to inevitable destruction. Israel was an artificial entity; the Jews were not a nation and had no rights to the land. Zionism was the personification of evil, a new version of colonialism, a drive for world conquest. Islam taught that Muslims could not accept nonbelievers' rule and would eventually overcome it with Allah's support, no matter how steep the odds.[12] Arab nationalism predicted and urged that all Arabs would eventually become a single state able to achieve all their goals.

On the other hand, the Palestinian activists explained Israel's existence by a quasi-Marxist theory of Western imperialist manipulation. It was inconceivable that the Jews, so long despised and quiescent in the Muslim world, could be the authors of this conquest. According to a Fatah document, "The 'Jewish State' was established in order to secure continued imperialist robbery and exploitation of our country."[13]

Thus, the revolutionary doctrine developed among Palestinians in the 1950s and early 1960s blended Islam not only with aspects of Marxism–Leninism but also with Third World radical nationalism. Mao Zedong and Che Guevara, Vietnam and Algeria, preached that guerrilla war was the way to build popular support and a political movement. All of Fatah's beliefs argued that victory was certain and, consequently, any compromise short of replacing Israel by an Arab state would be not only treasonous but also unnecessary. Further, the Palestinians were guiltless victims entitled to use any means to redress their grievances.

Palestinians hoped that Arab states, uniting behind Egypt's wildly popular Nasir, would lead the reconquest. For almost two decades, Palestinians had been willing to leave the issue in Arab rulers' hands. But while giving lip service to Palestinian rights, the Arab states used the cause to gain domestic legitimacy, further their own interests, and triumph over Arab rivals. Jordan had annexed the West Bank in 1950 and offered an alternative loyalty by giving Jordanian citizenship to Palestinians. The main factors suppressing a separate Palestinian identity in the 1950s and 1960s were Arab regimes and the appeal of radical Pan-Arabism. According to the prevailing arguments, victory for the Palestinian cause would have to await Arab unity; when Israel was destroyed, Palestine would be a province of a much larger Arab state. This is why Palestinians failed to revive their separate identity or seek sovereignty over the West Bank and Gaza during the nineteen years of Egyptian and Jordanian occupation between 1948 and 1967.

Both Shuqayri's PLO and Arafat's Fatah shared this belief that the Arab states would destroy Israel and set the stage for the refugees' return and the establishment of Palestine. But Shuqayri thought Arab governments would do this by themselves; Arafat argued that Palestinian guerrilla action was needed to push them into war.

Despite Fatah's links to Islamic radicals, to Pan-Arab nationalists, and to the intelligence agencies of Egypt and Syria, it also moved over the years toward favoring a separate Palestinian identity rather than a Pan-Arab or Islamic state. Arafat thus preached that Palestinians "had to be rescued from the stranglehold of Arab tutelage, inter-party discord, and regional Arab policies."[14]

Instead of a passive audience, Palestinians would be the vanguard; the Palestinian "battle for liberation" would not be the outcome of Arab unity but the source of it. "It is high time that the Palestinians should cease to be used as pawns to further personal or regional ends," Arafat insisted. "The Palestinian cause must now emerge on the international scene as a liberation struggle between the Palestinian people and an occupying state. All that we ask of the Arab governments is that they should be able to protect their own frontiers and to permit and support Palestinian action inside the occupied territories."[15]

Given this doctrine, Arafat's group was eager to launch an armed struggle in order to compete with Shuqayri's PLO. Algeria, which had just won independence from French colonial rule after a long battle, was Fatah's first patron and model. The Palestinian revolutionaries thought their people, like Algerians, could be mobilized by guerrilla warfare and that the Jews either would be defeated or, like the French settlers, would flee if faced with indiscriminate violence.

This tendency to overestimate Arab armed might and underestimate Israeli steadfastness would long plague both Arafat and Fatah. Actually, the Algerians had been militarily defeated and gained independence only because France tired of the conflict. Israel, by contrast, was not a colony whose mother country would give it up when the cost became too high. Its people were fighting for their own lives and independence. When Fatah finally did consider this point, it erroneously saw the United States as France's equivalent—as an imperialist sponsor which might be pressured into surrendering Israel to the Arabs. This misunderstanding of Israel's nature, U.S. policy, and the relations between these two nations contributed to the PLO's mistaken decisions and strategies.

Fatah began training in Algeria, but that country was too weak and distant to be its main sponsor. Since Egypt was already backing the PLO and Jordan opposed Palestinian nationalism altogether, Syria—the rival of both Egypt and Jordan—was Arafat's logical choice as patron. In 1964, having allied himself with Syria's military intelligence, Arafat moved his headquarters to Damascus.

New members of Fatah were recruited from student groups and refugee camps; funds were raised among wealthy Palestinians in Kuwait, where Arafat and his friends had many contacts. After a debate on whether to start by fighting or by organizing a mass political movement, Fatah's cadre decided that armed struggle was necessary to build a political struggle. Their first raid—an ineffective bomb attack on Israel's water system—took place on January 1, 1965. So significant was the resort to arms that Fatah would eventually consider this its official founding date, even though the organization had begun some six years earlier. But at the time, Fatah issued its first battle communique under the name of its military branch, al-Asifa, in order to be able to deny responsibility if its operations failed or brought bad publicity.

The earliest attacks were indeed unimpressive. Israel captured its first prisoner from Fatah when his rifle misfired; the first casualty was a member of Fatah who was killed by Jordanian soldiers while recrossing the border after an attack on Israel.[16] Fatah was already discovering the difficulty of cooperating with Arab states: Egypt and Jordan opposed the group; Syria used aid as a way to control it. Some Arab states called Fatah a Western agent and criticized it for not coordinating with them or for putting Palestinian interests above Pan-Arab nationalism. The Lebanese government briefly arrested some Fatah leaders who were trying to start operations there.

But the number of raids into Israel increased throughout 1965 and 1966. Syria, Fatah's main supporter, used the territory of weaker states bordering Israel—Lebanon and Jordan—to deflect reprisals from itself. It opened training camps and a command post on its border with Jordan to facilitate attacks from the Jordanian-ruled West Bank. Fatah and other Palestinian groups, seeking publicity and competing among themselves, exaggerated their military successes, starting a tradition which confused their own leaders about the achievements of this guerrilla strategy.

Israel also put pressure on Jordan to stop the Palestinian attacks. After three Israeli soldiers were killed by a Fatah mine on a road inside Israel in 1966, the Israeli army raided the village of Samu in the West Bank and blew up houses there. Several dozen Palestinian civilians hiding inside were killed. The Israelis also attacked the main Palestinian military camps on the West Bank, at Qalqilya and Jenin. Palestinians demonstrated, demanding that King Husayn arm them. Instead, as Israel had hoped, he restricted attacks from the armed Palestinian groups by deploying his army to block them.

Fatah came under pressure in Syria, too. After a 1966 coup which overthrew the government there, the newly dominant faction plotted to replace Arafat with a pro-Syrian Palestinian officer. When this man was killed, Syria accused Fatah, jailing Arafat, Abu Iyad, Abu Jihad, and eight others for forty days to compel their cooperation. But Fatah, learning to manipulate inter-Arab competition, responded by making an alliance with Egypt. In turn, Syria and Iraq countered by establishing small Palestinian groups as their own instruments.

Syria's willingness to take risks, however, was about to produce a much bigger clash. The regime's radicalism increased tension on the Syria–Israel border, intensified by competition among Arab states to see which could make the most extreme threats against Israel. In May 1967, amid rumors fanned by the USSR of an impending Israeli attack against Syria, Egypt, Jordan, and Syria made an alliance. Nasir loudly threatened war, demanded UN peacekeeping units be withdrawn from the border, built up his forces in the Sinai, and closed the Straits of Tiran to Israeli shipping.

Fatah's raids and Shuqayri's heated rhetoric intensified the crisis. Returning from Gaza in May 1967, Shuqayri told Nasir that the Palestine Liberation Army there was "in advanced positions, ready for battle." The Palestinian people were "straining for the fight . . . The army of Egypt . . . now stands face to face with the gangs of Israel," and the Arab nation was intent "on the liberation of the usurped homeland." War was inevitable, Shuqayri said, and the Palestinian army "will indeed be in the forefront of the fighting" to liberate all Palestine "from Israeli occupation." After victory all non-Palestinian Jews would "go back the way they came; they came by sea, and they will go back by sea," to their original countries.[17]

While Shuqayri articulated the Palestinians' emotions, Nasir expressed a view that would long dominate the PLO's thinking as well. Arabs, said Nasir in 1967, had three closely connected enemies: U.S. imperialism, Zionism, and conservative Arab regimes. These evil forces were "the enemies of liberation everywhere, the advocates of counter-revolution against all aspirations to liberty, progress and welfare . . . in the whole of the Third World" in order to keep it backward, dominate it, rob its wealth, and make it "a market for their wares." America, the conspiracy's leader, "implanted Israel in our territory [and] is supporting reaction and imposing backwardness upon us." Israel could not "live for a day without American economic and military aid," Nasir claimed. (Actually, Israel received little U.S. aid at this time.) The same could be said for the rulers of Saudi Arabia, Jordan, Tunisia, and "other stooges" (to use Nasir's phrase) whose people would overthrow them if they were deprived of U.S. protection.[18]

The first step in defeating this triple alliance and the only way to achieve Arab unity and development was, according to Nasir, "to prepare for the decisive battle, in Palestine and elsewhere . . . so that the Arab alone may be paramount in all Arab territories from the Ocean to the Gulf." Shuqayri told journalists in late May, "I promise you that zero hour has come. This is the hour our people have been awaiting for the last 19 years." He suggested that few Jews would survive the war.[19]

What happened, however, was quite different from the expectations of Nasir, Shuqayri, and Arafat. Israel attacked first, smashing the armies of Egypt, Syria, and Jordan in six days. Despite Shuqayri's bragging, the PLO and Fatah played little role in the fighting. Between 200,000 and 250,000 more Palestinians fled from the West Bank to Jordan. Rather than overseeing the Jews' deportation, Shuqayri had to beg Palestinians not to run away. At the end of the war, Israel had captured the rest of pre-1948 Palestine— the West Bank and Gaza—along with Egypt's Sinai peninsula and Syria's Golan Heights. The resulting humiliation and hopelessness inflamed the Arabs' worst fears that Israel would take over the region.[20]

The Arab states' threat to eliminate Israel was put to the test in the 1967 war. Their total defeat destroyed the Palestinians' faith that Arab rulers would be the principal instrument of Israel's destruction. Fatah, convinced it knew the way to retrieve Arab honor and victory, quickly blamed the defeat entirely on the Arab states' governments. The war, argued one Palestinian magazine, provided "evidence of failure, slackness and conspiracy, the setback was a new proof of the error of keeping the Palestinian people in particular, and the Arab people in general, remote from the field of battle." Regular armies were unreliable since the enemy, backed by Western imperialism, would always be superior in conventional weapons. Only guerrillas could win.[21]

What was distinctly not sought was moderation or compromise. Since the disaster had been so huge, no government would accept the results. The "progressive" military rulers in Egypt, Syria, and Iraq, shown to be no more effective than their conservative predecessors, would not be more politically yielding than regimes they had overthrown. The 1967 Arab summit agreed not to negotiate, recognize, or make peace with Israel.

"There are only two well-defined goals on the Arab scene," wrote the influential Egyptian journalist Muhammad Hasanayn Heikal, "erasing the traces of the 1967 aggression by Israel's withdrawal from all the areas occupied by it in that year and erasing the aggression of 1948 by Israel's total and absolute annihilation . . . The mistake of some of us is starting off with the last step before beginning the first."[22]

Shuqayri, however, warned against making peace even in exchange for Israel's withdrawal from the West Bank and Gaza, declaring it "absolutely false" that the Arabs would ever live with Israel "in peace as good neighbors." Peace would come only when Israel "ceases to exist." Israelis were urged to "return to your original countries, emigrate to where you will find a quiet life. For Palestine will not be a land of quiet and stability until its original people return to it."

Through war and terrorism the Arabs would show Israelis that they could not enjoy a normal life unless they left, Shuqayri declared. "You are surrounded by a hundred million Arabs, who will never let Israel alone." The Arabs would grow stronger; Israel would pass away like the Crusades, "after a terrible struggle, leaving behind them ruined fortresses and demolished castles." Characteristically, Shuqayri had entitled his 1966 book *Liberation, Not Negotiation.*[23]

But the United Nations suggested a diplomatic alternative on November 22, 1967, in the form of Resolution 242. This would become the Middle East peace process's central text. The resolution emphasized "the inadmissibility of the acquisition of territory by war and the need to work for a just and lasting peace in which every State in the area can live in security." It called for the "withdrawal of Israeli armed forces from territories occupied" in the 1967 war, "termination of all claims or states of belligerency," "achieving a just settlement of the refugee problem," and "acknowledgment of the sovereignty, territorial integrity and political independence of every state in the area and their right to live in peace within secure and recognized boundaries free from threats or acts of force." In other words, Israel would return territories captured in 1967—the West Bank and Gaza, the Golan Heights and Sinai peninsula—to Arab rule and, in exchange, obtain peace, recognition, and security guarantees.[24]

Fatah had two objections to this proposal: First, Fatah sought to destroy Israel, not negotiate peace with it, and Fatah wanted all the land, not just the West Bank and Gaza. Fatah declared that "occupied territory" meant not just the West Bank and Gaza but all of Palestine. "Withdrawal from the occupied territories [of 1967] will do no more in our eyes than eliminate the latest manifestation of aggression; the question of the source of the aggression . . . the alien Zionist presence in our land, will remain unaffected." The PLO also objected "to Israel's right to exist and to establish permanent, recognized frontiers." It did not want to end the war or give up demanding all of Palestine.[25]

Second, by identifying the problem of the Palestinians as a refugee issue, the resolution suggested the solution would be a return of the pre-1967 situation—Jordanian rule—rather than an independent Palestinian state. This outcome was precisely Fatah's great fear: that the Arab states would make peace in exchange for regaining their own territory, forever ending the Palestinians' chance to destroy Israel. The PLO had to stop negotiations to make sure that it—not Jordan—would represent the Palestinians and be seen as the rightful owner of the West Bank and Gaza. Ironically, while the PLO later argued that Resolution 242 required that Israel relinquish all these lands, at the time it also raised a third objection that the proposal would permit border changes in Israel's favor.

While the PLO just talked, Fatah sought to show itself as a group of self-sacrificing heroes transforming the Arab world's daze of defeat and fatalism into a revolutionary storm. Fatah criticized the PLO as lacking independence, strategy, or proper leadership. Shuqayri, discredited by the debacle, resigned as PLO leader in December 1967, to be replaced by another Palestinian lawyer, Yahya Hammuda.[26]

Meeting in Damascus just after the 1967 war's end, Fatah decided to continue fighting, and it staged the first postwar attack on Israel at the end of August. From bases in Jordan, it began a cross-border guerrilla war against Israel's army as well as terrorist attacks against Israeli civilians—both tactics designed to raise Palestinian morale, show that the enemy was weak, and prove that Fatah had the courage and strategy to lead the way for all Arabs. Before 1967 the goal had been to set off a new crisis in which the Arab states would go to war with Israel. Now an additional, more immediate, objective was to foster a radical upsurge able to stop any Arab regime from compromising with Israel.

The West Bank and Gaza Strip, now under Israeli occupation, were a key front for the PLO and Fatah. But at first, their residents were uninterested in the PLO and knew little about Fatah, whose own base of support was still small. The vast majority of people were passive peasants. Local politics was dominated by powerful families—who had cooperated with Jordan's regime during its presence—and were contested by their younger, more radical, members—doctors, lawyers, engineers, pharmacists, journalists, and students who had picked up Pan-Arab, Nasirist, Ba'thist, or Communist ideas at school and opposed the king. Most of them, on both sides, were not Palestinian nationalists.[27]

No one believed Israel's occupation would last long. Yet since it was in control, the local Palestinian elite, including younger activists, followed the usual practice of getting along with the authorities to protect their property and position. Pre-1948 contacts with Israeli Jews were reestablished; a tacit Israel–Jordan arrangement let West Bank produce be sent east across the river. Israel's authorities asked some from the great families to go to Amman to prepare the way for negotiations. Arafat had to act quickly lest Jordanian–Israeli contacts ultimately lead to an agreement.

To assess the situation, Arafat himself, in disguise and carrying false papers, crossed the Jordan river to the West Bank. But despite Fatah's constant talk of a people's war, he did not try to raise mass rebellion in the countryside or arouse demoralized refugees. Experienced local activists in Nablus, wedded to Jordan's regime or Pan-Arab nationalism, were uninterested in him. Excluded from society's top and bottom, Arafat had to work with the small middle, recruiting shopkeepers and artisans.

After making some progress on organizing in Nablus, he moved on to Ramallah, where conditions were even less favorable. The town contained every possible religious and political sect. Many of its people had emigrated to North or South America and sent back money or returned themselves to buy property and build houses. These Christian and Western influences gave Ramallah an easygoing atmosphere, quite different from its conservative environs. But despite this modernization, Ramallah was still an extended village, a hard place for Arafat to hide and build an underground movement. He spent most of his time and energy moving around simply to escape detection. It was not long before Palestinian informants for Israel's spreading intelligence network reported that a stranger was up to something mysterious in a quiet neighborhood. He disappeared shortly before a raid by Israeli forces, making his way back to Jordan.

This experience had a major effect on Arafat's thinking, on Fatah's strategy, and ultimately on the PLO. Arafat placed little confidence in people and conditions on the West Bank and Gaza. In contrast to the Marxists, he was uninterested in building an ideological cadre party. Instead, Fatah emphasized actions outside the land, and military rather than political struggle. More than a decade would pass before Fatah would begin seriously building a political network in the territories; it would be twenty years before that approach became preeminent.

Arafat's foray into the West Bank also gave a boost to his personal fortunes. As happened so often in Palestinian political life, actual failure was insignificant compared with symbolic success. Arafat was seen as a daredevil commander and effective underground operator who risked his life at the front and behind enemy lines. The resulting glory helped make him leader of the Palestinians.

During the three years after 1967, Fatah spoke with bravado, claiming to have "all its military bases [in] the occupied homeland" and to be making dozens of attacks daily. "No part of Israel, no Israeli installation, no Israeli target is out of their reach, and the Israeli regime may henceforth expect the steadily increasing disruption of its colonialist presence in the weeks and months to come." Israel, Fatah falsely charged, used "napalm bombings, strafings, evictions, summary executions, plundering, brutality, imprisonment, desecration, violations and countless other crimes" to suppress the "people's armed upsurge."[28]

Such propaganda was effective in mobilizing supporters but also dangerously self-deluding for the leaders, who it influenced to adopt and sustain an ineffective strategy. Like so much of the movement's history, public relations' success went hand in hand with debacle. Fatah's terrorist guerrilla operations inflicted civilian and military casualties but hardly destabilized the country. Israel defeated the offensive by mounting a focused, effective repression against activists and permitting a relatively normal life for Palestinians who refrained from involvement in the insurrection.

Those who tried to organize rebellion right after the 1967 war were deported. Since most of the protest was carried out by pro-Jordan or leftist activists, Fatah remained a minority movement in the territories. The elite's remaining members were able to hold onto their authority and to make a great deal of money in business by cooperating or being quiet. Workers and peasants could vastly increase their incomes by working in Israel.

Fatah's struggle, then, had to be waged from outside the West Bank, and the kingdom of Jordan was the best operational base. The Jordan river valley, which runs along the Israel–Jordan border, is hot and desolate, but the narrow stream creates a strip of oasis through a rocky wilderness. The mountains are close on both sides, and Israeli and Jordanian towns lying at their feet are in sight of one another. Along the river, the terrain varies from rolling hills to maze-like small canyons. Literally every night during the late 1960s, Palestinian terrorist guerrillas and Israeli patrols played a deadly game of hide and seek in this little amphitheater.

Even if the infiltrators succeeded in crossing the river, however, Israel's forces usually penned them up before they could cross the hills to the west. While unable to stop all the armed attacks or bombs planted in public places, Israel managed to keep them to a minimum. Its security forces quickly rounded up underground cells in the West Bank and Gaza and killed or captured most PLO fighters who tried to cross from Jordan.

"If the purpose of the terrorists had ever been to drive Israel from the territories it occupies or to inflict significant damage upon it," concluded a CIA study in 1968, "there could be no question that they have failed." Unable to damage or defeat Israel's army or to create an effective resistance, the PLO gunmen sought softer, civilian targets for their bombs and bullets. Between 1967 and 1970, 115 Israeli civilians were killed and 687 were wounded in Palestinian terrorist attacks.[29] Israel retaliated by attacking near-by Palestinian bases in Jordan to pressure Amman's government to close them down.

One of these operations, however, became a historic Fatah political victory that would mark a turning point in its fortunes. In March 1968 a large column of Israeli troops crossed the Jordan river to hit the main Fatah camp at Karama. Stung by public criticism over earlier passivity, Jordan's army battled this force. The Israeli column continued advancing, capturing the camp and a large number of prisoners. Arafat and Abu Iyad escaped. The Palestinians had fought back and Israel had lost 21 men, but the attack's objectives were achieved.

In the Arab world, however, the encounter became a legend. Karama means honor in Arabic, and Fatah's battle there appeared heroic next to the Arab armies' apparent cowardice and incompetence a year earlier. Jordan's role in the fighting was forgotten. To his West Bank visit, Arafat now added new credentials for leadership. Recruits poured into the movement, which gained great influence in the refugee camps in more tolerant Lebanon and Jordan, though not in totalitarian Syria or Iraq.

Support from Egypt, the most powerful Arab country, and Nasir, chief of the whole Pan-Arab movement and the PLO's real founder, helped Arafat take over the organization. At the fourth Palestine National Council meeting, held in Cairo in July 1968, Fatah and the smaller armed groups claimed half the seats, dominated the proceedings, and seized control. Yasir Arafat formally became the PLO's chairman in February 1969. From this point on, he would always be the virtually undisputed leader of the PLO.

Arafat was a centrist nationalist in his relative indifference to class struggle or Marxism–Leninism but was otherwise quite radical. He saw himself as a man of action reacting against years of windy Arab theorizing. "We do not have any ideology—our goal is the liberation of our fatherland by any means necessary." Palestine could be recovered only "by blood and iron; and blood and iron have nothing to do with philosophies and theories." He had contempt for politicians: "It is the commandos who will decide the future."[30]

In his opinions and appearance, the young Arafat was a fitting symbol of the new Palestinian generation and its revolutionary tactics. He wore a military uniform and carried a rifle or pistol to make him seem a fighter fresh from the field, who shared the risks and glory of battle directly, rejecting the soft life and endless talk of other Arab leaders. "Our new generation is tired of waiting for something to happen," Arafat said in 1969. "Isn't it better to die bringing down your enemy than to await a slow, miserable death rotting in a tent in the desert?"[31]

While Arafat's radical rhetoric and uncouth appearance made him seem unattractive and untrustworthy to Western audiences,

their reaction was secondary for him. Arafat was deliberately culti-
vating the appearance of being a man of the people. His Palestinian
headscarf *(kaffiya)* and unshaven stubble brought him closer to the
masses.

Although Arafat's style was very different from that of his older
rivals in the Palestinian elite, much of his ideology and many of his
goals were the same. The main change between Shuqayri's 1964
Palestinian Charter and Arafat's 1968 revised text was that the former made the PLO part of a struggle led by the Arab states, while
the revised version stressed the PLO's independent and leading role.

But the Charter's basic continuity reflected a consensus so powerful that the document would never really be formally annulled
or replaced.[32] It was a proudly, self-consciously radical platform
which, as Karl Marx had written at the dawn of another revolutionary movement, disdained to conceal its aims. The Charter claimed
all of Palestine and insisted that Israel be destroyed, rebuffing any
idea of compromise, negotiation, or coexistence with it. As a bow
to Pan-Arab nationalism, Palestine was called "an indivisible part
of the Arab homeland" and the Palestinians "an integral part of the
Arab nation." Palestinians, however, remained Palestinians regardless of citizenship.

The Charter defined Palestinians as "Arab nationals," and excluded Israeli Jews—except for the few who had lived there before
"the beginning of the Zionist invasion," at a date left undefined.
Thus, the great majority of Israelis would have no right to remain
in the country following a PLO victory. Zionism, rather than being
a Jewish nationalist movement, was described as imperialist, racist,
fanatic, aggressive, expansionist, colonial, and fascist. Israel was not
the realization of Jewish aspirations but "a geographical base for
world imperialism placed strategically in the midst of the Arab
homeland to combat" Arab liberation, unity, and progress. It was
part of the European colonialism then disappearing throughout Africa and Asia, and it would be eliminated, too. The nations of the
world should make support for Zionism a crime. The Charter rejected the 1947 UN plan to create both Israel and a Palestinian state.
Jewish immigration to Israel must be blocked lest it strengthen the
state's existence. Israel's insecurity and Arab opposition should be
maintained to ensure that the USSR prevent "the millions of Jews
in the Soviet Union" from emigrating there.

The problem was Israel's very existence—not rule in the West Bank and Gaza—since every inch of that country stood on occupied territory. The struggle was not merely, the Charter declared, to eliminate the consequences of the 1967 war but to destroy Israel, "the instrument of aggression." And that fight must continue, "until final victory is won, no matter how long this takes and regardless of the sacrifices involved."

The PLO never saw Israel as the sole adversary but rather as a dependent of "world imperialism, under the direction of the United States of America." Anti-Americanism was an integral part of its program and activity, but there was a contradiction since the PLO also spoke of isolating Zionism "from the centers of power"—in other words, persuading the West to abandon Israel.

Having identified the enemy, the Charter also declared the basic principle for Arafat's internal political strategy: "Conflicts among the Palestinian national forces . . . should be ended for the sake of the basic conflict that exists between the forces of Zionism and of imperialism on the one hand, and the Palestinian people on the other." The extremely high value set on unity was so vital precisely because of the persistence of bitter conflicts among Palestinians and Arabs. To preserve harmony, decisions on the new Palestine's political, economic, and social system were deferred until after victory.

On strategy, the Charter spoke clearly and definitively. Armed struggle was the only way to liberate Palestine, not merely a temporary phase in the battle but the proper road from beginning to end. As Arafat put it, "The guns will talk." Diplomacy was deprecated as surrender. In regard to the Arab states, the PLO wanted to have it both ways. An alliance of the Palestinian people and the Arab masses might circumvent the incumbent governments. But such "national liberation," "revolutionary," "progressive forces" siding with the PLO usually turned out to be small, uninfluential leftist groups. Thus, the PLO had to deal with existing regimes. It tried to overcome the power imbalance by claiming that Palestinian liberation was the necessary precursor, rather than—as Nasir and his counterparts held—the outcome of a utopian Arab unity.

The PLO claimed to be the vanguard that would determine the destiny of all Arabs and strove to convince the Arab states that Israel directly threatened them by planning to seize "vast areas of Arab territory in Lebanon, Syria, Jordan, Egypt, Iraq, [Saudi Arabia] and the states of the Arab Gulf." The invasion of Palestine was only a bridgehead, and the 1967 war a first wave of assault. Nasir told the February 1969 PNC meeting that Arab involvement in the issue "should be based not merely on affection for the Palestinian people, but should be seen as a matter of self-defense in any Arab homeland."[33]

Theoretically, the PLO had a priority over every other issue and a right to free use of Arab territory. In fact, as the future would show, Arab states did not accept the PLO's independence because the Palestine issue's very importance made it too valuable to leave in the PLO's control.[34]

Nonetheless, the PLO sought a total victory over its adversary. The Charter's Article 21 rejected "all solutions which are substitutes for the total liberation of Palestine." An independent Palestinian state in the West Bank and Gaza was explicitly called a Zionist plot, and anyone proposing such an idea was an enemy. Such a state would be "absolutely incompatible with the Palestinian Arab people's right to the whole of Palestine, their homeland."[35]

These goals were taken very seriously by PLO activists and their Palestinian supporters. A Fatah platform listed them as "the liberation of Palestine . . . the annihilation of the Zionist entity in all of its economic, political, military, and cultural manifestations; and the establishment of an independent democratic Palestine which would rule the entire land of Palestine." Popular armed revolution was "the definite and exclusive way to the liberation of Palestine. The armed struggle is a strategy, not a tactic."[36] In short, violence would muster Palestinian and Arab support, the enemy would be destroyed and uprooted, the dream of "the return" to Palestine would be fulfilled, and a new utopia built on the site. Revolution until victory.

The PLO saw the struggle between Zionism and Palestinian nationalism and between Israelis and Palestinians as a zero-sum game in which each sought the other's total destruction. Yet while the conflict originated in an inevitable clash of two people seeking to control the same land, the all-or-nothing nature of the post-1948 competition arose from a choice made by Arab and Palestinian leaders.

By the end of the 1960s, Fatah and Arafat had already achieved what would have been unthinkable a few years earlier. They had begun to reawaken Palestinian nationalism, initiated their own war against Israel, hammered out a consensus program, and taken over the PLO. The PLO seemed firmly entrenched in Jordan and Lebanon, from which it could attack Israel. While Egypt, Syria, and Iraq tried to control the PLO and would not let it attack Israel directly from their own soil, they pressed the two smaller countries to permit such raids.

If Jordan and Lebanon were not pleased to be the PLO's hosts or face Israeli counterattacks, they seemed to have little choice since the PLO was becoming a state within a state in both countries. Its armed forces rivaled their national armies, and the PLO enjoyed political support from local leftists, radical nationalists, many Muslims in Lebanon, and most Palestinians in Jordan.

These successes, of course, were not ends in themselves but merely way-stations for a movement with far larger ambitions. Arafat's assignment of responsibilities was that "Fatah will be the leader, the Palestinian people the vanguard, and the Arab masses the supporting base." But he had not quite succeeded in uniting Palestinian forces or winning Arab support, and the PLO's use of terrorism made it disreputable in the West. These three problems would soon lead the seemingly triumphant PLO into its first debacles.[37]

2 >> The Poisoned Fruits of Terrorism, 1969–1973

In May 1970 a squad from a PLO member group crossed the border from Lebanon and fired a rocket into an Israeli school bus. Nine children and three teachers were killed, and nineteen children were wounded. During the late 1960s and early 1970s, PLO operations against Israel were often terrorist attacks aimed at killing Israelis, making no distinction between civilians and soldiers. "Because," said Arafat in 1972, "civilians or military, they're all equally guilty of wanting to destroy our people."[1]

Except for the 1971–1974 period, Fatah generally considered international terrorist attacks on non-Israeli targets as a diversion from its priority of direct assaults on Israel and Israelis. In contrast, some of the smaller groups that were now members of the PLO — especially the Popular Front for the Liberation of Palestine (PFLP) — favored the former approach, considering the West an enemy equal to Israel and needing especially spectacular actions to compete with Fatah. In July 1968 a PFLP team hijacked a Rome–Tel Aviv flight of El Al, Israel's airline. During the next fourteen years, Palestinian terrorists seized twenty-nine more planes; attacked airports, starting with a December 1968 assault on an El Al plane in Athens which killed one bystander; and hid bombs on airplanes, beginning with a February 1970 Swissair Zurich–Tel Aviv flight which killed all forty-seven passengers.[2]

Whatever the internal debate among PLO member groups regarding the pros and cons of international terrorism, the use of such tactics against Israel was a well-considered choice by PLO leaders, not an uncontrollable emotional reaction to oppression or a natural outgrowth of Palestinian desperation. Few of the many groups throughout history which have faced great deprivation or oppression resorted to terrorism. But between 1969 and 1985 PLO groups committed over 8,000 terrorist acts—mostly in Israel, but at least 435 abroad—and killed more than 650 Israelis, over three-quarters of them civilians, and hundreds of people from other countries.[3]

At the same time, though, terrorism proved a mixed blessing for the PLO, failing to destroy Israel militarily or undermine it diplomatically. Looking back on the PLO's history, a Palestinian intellectual later wrote, "Too many of us feel that we have gained representation and media visibility at an exorbitant cost. We became known as hijackers and terrorists."[4]

Nonetheless, PLO leaders usually thought terrorism to be an easy, appropriate, and successful strategy. Operations induced a sense of achievement among Palestinians and PLO activists, mobilized Palestinian and Arab support for the PLO, raised the Palestine issue's international priority, coerced Arab states or other Palestinians into rejecting negotiations with Israel, and made many European states eager to appease the PLO.

When a PLO group seized four airliners in 1970, the British magazine *The Economist* commented, "The great hijack worked. The hijackers have succeeded in making 'Palestinian' an international household word." European countries were blackmailed into releasing terrorists they held prisoner. Layla Khalid, who killed an Israeli security guard in a 1970 aerial hijacking attempt, was captured by Israel and turned over to British police, only to be released in exchange for Western passengers held hostage during other hijackings in Jordan.[5]

George Habash, the PFLP's leader, declared that Khalid's deed made the masses "proud and more determined than ever to fight," and that such action was "good for our cause." The West's criticism was unimportant since liberation would "not be won through the sympathy of world public opinion; it will be won through our own masses," their willingness to fight, "and their preparedness to offer millions of victims until victory is won."[6]

Of course, the PLO argued that it was not committing terrorism, defining any military action advancing its cause as legitimate armed struggle. For the PLO, terrorism meant "wanton acts of destruction," in Arafat's words, and not—as in the Western sense—any deliberate attack on civilians. Purpose rather than target was the key element. The PLO came to see the Western idea of terrorism as a plot to single it out for condemnation. But the fact was that most of the PLO's armed struggle was purposefully aimed and waged against civilians.[7]

On conducting the first plane hijacking in 1968, the PFLP said it acted "under exceptional circumstances and against our will." A bomb was put in the Jerusalem food market in 1969, a PLO leader claimed, because the Israelis "drop napalm bombs on civilians and torture our prisoners in the occupied territories."[8] Standard PLO rationales for terrorism were to exaggerate Israeli actions and assert that since any institution in Israel, including a kindergarten, was part of an illegitimate state's existence and defense, all were legitimate targets.[9]

The PLO also adopted terrorism, however, because that was the best it could do militarily. The organization wanted to institute a people's war, following the example of Marxist–Leninist guerrillas in China, Cuba, and Vietnam. Its plan was to begin with hit-and-run cross-border raids in rural areas, gradually building to a higher level of combat: bigger units, the transfer of bases to the enemy's territory, the seizure and holding of "liberated zones," and finally a march on the cities and the enemy regime's collapse.[10]

PLO cadres avidly read Che Guevara and Mao Zedong, but these texts did not prepare them for fighting a determined, innovative Israel army backed up by a highly effective intelligence network (which Abu Iyad, the PLO's second most important leader, once mistakenly called "a myth").[11] Similarly, Arafat said of Israel's army in 1972, "In hand-to-hand combat, face to face, they're not even soldiers. They're too afraid of dying, they show no courage."[12]

The PLO's relationship to the Palestinian people also pushed the organization toward terrorism. Historical tradition tended to glorify a heroic group of heroes rather than patient organizing for a mass uprising. The PLO's natural constituency—Palestinians in the West Bank and Gaza Strip—would cheer on the PLO's fighters but were neither ready nor able to support a protracted guerrilla war. The majority of Palestinians were passive peasants or refugees demoralized by defeat and suffering. Equally, despite their rhetoric, PLO leaders were often traditionalists and elitists who had little interest in mass organizing during the early years of Fatah or the PLO. They also feared that local leaders in the West Bank or Gaza who emerged in such a process might try to take over the movement and perhaps even compromise with Israel or Jordan.

Arafat's 1967 visit to the West Bank had confirmed the difficulty of building a revolutionary underground. He admitted that Palestine's lack of remote jungles as in Vietnam made guerrilla warfare difficult, but argued that the PLO had two ways to win its struggle. The first was for the Arab states' armies to attack Israel. "We are not alone in the field," said Arafat in 1968. "We are an extension of the hundred million Arabs."[13]

Yet despite their hot threats, Arab states always put their own interests first, as they had done in trying to manipulate the PLO in its early years, and would not risk too much for the Palestinians. Although supposedly united against Israel, Arab states were often more interested in competing among themselves, given their conflicting interests and the desire of several rulers to lead the Arabs or dominate the region. Arab rulers had also learned from their defeat in the 1967 war how difficult and risky it was to go to war on Israel.

The PLO's other prospect was to wage war against Israel's civilian sector, to bring about the collapse from within of a country they appraised as a fragile, artificial entity. The revolutionary struggles on which the PLO modeled itself had aimed to overturn unpopular regimes by winning over the people. The PLO's target in Israel, however, was not merely a government but the people themselves. Thus, since the PLO was at war with a society—not an army or simply the post-1967 occupation—every aspect and member of Israeli society was a legitimate target. The PLO's aim "is not to impose our will on the enemy," explained the PLO's magazine *Filastin al-Thawra* in 1968, "but to destroy him in order to take his place . . . not to subjugate the enemy but to destroy him."[14]

Since all Israeli Jews were, by definition, settlers illegally occupying Palestine, the PLO deemed them to be appropriate targets. "There are [no] Israeli civilians," said a PLO official, "women and men, all are ready at any moment to use arms against us."[15] This view reflected the PLO's hatred and demonization of Israelis, but it was also a rational analysis. The PLO thought this formula had worked against the French colonists in Algeria and was necessary since Israel's destruction entailed its people's destruction, demoralization, or departure.[16]

Arafat was certain of Israel's inevitable breakdown. The Crusaders were victorious in the twelfth century and the Mongols in the thirteenth century, he recalled, until the Arabs defeated them at the battles of Hittin and Ayn Jallut, near "where we are today fighting the Zionists . . . The Zionists will be defeated in the same valley, in the same land." Two of the PLO's brigades were named after these great Arab triumphs.[17]

"The Israelis have one great fear, the fear of casualties," said Arafat, and this principle guided PLO thinking. He intended "to exploit the contradictions within Israeli society."[18] Killing enough Israelis by terrorism or war would force the country's collapse or surrender. A PLO official in 1970 said that the Jews could not long live under so much tension and threat; "Zionist efforts to transform them into a homogeneous, cohesive nation have failed," and so they would leave. "Any objective study of the enemy will reveal that his potential for endurance, except where a brief engagement is concerned, is limited," the 1968 Palestine National Council meeting concluded. Wearing down Israel "will inevitably provide the opportunity for a decisive confrontation in which the entire Arab nation can take part and emerge victorious."[19]

While eager to avoid the appearance of being antisemitic, PLO leaders often updated such historic prejudices by simply substituting the word "Zionist" for "Jewish." The PLO Charter suggested that Zionism was an international conspiracy against the world's peace and welfare. Abu Iyad commented in 1969, "The Zionists have put into effect their racial colonial plan under the slogan that God's Chosen People must dominate the earth." He even claimed that the Zionists had rewritten theology, "distorting and faking religious books to lead the Jews in all parts of the world into believing that their place is in the land of Palestine." A PLO official told a 1970 Christian meeting, "Talking of Zionist world domination, Gentlemen, we believe that Zionism has succeeded not only in infiltrating into all the institutions of society in the West, but also in penetrating the Christian Church and subjecting it, in many fields, to its wishes and whims."[20]

Arafat's mind was filled with similar conspiracy theories. He was convinced that Israel was a U.S. or Western "military base," not a real country. Israel, he once said, was the creation of a secret 1907 conference of Western leaders who decided to establish "a hostile, alien nation" to ensure the Middle East remained "disunited and backward." In 1968 he called Zionism "an embodiment of neo-Nazism . . . intellectual terrorism and racial exploitation" from which the PLO would liberate the Jews.[21]

Given this analysis, the strategy of terrorism was quite logical. The aim of the PLO's attacks, Arafat said in 1968, was to "prevent immigration and encourage emigration . . . To destroy tourism. To prevent immigrants becoming attached to the land. To weaken the Israeli economy and to divert the greater part of it to security requirements. To create and maintain an atmosphere of strain and anxiety that will force the Zionists to realize that it is impossible for them to live in Israel." By achieving these objectives, the PLO would "inevitably" prevent Israel's consolidation and bring about its disintegration and dissolution, paving "the way for a quick blow by the regular armies at the right moment."[22]

Even when the PLO lost faith in Arab armies, it still thought anticivilian terrorism alone could, as a PLO magazine wrote in 1970, make each Israeli feel "isolated and defenseless against the Arab soldier in his house, on his land, on the road, in the cafe, in the movie theater, in army camps and everywhere." Each Israeli would then be bound to value more highly "the life of stability and repose that he enjoyed in his former country" compared with "the life of confusion and anxiety he finds in the land of Palestine. This is bound to motivate him towards reverse immigration."[23]

Terrorism was not only a strategy to achieve victory, though; it was also intended as revenge for Palestinian suffering. Habash explained in a 1970 speech to Westerners taken hostage in hijackings: "For 23 years we lived in misery and suffering in camps outside our country, driven like sheep, neglected, and waiting for our rights to be restored. And nothing happened." Consequently, he continued, "We felt that we had the right to defend ourselves, bearing in mind our sufferings and our people . . . Our law is our revolution. It is our duty to defend it because it is a righteous cause and because we shall be victorious."[24]

In fact, it was not so clear that the PLO would be victorious through terrorism. Rather than weakening Israel from within, terrorism was beginning to shape the PLO from within by the late

1960s. One of the main problems was the proliferation of small groups—in 1969 there were fourteen of them—that did not accept Arafat's authority. Terrorism could easily be implemented and bring publicity and popular support for such factions. Each could also counter Fatah's Egyptian sponsorship and escape the larger group's control by obtaining Syrian, Iraqi, or Libyan backing.

Yet conflicts among PLO factions were not merely the product of manipulations by Arab states. The smaller contingents also had their own ideas on strategy. In contrast with Arafat's Fatah group, they demanded the PLO work to overthrow moderate Arab governments as the necessary precondition for the liberation of Palestine. These groups' leaders also considered themselves more qualified than Arafat to rule the PLO. Three of these men—Ahmad Jibril, George Habash, and Naif Hawatmah—would become particularly important, posing the main alternatives to Arafat's policies and often making him bend to their wishes to keep them in the PLO. They served as constant reminders that Arafat might lead but he did not control Palestinian politics.

Jibril had more impressive military credentials than Arafat. Born in a village near Jaffa in 1936, he went to Syria as a refugee twelve years later, graduated from its military academy to become an engineering officer, but was soon dismissed for his radical activities. After his Ba'th party allies seized control of Syria in 1963, he founded his own group and was ever after aligned with that country.

Habash and Hawatmah, both highly educated Christian Arabs, approached revolutionary politics from a different path than Arafat or Jibril. As with so many other Third World youths displaced from traditional society, a Western education guided Habash and Hawatmah not into a belief in Western democracy but into a yearning for the new dogmas of a Marxism adapted to their taste. They also grasped Pan-Arabism as a substitute for a Christian Arab community whose faith they no longer believed and whose dimensions were too narrow for their ambitions.

Hawatmah and Habash found their way to the Pan-Arab Arab National Movement and finally into a December 1967 merger with Jibril's faction to form the PFLP. The PFLP melded Pan-Arabism and Marxism but, after a complex series of debates, the non-Marxist Jibril left to form the Popular Front for the Liberation of Palestine-General Command (PFLP-GC) in 1968.[25]

The PFLP, too Marxist for Jibril, was not Marxist enough for Hawatmah. In 1969 he formed the Democratic Front for the Liberation of Palestine (DFLP). Hawatmah was not even a Palestinian but a Jordanian from east of the river, a background which inclined him to broaden the movement toward a Pan-Arab perspective. He was born in 1931, joined the Arab National Movement in 1954, and was exiled from Jordan three years later. He lived and was arrested in Iraq, then went to Beirut in 1963. The DFLP was funded by Iraq and Libya but kept its money in Kuwaiti banks. Close to the Soviets, Hawatmah undertook diplomatic missions at Moscow's request in Africa. He helped Gulf revolutionaries, Arab Communist parties, and Marxist South Yemen.

Habash, born in 1926, became a young refugee during the 1948 war and never forgot the trauma of fleeing his home in Lydda. He was a founder of the Arab National Movement. Jailed by Syria in 1968, he escaped when his supporters stormed the jeep carrying him to court. At various times the PFLP enjoyed Iraqi, Syrian, and Libyan patronage. It was particularly active in building terrorist cells in Europe and cooperated with foreign terrorists like the Venezuelan-born Ilich Ramirez Sanchez, better known as "Carlos."[26]

The PFLP preached a revolution to "rechannel history into its proper course," a course disrupted by Israel's creation and Arab disunity. A worldwide anti-imperialist movement—spearheaded by Algeria, Cuba, and Vietnam, aided by the USSR and China—would triumph over U.S. imperialism, the Third World's "number-one enemy." Palestinian resistance was an "alarm bell" to awaken and mobilize the Arab nation. And each terrorist act was a loud peal calling the people to arms.[27]

This trio—the pro-Syrian PFLP-GC, the Pan-Arab PFLP, and the Marxist DFLP—and their leaders remained Arafat's and Fatah's main rivals. Over the next twenty years they would alternately restrain or fight Arafat, marching in and out of the Fatah-dominated PLO and astonishing the world with acts of terrorism. Each of them proclaimed himself to be the most militant, anti-American fighter and opponent of compromise. Over the years, their fortunes rose and fell and passed through endless rivalries and alliances with Arafat, Arab states, and one another.

Fatah and other Palestinian groups inside and outside the PLO also competed in staging spectacular actions to gain recruits and prestige. The smaller the faction, the more it needed to use terror-ism to seize headlines in a grab for a share of power and glory. Because terrorism is best conducted by small, compartmented net-works, reliance on it increased the PLO's already excessive frag-mentation, preventing the imposition of discipline. Having con-ceded the propriety of terrorist armed struggle, Arafat and his colleagues could neither denounce it nor punish those seen as champions by the general Arab public.

While Fatah itself usually—though not always—preferred to concentrate its military efforts against Israel directly, the PFLP and several smaller groups were equally interested in attacking those whom they saw as Western imperialists who supported Israel or Arab reactionaries who interfered with the Palestinian struggle. The professed goal of regionwide and even worldwide revolution broadened their range of targets. "Our enemy is not Israel alone," Habash explained, but also "imperialism and the forces of reaction. It is thus natural that our military strategy should conform to our political definition of the enemy."[28]

Bad publicity in the West resulting from terrorist activities could be blamed on a failure to understand the justice of their cause. Ha-bash suggested that this predicament could be minimized by plan-ning operations to avoid "third parties being harmed" and ensure that the damage done "is restricted to the enemy and his interests." The propaganda used must "make it absolutely clear that right is entirely on our side in every operation we carry out." Hawatmah would call a 1978 bus hijacking in which thirty-four Israeli civilians were killed "a heroic operation stemming from the right of our people and our revolution to employ all forms of struggle."[29]

Arafat was frustrated by the fact that his domination over the PLO did not extend to these groups. He tried but failed to establish a Permanent Office for Commando Action in 1968 and a Unified Command of Palestine Resistance in 1970. But all PLO member groups retained operational and ideological autonomy, free to ally with whatever Arab states they chose. They sometimes even made conflicting claims for credit on individual terrorist acts.[30]

PFLP ideology also made Fatah nervous by inciting class struggle and revolution against conservative Arab rulers, ideas contrary to the PLO's prime directives for survival: maintaining Palestinian unity and the Arab rulers' support. While the PFLP claimed that conservative regimes only pretended to support the Palestinians, Arafat wanted to work with all the Arab governments. Defeats in the 1948 and 1967 wars, said the PFLP, proved the Arab world's whole structure had to be changed. "Petit-bourgeois" leaders like Arafat inevitably failed, said Habash, because they did not adopt Marxism, transform conventional war into peoples' guerrilla war, or overthrow the Jordanian, Lebanese, and Saudi regimes.[31]

The PFLP urged class struggle; Arafat sought to bring all Palestinians together in a broad nationalist struggle. The PFLP feared that the West Bank/Gaza elite would make peace with Israel in exchange for a Palestinian state in the territories. While young men from refugee camps were fighting Israel, it charged, "The merchants on the West Bank were seeking to link their interests anew with the enemy state." Instead of Fatah slogans like, "We are all commandos!" or "No rich and no poor so long as we remain homeless!" the PFLP insisted that workers, peasants, and refugees must be the leading forces.[32]

Abu Iyad ridiculed the PFLP and other smaller PLO member groups as demagogues and adventurers. He insisted that class conflict and Marxism were irrelevant for the Palestinians. The PLO's victory, Abu Iyad argued, would automatically bring social revolution and transform the Arab states. The struggle itself was transforming Palestinians from "poor helpless refugees" into heroic combatants. At any rate, Fatah's goal was not to overthrow Arab regimes, he said, but to stop them from dominating the Palestinian cause.[33]

Yet Arafat always found the threat from Arab states as difficult to resolve as the smaller groups' challenges. The PLO insisted Arab states stay out of its affairs while demanding the right to intervene in any Arab state when its own interests were affected. But Arafat always had to worry either about radical Arab states supporting his rivals or about moderate Arab states betraying him in seeking better relations with the United States.[34]

After the 1967 war, sporadic fighting broke out between Israel and Egypt along the ceasefire lines on the Suez Canal. This War of Attrition continued until both sides accepted a U.S.-sponsored truce in July 1970. When Fatah's radio station in Egypt dared to criticize Nasir for accepting the ceasefire, he shut it down.

Next, UN and U.S. efforts to make peace between Israel and its

Arab neighbors began in the framework of UN Resolution 242. To the PLO, these events seemed a first step toward its old fear of Arab states' recognizing Israel. A return of Jordanian or some form of Palestinian rule in the West Bank and Gaza would destroy forever its chance to regain all of Palestine. Consequently, the PLO harshly criticized Egypt and Jordan and reconfirmed its own exclusive reliance on armed struggle. "Peaceful settlements," Arafat proclaimed, "can have only one meaning—surrender." The PLO opposed any compromise; it was fighting to liberate "every inch" of Palestine.[35]

Habash agreed with Arafat, claiming that "reactionary" Arab regimes were planning to destroy the PLO as a necessary prelude to peace with Israel. He announced that the PFLP would destroy them first. The PLO turned this fear into a self-fulfilling prophecy, stumbling into confrontations with Lebanon and Jordan.[36]

In Lebanon, however, the PLO seemed to have won. After PLO clashes with the Lebanese army in April, October, and November 1969, Nasir mediated a deal which ended Lebanon's ability to control the PLO. PLO committees ruled the refugee camps; Lebanese authorities had to facilitate the PLO's armed struggle against Israel by giving it frontier crossing points and bases. The PLO's role as an autonomous power in Lebanon would be one of several factors pushing that once prosperous, peaceful country toward civil war and disintegration.

A very different pattern unfolded in Jordan, the PLO's main base of operations, where Israeli reprisals and the Palestinian entanglement in Jordanian politics brought mounting antagonism between unwilling host and ungrateful guest. There, too, the guerrillas' rowdy behavior and the Marxist groups' open call for revolution created friction. With Amman's streets full of armed, undisciplined guerrillas, Jordan's army and gentry found themselves challenged by a competing authority. They were not ready to cede to Arafat their own claim on the West Bank, Jordan's most valuable land, much less the whole country.

But in Jordan, the state and military were stronger and more united than in Lebanon. The PLO's intention to turn the Middle East into a second Vietnam threatened to embroil Jordan in war and destruction regardless of what its people or rulers wanted. Particularly dangerous was the PLO's active effort to undermine the loyalty of the Palestinian majority among Jordan's citizens. When the guerrilla groups proclaimed their belief that the Palestinians and Jordanians "are one people," they were filing a claim to rule Jordan, too. Thus, Jordan's leaders and army opposed the PLO not because of reactionary, imperialist conspiracies but from motives of patriotism and self-preservation.[37]

Clashes between Jordanian and PLO soldiers broke out frequently. In April 1970 violent demonstrations greeted the visit of U.S. Assistant Secretary of State Joseph Sisco, despite a prior PLO promise to restrain them. The king's men organized a Palestinian front group, the Victory Battalions, to put the PLO in its place. But the PFLP and DFLP were drunk on revolutionary rhetoric and miscalculated adventurism. Fearful that Jordan would betray the PLO and eager to preserve Palestinian unity, Fatah supported its colleagues. The PLO demanded the dismissal of popular Jordanian army officers who opposed it, foolishly expecting the army—made up of bedouin troops fiercely loyal to Husayn—to desert the king or the masses to rise up in support of the PLO.

At this moment, the PFLP escalated tension by the most spectacular terrorist action to date. On September 6 it simultaneously hijacked a TWA, a Pan American, and a Swissair passenger plane, landing two of them at an old airfield in Jordan and blowing up the third at Cairo airport. A fourth kidnapped British plane was added to the collection on September 9. They held the passengers hostage to demand the release of Palestinian terrorists imprisoned in Europe. The PFLP blew up the planes three days later and kept fifty-four of their passengers, including about twenty American Jews, as prisoners.

This was the last straw. The PLO had forced a confrontation it had no chance to win. On September 15 Jordan's army attacked the Palestinian forces, and full-scale fighting raged in Amman's streets for ten days. Army units surrounded the capital to block reinforcements from PLO bases in the countryside or Lebanon. Jordanian artillery and tanks blasted PLO positions in refugee camps. PLO leaders, including Abu Iyad, were captured; PLO forces were outgunned and cut off, deprived of food and supplies.

The PLO had expected its allies to save it. Indeed, on September 20 Syrian tanks crossed into Jordan. But Jordan's willingness to fight—backed up by secret U.S. and Israeli promises to intervene if necessary to save the king—stopped them in their tracks. Moreover, General Hafiz al-Asad, Syria's defense minister and air force commander, was planning to seize power in Damascus and refused to provide air support for the army. The Syrian forces backed down and withdrew; an Iraqi division stationed in Jordan stood by and did nothing.

Nasir was the PLO's last hope. On September 27 he mediated a fourteen-point agreement ending the fighting in a virtual PLO surrender to the Jordanian authorities. The Western hostages were freed in exchange for seven terrorists held in British, West German, and Swiss jails. This would be Nasir's last service to the PLO, however. He died shortly after the meeting of a heart attack, the last casualty, in a sense, of fighting that left two thousand dead, mostly Palestinians.

The Jordanian army also captured many PLO fighters, and over two hundred more preferred to cross the river and surrender to Israel rather than submit to King Husayn's enraged, vengeful troops. Jordan's army later captured the PLO bases in the north without interference or objection from the Arab world. By July 1971 PLO forces and offices had been completely expelled from the country.

As these events were still going on, Abu Iyad made a brilliant analysis of the mistakes that had produced the debacle. The profusion of small groups "practically strangled us," he complained, because the PLO was a weak confederation of sovereign entities, an orchestra in which each musician played a different tune. In Algeria, China, and Vietnam a single party or front had led the revolution. "I can assure you that we are on the way to unifying everyone," he pledged. But nothing changed in the PLO. Its Executive Committee in 1971 had members from Fatah, the Palestine Liberation Front, the pro-Iraq Arab Liberation Front, the pro-Syria al-Sa'iqa, the DFLP, the PFLP, the Palestine Salvation Front, and the Palestine Liberation Army (virtually a faction in itself).

Abu Iyad said a second major mistake was that "our slogans went beyond . . . the reach of our swords." The leftist, independent-minded Syrian intellectual Sadiq al-Azm pointed to "the oscillation between grandiose claims to achievement and abysmally low levels of performance." The masses were confused by the PLO's excessive ambition, wild claims, and ideological diversity. Was it fighting a nationalist or a class war? Was its struggle guided by Palestinian interests or by those of the whole Arab nation? One day, said Sadiq al-Azm, the PLO's leadership would denounce the king and demand his overthrow; the next, Arafat would kiss him at a banquet.

The third mistake was massive corruption and personal aggrandizement. "We came to love offices [and] ostentation," Abu Iyad noted. In Amman alone there were 250 separate offices.

Fourth, the PLO seemed unable to avoid strife with Arab states. Its need for bases free of its host's control brought it into collision with governments determined, at most, to control the organization and, at least, to rule their own territory. The PLO's effort to find local allies and popular support to constrain or counter the rulers only intensified the conflict. Fatah, Abu Iyad noted, had a "slogan of 'non-interference' in Arab politics and at the same time interfered without interfering."[38]

Yet despite their own mistakes, the PLO leaders blamed Jordan's government for the most unforgivable sin: betraying Arab solidarity and aligning with Zionism and imperialism. The PLO claimed that 20,000 Palestinians had been slain and vowed revenge on Jordan through both political action and terrorism. PLO meetings in the early 1970s called Jordan and Palestine one ethnic and geographic unit and demanded that a nationalist regime replace King Husayn. The PLO was claiming Jordan as a piece of its Palestine, while Amman claimed that part of Palestine, the West Bank, belonged to it.[38]

The behavior of the "progressive" Arab camp—Egypt, Syria, and Iraq—was almost equally unsettling. These regimes had done little or nothing while Jordan "massacred" Palestinians. Arab states spoke often of brotherhood with the Palestinians, yet had a notion of fraternity which seemed based on Cain's behavior toward Abel.

The PLO dubbed the confrontation in Amman "Black September," a setback so serious that Abu Iyad said the PLO was threatened "by total collapse."[40] Deprived of its main bases, with hundreds of its activists arrested, blocked from attacking Israel, and having suffered a great loss of prestige, Fatah turned to international terrorism to open a new front.

The era between 1971 and 1974 marked the peak of the Palestinian international terrorist campaign, including plane hijackings, letter bombs, and assassinations. Jordan was the first target for revenge. On November 28, 1971, Jordan's Prime Minister Wasfi al-Tal was returning from lunch with the Arab League's secretary-general

when a six-man Palestinian hit squad from a mysterious group
called Black September shot him down in the lobby of Cairo's high-
rise Sheraton hotel by the Nile. One of the assassins lapped his
blood. "Are you happy, Arabs?" his wife screamed as she stood over
the body. "Palestine is finished!" But the assassins were freed on
low bail and allowed to leave Egypt. Arafat claimed responsibility
for the killing. A month later, Black September wounded Jordanian
Ambassador Zayd al-Rifa'i in London. The gunman fled to France,
which released him. More attacks on Jordanian diplomats ensued,
including a plot to overthrow King Husayn in 1972 and an attempt
to assassinate him at the Rabat Arab summit in October 1974.[41]

Black September was the cover name Fatah used for its international terrorist operations under the supervision of Abu Iyad between 1971 and 1974. Financial and logistical help came from
Libya, Syria, and Algeria.[42] At the 1972 Olympics, held in Munich,
eight Black September terrorists seized the Israeli team's com-
pound, killing two athletes and taking others as hostages. The West
German authorities promised them safe passage out of the country.
But as terrorists and hostages were heading to the airport, police
snipers tried to shoot the kidnappers. The terrorists blew up their
own bus. Five terrorists and nine more Israeli athletes were killed.
In another operation, sympathizers from the terrorist Japanese Red
Army group, collaborating with the PFLP, murdered twenty-six and
wounded eighty civilians at Israel's Lod airport in May 1972.

In March 1973 Black September terrorists invaded the Saudi embassy in Khartoum, Sudan, during a party and seized diplomats as
hostages. Arafat asked the Sudanese government to attempt no rescue and to await the arrival of PLO mediators. But the kidnappers
murdered the American ambassador, charge d'affaires, and a Bel-
gian diplomat before they surrendered. Sudan blamed Fatah for the
attack, and one of the captured terrorists admitted it was a PLO
operation ordered directly from Arafat's headquarters and planned
by the director of Fatah's local office, who left on a Libyan plane a
few hours before it began. According to a secret U.S. State Department report, the terrorists were indeed under the control of PLO
headquarters in Beirut and only murdered the hostages on "receiving specific codeword instructions."[43]

These bloody terrorist acts helped the PLO join a global network
of such groups and gain Soviet bloc support. PLO soldiers were

trained in China, Vietnam, North Korea, Pakistan, and India, as well as in Arab states. At first the Soviets had attacked the PLO as "adventurist" and "ultra-revolutionary." Moscow's interests lay with the Arab states, not with small, quarreling groups that might undermine Soviet allies or ignite a new war. After Arafat's visit to Moscow in October 1971, however, relations began to improve. The PLO became a Soviet client, though never a puppet. The USSR gave the PLO arms and training in order to weaken U.S. influence and undermine Israel.[44]

Arafat met Romanian dictator Nicolae Ceausescu in October 1972 to exchange his organization's experience in conducting kidnappings and assassinations for Romanian advice on running disinformation and influence-buying operations to improve the PLO's political standing in the West. Romania also provided forged passports for PLO terrorists and trained them on its military bases. A 1979 agreement between the PLO and East Germany set terms for exchanging intelligence on the United States and Israel, with the Communist regime providing a safe haven for terrorists, training facilities, electronic equipment, and explosives.[45]

Nonetheless, for Fatah, in contrast with the smaller groups, international terrorism was largely an interim strategy to keep world attention focused on the Palestinian question while it built bases in Lebanon for launching direct attacks on Israel. Moreover, raids outside of Israel were relatively ineffective at hurting Israelis. Between 1968 and 1973, Palestinian attacks killed only thirty-two and wounded twenty-four Israelis outside the country's borders. Such assaults also won Israel international sympathy, making it harder to undermine Israel's support from the West. "Public relations . . . has not been one of our strong points—we are primarily an action organization," Arafat admitted. "However, we realize that one of the main reasons for Arab failure has been in our inability to match the Zionist propaganda machine and to explain our case to the world."[46]

In November 1973 PLO leaders held a secret meeting with deputy CIA director Vernon Walters in Morocco and promised not to attack Americans. Ali Hasan Salama, one of Black September's leaders, was the organization's liaison to the CIA. After about 1975, the PLO helped protect U.S. diplomats in Beirut.[47]

By 1974, then, Fatah deemphasized international terrorism, preferring to attack Israel directly from Lebanon. The use of Black September as a front group was discontinued, and some Fatah members walked out in protest, continuing their vocation as international terrorists independently and even attacking the PLO. One of them, Abu Nidal, formed his own group—the Fatah-Revolutionary Council—that year. The PLO ineffectively sentenced him to death for allegedly plotting to kill Arafat. He did slay a number of PLO officials in later years, plus murdering over 300 and injuring 650 people in other terrorist attacks, two-thirds of them in Western Europe.[48]

To counter the PLO's image as a terrorist group seeking the destruction of Israel and its people, the DFLP proposed a new plan, which was adopted at the Eighth Palestine National Council session in 1971. The PLO still aimed to reconquer all of Palestine and destroy Israel but now promised "to set up a free and democratic society in Palestine for all Palestinians, including Muslims, Christians and Jews." The Jews would allegedly benefit by being liberated from Zionist domination.

Arafat called this "a humanitarian plan which will allow the Jews to live in dignity, as they have always lived, under the aegis of an Arab state and within the framework of an Arab society."[49] Yet literally no Israeli Jew took seriously—after twenty years of conflict and terrorism—a paper promise of limited rights if they surrendered. The Arab record on democracy was not encouraging, and many Israelis from Arab countries did not have such happy memories of their lives there. As if this were not enough, PLO leaders made it clear that Jews would never be allowed to outvote the Arabs. In short, it was not surprising that Israelis did not respond to this tremendously transparent ploy or to Hawatmah's call to join in the armed struggle.[50]

For its part, the PLO still rejected a Palestinian state on the West Bank and Gaza Strip as a solution because it knew that Israel would stop that territory from being used as a base for further attacks. Thus, such a deal was said to constitute a sell-out, an acceptance of Israel's continued existence. The PLO was still struggling to reverse the events of 1948, not the 1967 defeat. "We are certainly not opposed to total Israeli withdrawal from the occupied territories," explained a 1971 PLO statement, as long as this did not preclude "the Palestinian right to struggle for the full liberation of Palestinian soil . . . since our struggle did not begin in 1967 but in 1965."[51]

Arafat swore never to commit the crime of permitting Israel's existence: "Shall we pass on this blemish to our children?" Abu Iyad explained that even if his own generation could not win, it had "no right to abandon the cause" or negotiate a settlement binding future generations. The highest duty was to preserve the option to regain all Palestine "even if they cannot liberate a single inch." Otherwise, the Arabs would permanently lose Palestine as they had lost Spain in the fifteenth century.[52]

Certainly, Arafat agreed with Habash's 1969 statement that giving up the claim to all Palestine "means, as far as I am concerned, that I shall never again see Lydda, my home town. Every Palestinian feels this way."[53] In a 1972 interview, Arafat proclaimed, "The end of Israel is the goal of our struggle, and it allows for neither compromise nor mediation . . . We don't want peace. We want war, victory. Peace for us means the destruction of Israel and nothing else."[54] Thus, the PLO refused to offer Israel peace or recognition, not from fanaticism or foolish stubbornness but because its objective remained the conquest of every inch of Palestine and its conversion into a Palestinian Arab state.

Terrorism had gained the PLO prestige with its Arab audience, discouraged any resolution of the Arab–Israeli conflict, and rebuilt the organization after its defeat in Jordan. The more audacious and horrifying an act was to the West, the more it impressed Arab people and countries, since each one seemed to demonstrate that Israel was being fought and defeated, revenge was being taken, and Palestinian action outshone Arab leaders' speeches. Similarly, the PLO's military defeats and bad image in the West did not weaken its growing entrenchment in Lebanon. This onslaught did not bring Israel's destruction nearer, but it was a substitute for progress, an emotionally satisfying spectator event for Arabs and Palestinians.[55]

Nonetheless, the PLO's underestimation of Israel had serious long-term costs. Refusing to believe Israel had any reason for existing, the PLO could not understand the commitment of that country's people. Abu Iyad insisted that "the colonialist Zionist military institution would collapse," claiming that three hundred Israeli soldiers refused to fight at the battle of Karama. Israel was not a real country, having failed to fuse the immigrants into a nation. All its citizens had in common was a feeling of persecution. "Such a conglomeration," Abu Iyad concluded, "cannot be a viable human society." This set of beliefs encouraged the feeling that terrorism—strik-

ing directly at demoralized people already on the edge of panic—
would trigger disintegration.[56]

Without realizing it, Abu Iyad had explained this theory's fallacy
back in 1969. If the PLO, he suggested, could only convince Israeli
soldiers "that in reality we are not, as the Zionists would have him
believe, barbarians who want to kill him and throw his women
and children into the sea," the PLO might turn Israeli Jews against
Zionism. Yet he himself said the solution was for the Jews to return
to the countries from which they or their ancestors had emigrated,
and PLO actions seemed to show precisely that murder or expulsion
were the options it offered.[57]

Both the PLO's belief in terrorism's efficacy and in Israel's disap-
pearance proved durable. The size of Palestinian losses, said Arafat
in 1968, "will be nothing compared with the great goal."[58] Without
the goal of total victory, the PLO might have been unable to mobilize its supporters, maintain its unity, and survive the Arab states'
efforts to subordinate it. Yet by setting an unreachable goal, it also
created a situation in which victory was impossible, unsuccessful
struggle endless, and Palestinian suffering extensive. These contradictions would only even begin to become clear to PLO leaders,
however, under the burden of many more years of exertion and
defeat.

3 >> A Bastion in Beirut, 1973–1983

After being expelled from Jordan in 1971, the PLO moved its political and military headquarters to Lebanon. For the next decade, Lebanon's weakness allowed the PLO a greater degree of independence and influence than it knew before or afterward. During this era the PLO gained leadership over the Palestinians, an alliance with Moscow, and considerable sympathy in the West. The Lebanese, however, fared worse from the PLO presence, which contributed to their devastating civil war and foreign interventions. Conflicts among Lebanese, among Palestinians, and between Lebanese and Palestinians built the critical mass for an explosion.

Lebanon was once the happiest of Arab countries; its capital, Beirut, was known as the Paris of the Middle East for its high cultural level. The basis of Lebanon's stability was a political compact apportioning power proportionately among Maronite Christians, Sunni and Shi'a Muslims, and Druze through the elite families that led them. A Maronite president shared power with a Sunni prime minister. Parliamentary seats were divided along communal lines, as were civil service and army posts. A Lebanese joke described an army unit that stopped fighting in the 1948 war after a Druze soldier was wounded, awaiting equivalent Maronite, Sunni, and Shi'a casualties before resuming battle.[1]

So pleasant was the country and seemingly successful its brand of intercommunal balance that Arafat called Lebanon his model for a future Palestine where Arabs and Jews would live together in peace. From the late 1960s on, the PLO built there an infrastructure approximating that of a state. Lebanon's government surrendered control over large parts of the country in 1968 and 1973 after armed clashes with the PLO. PLO offices proliferated in Beirut, and its control over Lebanon's poor, remote southeast was so complete that Israel called the area "Fatahland."[2]

PLO groups ruled the refugee camps, with about 150,000 Palestinian inhabitants, running everything from trade unions to garbage collection, cultural centers and youth groups. Fatah set up a network of economic enterprises employing as workers about 3,000 people in the camps. It also established hospitals, orphanages, schools, a police and judicial system, and a relief fund for "martyrs'" families. The Palestinian groups recruited fighters, organized supporters, and set up military bases in the camps. Young men with few other prospects for employment swelled the armed groups' ranks. Fatah, for example, built regular units—the Qastel, Karama, and Yarmuk brigades, with 1,500 men each—plus about 1,000 commandos for guerrilla or terrorist operations, and perhaps 10,000 more armed militiamen among the refugees.

Lebanon's government was unable to regulate the PLO because it enjoyed Egyptian and Syrian support, prestige for its battles against Israel, and reinforcement by thousands of its men expelled by Jordan. Despite Arafat's caution, however, the smaller PLO groups wanted to intervene in local politics. To some extent, the PLO's own needs and local conditions made this outcome unavoidable. Fatah now faced the same dilemma as in Jordan.

By the 1970s Lebanon's delicate balance was also subverted among its own citizens. The Muslim population outgrew the Christians, and the Shi'a became the largest single group. New ideas also challenged the status quo: Radicals urged social revolution against the class structure and communal bosses; each community demanded a bigger share of power; ideologues advocated Lebanese Christian nationalist, Arab nationalist, Marxist, or Islamic doctrines.[3]

In this context, the Palestinians' numbers and political interests added to the destabilization. The smaller PLO member groups outside of Arafat's control supported Lebanese radicals whom they saw as fellow revolutionaries, while clashing with one another, with Fatah, and with Lebanese militias. In April 1972 Arafat made his most serious, but still futile, effort to coordinate operations under a

Higher Military Council. Even in Fatah, however, many activists opposed centralization. Blood was periodically spilled in internal clashes.

In addition to problems created by this partisanship and factionalism, the PLO international terrorist and cross-border attacks were dragging Lebanon into a conflict with Israel which few Lebanese wanted. In December 1968 Israeli forces raided Beirut airport, to retaliate for PLO attacks on its airliners, and destroyed thirteen planes. Israeli forces also staged air and ground raids on the south and, in a daring April 1973 operation, assassinated three key Fatah terrorist leaders in Beirut. Tens of thousands of Shi'a Muslim residents fled northward to avoid fighting in the south, further upsetting the communal balance and bringing new recruits to the growing Shi'a militias.

The PLO's urgent need to escalate operations from Lebanon was also influenced by events which further thwarted any hope that Arab states might reconquer Palestine for the PLO, while raising fears that they might bargain with Israel without it. In 1972 King Husayn, the PLO's main rival, proposed a plan to regain the West Bank from Israel and return it—albeit with some Palestinian autonomy—to his own rule. The PLO feared that the king, who was still popular among West Bank Palestinian politicians, would succeed.

Even the occurrence of an Arab war with Israel, which the PLO had wanted, seemed to threaten its interests. In October 1973 Egypt and Syria launched a surprise attack, stunning Israel and challenging its assumed military superiority. Israeli forces counterattacked and forced the Arab armies back to the prewar lines and even further back by the time a ceasefire ended the fighting after three weeks. Still, many Arabs thought the war regained honor lost in their 1967 military defeat. This new battle was the very crisis the PLO had been trying to provoke, yet the organization played no role in it. When Egypt and Syria made disengagement agreements with Israel in early 1974, they neither consulted the PLO nor showed any concern for its interests.

As always, Arafat put the best face on the situation. The 1973 war, he proclaimed, "has given us part of Palestine, and the fifth war will give us Tel Aviv."[4] Nonetheless, the behavior of Jordan, Egypt, and Syria made the PLO see a potential new conspiracy. Perhaps Israel might return the occupied West Bank to Jordan's rule;

Egypt and Syria might abandon the struggle to destroy Israel in exchange for their territory captured by Israel in 1967. In that case, Jordan would regain the West Bank; Egypt, the Sinai peninsula; Syria, the Golan Heights; the PLO, nothing.

To avert this alleged danger, the PLO developed a new strategy to gain a veto over any peace settlement and avert an Israel–Jordan agreement. The program produced by the 1974 PNC session became, next to its Charter, the basic policy guideline. It outlined a two-stage process: first, creation of a Palestinian authority on the West Bank and Gaza Strip, then using that entity as a liberated zone for liquidating Israel.[5]

In Arafat's words, "Any decision taken now must take into account how the revolution is to continue and how the rest of Palestine is to be liberated." The PLO's theoretician, Khalid al-Hasan, posed the main question as, "How will the revolutionary Palestinian and Arab struggle to eliminate the Zionist entity and to establish the Palestinian democratic state continue?"[6]

The resolution answered this question by ordering an armed struggle, supplemented by diplomatic efforts, "to liberate Palestinian land and to establish the people's national, independent and fighting authority on every part of Palestinian land to be liberated." The PLO's plan was to keep any part of Palestine from Jordan's hands and gain an operational base outside of any Arab regime's control.

In no way was this resolution intended to propose peace with Israel, since the main task of the proposed "independent and fighting authority" would be to continue battling for full victory until all Israel was conquered and supplanted by Palestine. But the resolution stipulated that the PLO would reject even an Israeli offer of the West Bank and Gaza Strip if the price was acceptance of "recognition, conciliation, secure borders" for Israel or a renunciation of the PLO's claim to all Palestine and the return of all Palestinian refugees to Israel with a right to dissolve the Jewish state.[7]

Lest any of this language be misunderstood by Palestinians or Arabs, the resolution flatly proclaimed that obtaining the West Bank and Gaza Strip would merely be a way-station in "the PLO strategy for the establishment of the Palestinian democratic state." The first duty of any Palestinian authority would be to ensure the unity of Arab states fighting Israel to complete "the liberation of all Palestinian soil."[8]

Arafat also insisted that the PLO, not Jordan, would represent the Palestinians if U.S.-proposed talks took place in Geneva. But the idea of accepting any cooperation with the United States was so repugnant to the PLO's two Marxist member groups—the PFLP and DFLP—that they walked out of the organization. Three years later, however, they approved a 1977 PNC resolution virtually identical to the 1974 version. While the PLO publicized this program in the West as proof of its moderation, Abu Iyad minced no words about its intention: "An independent state on the West Bank and Gaza is the beginning of the final solution. That solution is to establish a democratic state in the whole of Palestine."[9]

While making only minor, tactical adjustments in its program, the PLO took some big steps forward in its status in the Arab world and internationally. The October 1974 Arab summit recognized the PLO, over Jordan's objection, as the Palestinians' "sole, legitimate representative." This phrase would appear in almost every subsequent PLO document, claimed as a license to lead the Palestinian people and to make all political decisions on their behalf.[10]

Yet this resolution was also a mixed blessing. By ceding the PLO a right to represent the Palestinians, the Arab states were also divesting themselves of responsibility for that struggle. In retrospect, this stand signaled not so much an intensified commitment to the PLO as the Arab regimes' withdrawal from the battle, at least from the standpoint of Palestinian interests.

Nonetheless, the PLO's efforts were also soon rewarded with its greatest diplomatic triumph to date. On November 13, 1974, Arafat addressed the UN General Assembly, speaking about his dream of a united Arab Palestine.[11] Shortly thereafter, the PLO became an official observer at the UN. A year later, the UN General Assembly passed a resolution equating Zionism with racism, one of the goals set by the PLO Charter.

Other diplomatic successes were achieved with help from the Soviet bloc and the influence of Arab oil money. The PLO gained full membership in the Nonalignment Movement in August 1975 and in September 1976 became a full member of the Arab League. Many Third World countries, often having no diplomatic relations with Israel, recognized the PLO. In 1985 Spain was the first West European state to grant it full diplomatic status.

Arafat had ended his UN speech by saying that he had come "bearing an olive branch and a freedom-fighter's gun. Do not let

the olive branch fall from my hand." Still, the PLO's military operations were meant to undermine a Middle East process which both
ignored the PLO itself and undermined its goals. The overwhelming
majority of these operations were stopped by the Israeli army, but
the methods and intentions were shown by several major successes.

On May 15, 1974, three DFLP terrorists crossed into Israel and
fired on a van bringing Arab women home from work, killing two
and injuring one. They then entered the town of Ma'alot and killed
three people in their home. Neighbors sounded the alarm, but before troops could arrive the terrorists moved to the school, where
they shot the janitor and herded over ninety schoolchildren from
the dormitories, kicking and clubbing them. Twenty escaped
through a window. The kidnappers sent out a teacher with a message demanding that twenty-three Arab prisoners be released
within a few hours and allowed to go to Syria. When the terrorists
refused to extend their deadline, Israeli troops stormed the building. One terrorist was shot as he ran to detonate explosives, the
two others fired at the children before being shot down. Twenty-
one children were killed and sixty-five injured.

A similar drama unfolded in Israel's northern city of Kiryat
Shemona in November 1974—about the same time Arafat was
speaking to the UN—when three PFLP terrorists killed eighteen
people, mostly women and children; a bomb went off in Jerusalem's Ben Yehuda street at lunchtime, wounding thirteen; and
three DFLP terrorists killed four Israelis in Beit-Shean. The next
month, two Israelis were killed and fifty injured by a hand grenade
thrown outside a Tel Aviv movie theater, an act the PLO said was
in retaliation for an Israeli air force attack on a PLO office. In March
1975 terrorists in two dinghies landed near Tel Aviv, shot at a crowd
leaving a theater, and seized ten hostages in the Savoy Hotel. Israeli
forces stormed the building. Eleven Israelis and most of the terrorists were killed.

Even the first anniversary of Arafat's UN speech, coinciding with
the passage of the resolution equating Zionism with racism, was
commemorated with the explosion of a 23-pound bomb in front of
a coffee house in downtown Jerusalem, killing seven and
wounding forty people. This terrorist act by Fatah was a curious
but appropriate symbol of PLO strategy: a massacre to celebrate a
diplomatic victory. Between 1971 and 1982 Palestinian attacks
within Israel killed 250 civilians and wounded 1,628.[12]

The PLO's heightened activity in Lebanon also increased tensions there. In April 1975 Lebanon burst into flames after a series of escalating clashes. Three bodyguards of Pierre Jumayyil, leader of the largest Christian party, were killed at a church gathering. Blaming the PLO and its Lebanese allies, Jumayyil's supporters retaliated by attacking a bus carrying Palestinians and Muslim Lebanese to a rally celebrating the first anniversary of the terrorist attack on Kiryat Shemona.

Fighting escalated steadily; each round of killing provided new causes for revenge. Soon Lebanon, with one-third New York City's population, had over seventy private armies. There were too many sides in the civil war for anyone to win. Hundreds of thousands of Lebanese became refugees; tens of thousands left the country; thousands were killed or wounded. Cities became battlefields, and the once-strong economy was in ruins.

The PLO was by no means wholly responsible for this breakdown. Arafat, in contrast with the PFLP and DFLP, did not want to intervene in Lebanon's internal politics. But the PLO had played some role in provoking civil war by weakening the central government's authority, escalating armed conflict, arming Lebanese revolutionaries, and provoking the Christians. The PLO's virtual rule in the south incited Israeli counterattacks and outraged Shi'a Muslims who lived there. If the PLO had helped the south Lebanese villagers, charged a Palestinian intellectual, they would have fought alongside the PLO. "Since such was not the case, they turned against those who had brought these reprisals upon them."[13]

Even the leader of the PLO's allies, Kamal Joumblatt, admitted the Palestinians "exposed themselves to criticism and even hatred . . . I never saw a less discreet, less cautious revolution." The PLO groups detained Lebanese citizens and officials, allowed corruption and undisciplined behavior by their forces, mistreated Lebanese people, and broke repeated promises to remove offices and military units from residential neighborhoods.[14]

Both sides in the civil war committed massacres and mistreated civilians. In January 1976 Christian forces besieged the Palestinian refugee camp at Tel al-Za'tar and, in response, a Muslim-leftist force including some PLO member groups attacked the largely Christian town of Damur. Damur fell within three weeks and was looted. The Christians, supported by the Syrian army, continued the encirclement of Tel al-Za'tar. Arafat's appeal for help to Egypt, Jordan, and the UN brought no response, and Tel al-Za'tar fell in August. An estimated 4,000 Palestinians had been killed in the battles.

At first, the PLO's Lebanese allies had the upper hand in the war with Lebanese Christian forces. But just as they seemed about to triumph, an unexpected savior rescued the Christians. Worried that a leftist-PLO takeover would block him from dominating Lebanon, Syrian President Asad sent in pro-Syrian units of the Palestinian Liberation Army and his own troops. The PLO, he proclaimed, "does not have any right to interfere in the internal affairs of the host country." Syria accepted no such limits for itself. By the end of 1976, it occupied two thirds of Lebanon and put severe restrictions on the PLO's presence there.[15]

Syria had always wanted to control the PLO, and Asad hoped to replace Arafat with a pro-Syrian leadership. While demanding that Jordan and Lebanon give the PLO a free hand on their territory, Asad kept it under tight control in his own country, where Palestinians could not wear uniforms, carry guns, or hold rallies without government permission.[16]

But PLO officials and supporters, shocked that fellow Palestinians would kill their own people at Syria's command, had already rejected this takeover bid. Al-Sa'iqa, Syria's main puppet group in the PLO and the organization's second-largest faction, had lost most of its supporters; Palestine Liberation Army officers who fought on Syria's side against the PLO had been expelled from the organization. Although badly shaken, the PLO nonetheless survived and kept its foothold in parts of Lebanon not occupied by Syria, particularly in the far south.[17]

The PLO's 1976 military defeat at Syria's hands was quickly followed by an equally dangerous challenge from Egypt, the other leading Arab state. Weary of war and facing mounting economic difficulties, Egypt's President Anwar al-Sadat was seeking a way out of the Arab–Israeli deadlock. In 1976 he revived King Husayn's idea for a Jordan–Palestinian federation. Along with the new U.S. president, Jimmy Carter, Sadat secretly urged the PLO to accept UN Resolution 242 if it was altered to refer to Palestinian rights. Egypt and Saudi Arabia covertly transmitted messages between Arafat and Washington. The PLO refused this proposal, however, since the UN resolution also recognized Israel's existence.

Sadat did not give up easily. In November 1977 he made a speech to Egypt's parliament that changed the course of Middle East history. As Arafat looked on in shock, Sadat offered to go to Israel and make peace. An Arab leader had again made a major decision on the Arab–Israeli conflict without consulting the PLO. Arafat's reacted angrily to Sadat's announcement: "Our strategic line has been and remains the total liberation of our national Palestinian soil. Palestine will remain Arab, Arab, Arab no matter how long it takes and how grievous the sacrifices may be." Every Arab state should be made into "a Hanoi for the Palestine revolution."[18]

Sadat visited Jerusalem, prayed at the al-Aqsa mosque there, and spoke to Israel's parliament. Egypt and Israel signed the U.S.-mediated Camp David peace accords in September 1978, followed by a peace treaty in March and the normalization of relations in August 1979. The PLO fought back, working with Syria and Iraq to expel Cairo from Arab counsels and totally rejecting the Camp David treaties. Speaking in the captured town of Damur, Lebanon, Arafat threatened that Carter's signature on the treaties "will cost him his interests in the Arab region."[19]

Although the PLO's diplomatic contacts with West European and Third World countries were steadily increasing in the mid-1970s, the PLO's terrorism and ideology prevented it from making headway with the U.S. government. U.S. policy, first formulated by Secretary of State Henry Kissinger in 1975, was to refuse to deal with the PLO until it accepted UN Resolution 242, abandoned terrorism, and recognized Israel's right to exist. These conditions were designed to provide proof that the PLO had genuinely changed its position so as to make possible successful talks and a stable settlement. There were some secret contacts between U.S. embassy officials and the PLO in Lebanon for security purposes and indirect exchanges in which Washington tried to persuade the PLO to meet the conditions. The U.S. Ambassador to the UN, Andrew Young, had to resign in 1979 after he saw his PLO counterpart in a brief, unauthorized meeting.

The PLO, however, had not met these criteria. Israel refused to negotiate with the organization, and Jordan saw it as a prime threat. Consequently, the Camp David accords were designed to bypass the PLO. It was not surprising that the PLO saw the accords as a plot to exclude it and to eliminate the Palestine issue. But the agreements also provided an opportunity the PLO could have exploited, by providing for Palestinian autonomy in the occupied territories to be followed by negotiations over their future. The PLO could have used this provision to organize Palestinians in the West Bank and Gaza, take control of the proposed local self-government bodies, and then be well-positioned to demand self-determination at the end of the transition period.[20]

This was not, however, the PLO's political style. By nature, Arafat was cautious, and he lacked the power or will to make or accept any major diplomatic initiative. "I am not independent," he commented in 1977, "and I cannot make contacts without referring to our brothers in the Arab area."[21]

Even at his most militant, however, Arafat could neither depend on radical Arab states nor resolve internal factionalism. The PLO's rapprochement with Syria in the anti-Sadat coalition made Iraq jealous. Baghdad hired the anti-Arafat Palestinian terrorist Abu Nidal to assassinate PLO men in the late 1970s. Fatah responded by shooting Iraqi officials in Britain, France, Pakistan, and Lebanon. In 1978, frustrated at a long series of setbacks, Fatah radicals in Lebanon also challenged Arafat's authority. Abu Jihad defeated the rebellion, but it was one more warning of the limits on Arafat's ability to centralize power.

The PLO did, however, receive enough financial backing to carry on its battle. Money came from a wide variety of sources, including taxes paid by Palestinians working in the Gulf. In exchange for the PLO's promise to keep things quiet there, the United Arab Emirates sent protection money. Saudi Arabia contributed $40 million a year. Some minor sources of funding were more unusual: Palestinian students in the United States apparently donated $5 million made from fraudulent insurance claims in the 1970s, and elements in the PLO may have been involved in drug smuggling from Lebanon through Bulgaria.[22]

Arms were also available, mostly from the USSR, Eastern Europe, China, and North Korea, sent through Arab countries. Libyan ships delivered munitions through the Lebanese port of Tyre, and Qadhafi also provided a radio station, vehicles, and guns. Iraq and Saudi Arabia gave arms, the latter perhaps illegally including M-16 automatic weapons sold to it by the United States. Czechoslovakia gave explosives; Polish experts helped build factories to manufacture antitank guns and shells at Palestinian refugee camps. Fatah officers were sent to the Soviet Union for training.[23]

Given its stable—if not improving—condition as the 1980s began, the PLO still refused to consider recognizing Israel or accepting a compromise. To do so, Khalid al-Hasan warned, would be to surrender any hope of regaining all Palestine and the PLO's claim to represent all Palestinians—including those living as citizens in Israel. A PLO Executive Committee member might admit, but only privately, that terrorism was counterproductive, taking energy away from organizing in the West Bank. A few intellectuals and PLO diplomats—like Ibrahim al-Sus, director of the Paris office—began asking whether a more moderate policy would be better, but they backed down when militant critics accused them of treason. The PLO's main asset was support from the Palestinians, and the vast majority of its constituents endorsed a tough line.[24]

To many Western observers, however, this PLO intransigence seemed irrational. Since they could not understand why the PLO acted as it did, the most minimal gesture by a PLO leader was often enough to persuade the Western media that the organization's policy was softening. For example, *Time* magazine commented in 1981 that the PFLP had "taken a step towards a more moderate strategy" by accepting a West Bank/Gaza state "at least as a first step" toward fulfilling Palestinian demands. Western visitors, hearing Arafat make private professions of moderation, excitedly spread news of "breakthroughs" on returning home, only to hear the PLO publicly deny them the next day.[25]

Instead, Arafat tirelessly repeated futile calls for rebellion, anti-American action, and total victory. "How long," Arafat asked, would the Israelis "stay in our country? Seventy years? Already thirty have passed. At one time an Arab bedouin was told it had taken forty years for him to take revenge. He replied 'I must have been in a hurry.'" "I am with the current of history," Arafat added confidently, "and those with the current of history will win. Those against it will vanish."[26]

Nevertheless, the PLO did not seem to be riding the tide of history in the region as a whole or in Lebanon. The PLO's encounter with Iran's Islamic insurrection and its aftermath showed Arafat's continuing high expectations for radical change and ensuing disappointments. The Shah, a friend of Israel and a U.S. ally, was overthrown in February 1979 by Ayatollah Ruhollah Khomeini, a supporter of the PLO who hated the United States and Israel. For Arafat, the unsuccessful revolutionary, Khomeini's success in realizing his own dream brought new hope. If Khomeini could rise from obscurity, exile, and leadership of a tiny group to conquer a seemingly mighty foe and rule a nation, so could Arafat.[27]

Arafat arrived uninvited in Tehran in February 1979, a few days after the Shah had fled and Khomeini's forces had taken over. As his plane approached Tehran's Mahrabad airport, Arafat said, "I felt as if I was landing in Jerusalem." His entourage carried Khomeini's picture and chanted, "Today Iran, tomorrow Palestine." Symbolically, the new Iranian regime gave the PLO the former Israeli embassy. After over two decades of struggle, this was the first piece of Israeli real estate Arafat had captured.[28]

Arafat was ecstatic. He was warmly received in Iran and envisioned himself as brokering a new regionwide alliance of Arabs and Iranians ready to battle Israel and America. The era of conflict between Arabs and Iranians was at an end, he announced. Iran's revolution had shifted the strategic balance decisively against his enemies. "Iraq can now throw its army fully into the battle against the Zionist enemy. And there is no Persian pressure any more on Saudi Arabia and the Gulf states."[29]

But both Iran and Iraq had their own quarrels which took priority over any struggle to liberate Palestine. Arafat's attempts to mediate between Baghdad and Tehran made both sides angry. Accusing the PLO leader of being pro-Baghdad, Iran cut off support and advised Arafat and the PLO to turn toward Islamic fundamentalist doctrine instead of nationalism. In August 1980 Iraq invaded Iran, starting an eight-year war that cost a million casualties. Iraq's dictator, Saddam Husayn, pressured Arafat into supporting him.[30]

In Lebanon, too, the PLO's high hopes for armed struggle and revolution turned to ashes. Its cross-border attacks against Israel had no military value; the great majority of terrorists were captured or killed. The murder of Israeli civilians reduced Western support for the PLO or sympathy for the Palestinians. The hijacking of an Air France plane to Uganda by a dissident Palestinian group in conjunction with West German terrorists only led to a spectacular July 1976 Israeli rescue at the Entebbe airport that was cheered around the world.

In March 1978 a Greek freighter dropped thirteen Fatah terrorists from Lebanon near Israel's coast. They landed on a beach in two dinghies, murdered an American woman taking photographs there, fired at cars on Israel's main highway, killed a taxi driver, and seized a bus and kidnapped its passengers. As the terrorists drove the bus toward Tel Aviv, shooting at cars along the way, the Israeli army tried to rescue the hostages. In the shoot-out, thirty-four Israelis were killed and eighty wounded. Israel retaliated by launching its largest raid into Lebanon. Thereafter, a UN force was established to monitor the Lebanon–Israel border.

Meanwhile, the civil war in Lebanon intensified, leaving the country with no effective government or army of its own. Authority was in the hands of Maronite Christian, Shi'a Muslim, Druze, and Palestinian militias or the Syrian army. PLO groups ruled large areas of the south, dominating and sometimes abusing the Lebanese residents, many of them Shi'a Muslims. Behind slogans of revolutionary solidarity with the Lebanese people, Palestinians sometimes took revenge for years of discrimination and ridicule from them. Local officials had to submit or resign. Houses, farms, crops, merchandise, and cars were seized—often for personal profit—by gunmen belonging to PLO member groups that sometimes acted as glorified street gangs. After some Fatah soldiers shot the independent-minded Islamic cleric in the village of Haruf, Arafat told the man's son that the Zionists had done it and gave him a pistol so he could take revenge on Israel.[31]

Musa al-Sadr, the charismatic founder of the Shi'a community's Amal militia, complained that the PLO "is not a revolution . . . It is a military machine that terrorizes the Arab world . . . The Shi'a have finally gotten over their inferiority complex vis-à-vis the Palestinian organizations."[32]

At Ayn Hilwe refugee camp, guns were installed on the hospital roof. PLO arsenals, gun emplacements, and military headquarters were set up in Lebanese neighborhoods. The UNRWA in Lebanon became, due to sympathy or intimidation, a virtual subsidiary of the PLO. Its facilities were used as military bases and training centers.[33] The PLO's soldiers enjoyed a high status in their communities and good pay. Subsidies from Arab oil-producing states let PLO groups recruit non-Palestinian, and even non-Arab, mercenaries. More than 3,000 terrorists from all over the world trained in PLO camps. Arafat hired out his own men for several causes, including as bodyguards for Ugandan dictator Idi Amin.[34]

For the PLO, armed struggle from Lebanon became, as one observer put it, "a veritable end in itself." By 1980 the combination of Israeli reprisals, the lack of military success against Israel, and growing clashes with Lebanese militias made Fatah shift to a new strategy. It sought to transform its forces in south Lebanon into a regular army, reinforced by several thousand soldiers and supplied with Soviet-made anti-aircraft weapons, mortars, artillery, tanks, and rocket launchers. In the spring of 1981 it launched a new kind of offensive, firing scores of rockets at northern Israel. While few of them hit anything, thousands of Israeli civilians fled and tensions were high until U.S. Ambassador Philip Habib arranged a ceasefire in July.

Eager to calm the region further, repair the Arab breach with Egypt, and preserve their own good relations with the United States, the Saudis presented a peace plan at the October 1981 Arab foreign ministers' meeting. It demanded that Israel withdraw from the territories, to be replaced by UN control there. A few months later, this land would become an independent Palestinian state under PLO rule. The UN Security Council would guarantee this agreement and peace among all states, including Palestine.

The PLO, Syria, Libya, South Yemen, Iraq, and Algeria rejected the proposal for even indirectly hinting at the recognition of Israel. In vain, the Saudis defended the plan as a public relations' move intended "not to communicate with the enemy, but rather with the international community, and especially with the United States and Western Europe." For Arafat, however, Israeli towns like Eilat, Jaffa, and Haifa were still "occupied Palestinian cities." The plan was adopted by another Arab summit in September 1982, only after being amended to undercut any recognition of Israel.[35]

By then, though, another Arab defeat had already taken place. Lebanon's seven-year-old civil war had made the PLO politically and military vulnerable. In the spring of 1982 there were fierce Amal–PLO battles in south Lebanon and Lebanese–PLO clashes in some cities. Walid Joumblatt, leader of Lebanon's pro-PLO leftist coalition after Syria assassinated his father, warned the PLO that it might lose all local support if it did not improve relations with the Lebanese groups.[36]

The PLO build-up in south Lebanon had made Israel determined to remove it permanently. Arafat kept the ceasefire, but smaller groups were pressuring him to lift it, and this situation could not last indefinitely. Israel's conservative government was concerned that the PLO was winning Western support and eagerly sought an opportunity to destroy the organization's base in Lebanon. Israeli Prime Minister Menahem Begin and Defense Minister Ariel Sharon agreed with the main Christian militia to expel the PLO from south Lebanon and install the energetic, brutal Bashir Jumayyil as a strong, anti-Syrian president in Beirut.[37]

On June 6 Israeli forces crossed into Lebanon, swept through the PLO positions, and advanced northward. Some of Arafat's top lieutenants deserted their posts and fled. The PLO received no help from Syria's army, from the USSR, or from any Arab state or Lebanese militia. Lebanese Christians cooperated tacitly with Israel, and many Lebanese Shi'a in the south openly welcomed the arriving Israeli soldiers. Israeli forces besieged Beirut for several weeks but did not want to enter the city in order to avoid high casualties and even more adverse international reaction. Lebanese politicians urged the PLO to leave to avoid a battle over the city, but Libyan leader Muammar Qadhafi advised the PLO to fight to the last man. If the Arab states had kept their promises, Arafat angrily replied, the PLO would never have been in such a desperate situation.[38]

Once again, Arafat had to retreat in order to survive. He agreed to leave Beirut if the PLO forces and their weapons received safe passage plus a U.S. promise to protect the Palestinians left behind. But he obtained neither binding guarantees for Palestinian civilians nor any political gain. No Arab diplomat came to see Arafat off as he sailed away in defeat. The PLO's presence in Lebanon as a $1 billion-a-year enterprise commanding 30,000 well-equipped fighters was at an end.[39]

Events followed with dizzying speed. On September 1 the PLO and Syria completed the evacuation of over 14,000 soldiers. Nine days later the U.S. Marine force overseeing their departure left Beirut. Bashir Jumayyil, Israel's ally, was elected president, then assassinated by Syrian agents in a bomb blast killing twenty-seven people. Israeli forces took over west Beirut, and four days later Lebanese Christian soldiers took revenge against the PLO by massacring over 600 residents of the Sabra and Shatila refugee camps there. Once again, the Palestinians' horrible suffering evoked both anger and frustration. Neither U.S. guarantees nor PLO forces had been able to protect them.

In Israel, the tragedy provoked protest and soul-searching. An investigation found Minister of Defense Ariel Sharon and several commanding officers guilty of serious negligence for allowing the Christian militia to enter the camps. Criticism about the war's conduct and heavy casualties led to Prime Minister Begin's resignation.

Arafat weathered the debacle better. Trying to transform military disaster into political success—as he had done a dozen years earlier with his defeat at Karama—he called the war a victory. The PLO, Arafat said, had fought bravely against a U.S.-directed attack, held Beirut for over two months, and yielded only because of a lack of Arab support. It had been, said Arafat, "a relative military victory but it was an absolute political victory." Khalid al-Hasan modestly proclaimed, "We should not become arrogant in the future as a result of this victory."[40]

In fact, Palestinians were traumatized and isolated. The PLO forces and offices had no place to go. Syria would not let armed PLO forces into areas of Lebanon it controlled. Egypt was boycotted by the Palestinians because of its peace with Israel; and the PLO was unwelcome in Jordan. Arab states that had long boasted they would sacrifice anything for the Palestinians failed to help. The PLO considered going to Greece, said Abu Iyad, "to make the Arab world look silly." Only far-off Tunisia would host the PLO's headquarters, and its media center had to move to Cyprus because no Arab country could be relied on to let it operate freely. For the first time in history, Abu Iyad noted sarcastically, the Arab countries had all agreed on something: to betray the PLO.[41]

Recriminations were extensive and bitter. Abu Iyad accused conservative Arabs of being accomplices to the attack. Khalid al-Hasan condemned Syria at a mass meeting for not fighting hard enough and asked why Damascus had not opened another front by attacking Israel in the Golan Heights. "The Arab silence around the besieged revolution and around the people who were exposed to extinction," stated PNC chairman Khalid al-Fahum, "was overwhelming and heartless."[42]

Internal problems for the PLO stemming from the defeat in Lebanon were as serious as the disillusion with Arab states. The PLO's institutions and operations were disrupted. Those evacuated from Lebanon were angry, horrified at the murder of countrymen and relatives in Sabra and Shatila, stunned by defeat, and eager to return to battle. Even within Arafat's own Fatah, there was unprecedented criticism of incompetence and corruption. Arafat faced a desperate battle to maintain his leadership of Fatah, Fatah's rule of the PLO, and the PLO's command of the Palestinians and independence from Arab states.

The great asset securing the survival of Arafat and the PLO was support from the overwhelming majority of Palestinians. They knew that disunity would forever end their dream of reconquering Palestine and that domination by any Arab state could crush their independence. But they equally opposed any concessions on the PLO's traditional goals and methods. Thus, the PLO was both unwilling and unable to change course.

The September 1982 U.S. peace initiative emerging from the war, however, offered another opportunity to do so. Neither an independent Palestinian state nor permanent Israeli control of the territories could ensure peace, said President Ronald Reagan. Self-government by the Palestinians of the West Bank and Gaza in association with Jordan offers the best chance for a durable, just and lasting peace." Israel would yield territory; the Arabs would recognize and make peace with Israel. There would be a five-year transition period for negotiations and implementation.

The PLO itself had often spoken of a federation between Jordan and a Palestinian state. But the PLO did not see itself as a junior partner. It opposed any Jordanian or West Bank/Gaza Palestinian role as negotiators with Israel. The PLO feared King Husayn would again control the Palestinians and repress the PLO and that local Palestinian leaders would either supplant it or become the vassals of Israel or Jordan.[43]

Despite the plan's disadvantages from the PLO's standpoint, it again offered a chance to take over power in the territories during the transition period, gain U.S. support, and then propose itself as their rightful ruler. Fearing such an outcome, Israel's government rejected the plan.

Yet the PLO also saw the proposal as a threat. Habash called the Reagan plan a "political bomb no different from the cluster bombs which our fighters confronted bravely in Beirut." Hawatmah called it an "imperialist American–Zionist plan." Arafat, too, scorned the proposal. "I have not heard a single Palestinian say that he accepted Reagan's plan," said his ally Abu Iyad.

The February 1983 PNC meeting echoed this rejection. The PLO put ensuring its own domination of the Palestinians before ending the Israeli occupation. It trusted armed struggle more than diplomatic compromise and preferred continuing to claim all Israel—saluting "the steadfastness of [Palestinians] living in the areas occupied in 1948"—rather than seeking a West Bank/Gaza state as the most realistic and quickest route to securing a Palestinian homeland.[44]

Isam Sartawi, the PLO's leading moderate, offered a different perspective. Stressing a need for realism, he noted some positive points in Reagan's proposal, suggested cooperation with the Israeli peace movement, and demanded an investigation of the PLO's poor performance in the Lebanon war. He urged the PLO to "wake up" and leave the "path of defeat" that had led to the 1982 debacle. Sartawi realistically but hopelessly ridiculed the wishful thinking that claimed that war to be a PLO victory. "Another victory such as this," he joked, "and the PLO will find itself in the Fiji Islands."[45]

Yet practical as Sartawi's advice was in the context of the wider world, it was not so pragmatic in the framework of PLO politics. Arafat wanted to placate hardliners and avoid any examination of his own mistakes. When Arafat refused to let him speak, Sartawi tried to resign. Two months later, he was murdered by the Syrian-backed anti-PLO Abu Nidal terrorist group.[46]

Ignoring Sartawi's warnings, Arafat had closed the 1983 PNC meeting by again celebrating the war as a PLO success. Although the United States had helped save the PLO from complete destruction in Beirut, Arafat claimed the war was a U.S. plot "to destroy the PLO" and that U.S. warships had convoyed Israeli troops into Lebanon. These lies made the PLO's alleged triumph seem more impressive. Some thought Israel's army unbeatable, said Arafat, "but, brothers, by God I have not found it invincible . . . I wish all my nation was with me to see the feebleness of this army."

In order to keep his options open, though, Arafat persuaded the PNC meeting to let him resume contacts with King Husayn. The king urged Arafat to accept a plan that allowed Palestinian negotiators other than the PLO, a Jordan–Palestine federation prior to any independent Palestinian state, and the Reagan plan as a possible framework for a peace process. "Arafat's never had to make a decision," Husayn told a journalist. "But this time he's going to have to. I've tightened the screws everywhere as much as I can." The king smiled, "Arafat's veering off in the right direction; he just needs a push."[47]

But this was wishful thinking. Far more powerful forces were pushing Arafat in the opposite direction. "You're asking me to kill myself," Arafat allegedly told Husayn. In April 1983, when the king made concessions he hoped would allow agreement, Arafat requested forty-eight hours to consult with a Fatah Central Committee meeting in Kuwait. Five days later, two Arafat emissaries brought the king a new draft making no mention of the Reagan plan and rejecting Husayn as a negotiator. The next day the king gave up. Blaming Arafat for the diplomatic failure, he proclaimed the Reagan plan dead.[48]

At most, the PLO was barely beginning a reevaluation. In 1983, for the first time, Arafat met with a group of Israeli doves. But there was far less serious debate about changing course than such a major debacle merited, and few challenged the central principle of PLO doctrine: "The confirmation of the legitimate rights of the Palestinian people," said the PLO's magazine in November 1982, "contradicts the existence of the Zionist state."[49]

Thus, Arafat seems to have been toying with the king to block any unilateral action by Jordan, rather than seriously seeking an accord. Nonetheless, these maneuvers horrified PLO leaders who took them seriously, adding to angry complaints in Fatah and the smaller PLO groups over the handling of the 1982 war and to Syrian concerns that Arafat might throw in his lot with Jordan and the United States. Arafat had violated his own two key rules for keeping power: preserving the best possible relations with Arab states and satisfying even the hardest-line minority in the PLO to preserve unity. Dissatisfied rebels, fed up with incompetence and wary of moderation, joined hands with Syria.[50]

After the PLO was weakened in the Lebanon war, Syrian President Asad saw the situation as a golden opportunity to take over the organization. As a Syrian leader explained his regime's claim to a veto power over PLO decisions in 1983, "Arafat fancies that his cause is exclusively Palestinian and that our role, as Arabs, consists of supporting him blindly. But Palestine is our raison d'etre as well, and we have the right—especially after the heavy sacrifices we have made for the cause—to discuss, contest, and even to oppose this or that action of the PLO." Asad refused to receive Arafat in November 1982, when the Fatah Central Committee met in Damascus, while encouraging PLO radicals to attack him.[51]

Arafat's Palestinian critics blamed him for the PLO's expulsion from Jordan and Lebanon. They accused him of betraying the revolution by dealing with Jordan and Egypt, of letting Sartawi make secret contacts with Israeli doves, and of promoting officers who were corrupt, inept, and cowardly. The DFLP and PFLP, both headquartered in Damascus, suspended activity in the PLO to protest Arafat's contacts with Husayn. In January 1983 Abu Musa, a senior Fatah military officer, castigated Arafat at a high-level Fatah meeting.[52]

A man respected for courage and military ability but not political sophistication, Abu Musa led the May 1983 anti-Arafat revolt in Fatah. As an officer in Jordan's army, he had graduated from Britain's Sandhurst military academy. After deserting King Husayn during the 1970 civil war, Abu Musa rose in the Fatah ranks to become deputy chief of military operations, head of the Yarmuk brigade, and a chief architect of Beirut's defense in 1982. Several of his supporters were also ex-Jordanian officers who held a grudge against King Husayn and whose professionalism was offended by Fatah's military incompetence. Among political leaders, the rebels included the pro-Syrian PNC chairman Khalid al-Fahum, and Abu Salih, a Marxist founder of Fatah who had been the PLO's liaison and arms supplier to the Lebanese left.[53]

Many activists shared the dissidents' views, which expressed the emotive power of Palestinian radicalism, but rejected their deeds in splitting and attacking Fatah while acting as Syria's pawns. Abu Musa explained, "We are the conscience of Fatah." His own father had fought against Israel's existence, Abu Musa declared. Could anyone in the PLO dare say it was now "fighting in order to recognize Israel"? Arafat knew many others could ask such hard questions. A movement whose whole purpose was to reconquer all of Palestine and which had equated compromise with treason for fifty years could not easily reverse itself.[54]

Abu Musa made another valid point in arguing that "in the stages of retreat, revolutionary movements adhere more closely to principles." The PLO's defeats had produced, in reaction, a tighter ideological rigor. Chased from so many geographical positions, the PLO was less able to abandon theoretical ones, especially since weakness undermined its confidence about its ability to bargain successfully.

Despite grumblings about Arafat's leadership within Fatah, rank-and-file Palestinians overwhelmingly condemned the rebels and backed him. "What Israel failed to accomplish in its 1982 war against the Palestinians in Lebanon is now being done by a handful of disgruntled Fatah officers aided and abetted by Syria and Libya," grumbled a Palestinian intellectual. "Once again, the Arab governments prove to be much more dangerous to Palestinian nationalism than the State of Israel. And again, the Palestinians themselves prove to be their own worst enemies."[55]

Syria helped the rebels seize PLO assets in Syria and Lebanon, but the insurgents' dependence on Syria undermined their credibility. Abu Iyad correctly commented, "By raising arms against their brothers and shedding Palestinian blood, the dissidents made a big mistake." Ironically, by becoming clients of Syria, the rebels also discredited the demand for reform. It was, wrote a Palestinian intellectual, "a Catch-22 situation: the leadership of both the PLO and the individual organizations has remained unchanged regardless of certain basic shortcomings, but conversely any change in the leadership necessarily threatens the wider political gains." Those responsible for the PLO's corruption and incompetence were able to portray themselves as patriotic defenders of Palestinian independence. The rebels also forced Arafat to prove that he was not a secret moderate and thus made it harder for him to be flexible in any future diplomacy or criticism of Palestinian terrorism.[56]

Nonetheless, Asad, determined to remove Arafat's men from Lebanon, was not to be appeased. Arafat had returned to rally the remaining PLO forces, especially in their relatively untouched strongholds in the north. But Syria's army, along with its clients among Arafat's Palestinian enemies, besieged his remaining forces. In December 1983, for the second time in eighteen months, Arafat's men were evacuated from Lebanon, saved again by U.S. and Israeli guarantees of safe passage.[57]

Sailing away from Tripoli in his camouflage uniform, Arafat was at the nadir of his career. Only a daring act could save him from

Syria's assault and his own isolation. Deprived of his main base and deserted by some of his closest comrades, Arafat was now forced to flee by the Arab regime that had been his best friend, and to seek help from the one which had been his worst enemy. On December 22, 1983, Arafat arrived in Cairo to meet President Husni Mubarak. The PLO had led the effort to isolate Egypt as punishment for making peace with Israel. Now Arafat swallowed the humiliation of unilaterally ending the ban. Boycotting the moderates, Egypt and Jordan, had made him dependent on Syria. Now he turned toward Cairo and Amman to save him from Syria.

Arafat's action stirred tremendous criticism in Palestinian ranks. His old comrade Khalid al-Hasan had branded earlier contacts with Egypt "political suicide." Now pro-Syrian Palestinians called the trip evidence of Arafat's treason. The PFLP expelled a member of its Political Bureau, Bassam Abu Sharif, for participating in the meeting; some PFLP officials called for overthrowing Arafat. Even usually loyal friends complained: Abu Iyad said that Arafat had violated PLO rules and PNC decisions; Abu Jihad approved an official censure of Arafat as having violated "the principle of collective leadership."[58]

Thus, even many of those among the large majority who remained loyal did not want Jordan as partner or the United States as mediator. "U.S. imperialism," said Hawatmah, "is [our] biggest mortal enemy." The smaller PLO groups agreed with Abu Musa's criticisms of Arafat, his demand for internal democracy, and his commitment to traditional goals, but they rejected the rebels' subservience to Syria and refusal to work within the PLO. Considering Arafat and Abu Musa to be equally at fault, they were neutral in the dispute. The USSR took a similar stand to avoid antagonizing its ally Syria.[59]

Several leaders within Fatah, led by Abu Iyad and Qaddumi, also accepted some of Abu Musa's criticisms. But they even more bitterly condemned his behavior. They regretted losing compatriots who also rejected any retreat or detente with Egypt, Jordan, or the United States. When a Soviet delegation said it regretted the fighting between the rebels and Arafat's men in Lebanon, calling it "fratricide," Abu Iyad replied that Abu Musa's men were not brothers but "criminals and renegades." There was no need to break with Arafat, said Abu Iyad, when hardliners like himself could always restrain him. Arafat "cannot act alone at all," he explained, noting how easily the Fatah Central Committee wrecked the 1983 PLO–Jordan talks.[60]

Abu Iyad was right. Arafat was the PLO and Palestinian leader, yet did not lead them anywhere, given his character and political situation. His legitimacy rested on a weak consensus and his continued image as an unbending militant. Consequently, Arafat repeatedly solicited Western concessions, made promises, and was then unable to deliver even Fatah, much less the PLO. Missing chances to use diplomacy did not undermine Arafat's power; defying Arab states and PLO factions did. The result was the same whether Arafat so acted because his claimed moderation was merely a public relations' ploy for the West or because he did not fully control the PLO.

The 1979 Egypt–Israel peace, the 1982 Lebanon war, and the 1983 split had deprived the PLO of its strongest Arab allies and main base for operations. Preoccupied for eight years by the Iran–Iraq war, Arab states neglected the PLO even more. The Arab world was so badly disorganized and divided it was incapable of even holding a summit meeting between September 1982 and November 1987.

"I was standing in Tyre, Lebanon when the Iranian revolution took place [in 1979]," Arafat later recalled, "and I declared that the PLO's strategic depth extends from Tyre all the way to Iran. Then came the Iran–Iraq war." By 1983, with the PLO being besieged by Syria, "the huge strategic depth of the PLO shrunk to the size of a few kilometers."[61] Unable to win a military victory or make a diplomatic compromise, the PLO had hit the lowest point in its history.

4 >> In Search of a
Program, 1984–1987

Although Arafat claimed them as victories, many Palestinians realized the extent of the PLO's disasters in Lebanon during 1982 and 1983. Israel had failed to install a new political order there but had largely succeeded in driving PLO forces from the border area. And while Syria had not destroyed the PLO, it had managed to drive from Lebanon forces still loyal to Arafat and to split the organization. In effect, there were now three PLOs: one headed by Arafat; the Syrian-controlled Palestine National Alliance, consisting of the Fatah rebels and three Syrian-controlled groups; and the Democratic Alliance, including the DFLP and PFLP along with two Iraq-sponsored (and, hence, anti-Syria) groups.

Neither the PLO's effort to act as a fuse setting off an Arab–Israeli war nor its attempt to lead a people's war had come close to destroying Israel or creating a Palestinian homeland. The organization was deadlocked and divided, and more isolated than it had ever been. Seeking a way out, Arafat began rethinking his situation. Because he lacked a secure base on Israel's border, a promising military option, or any reliable Arab state as sponsor, diplomacy seemed a logical alternative. Yet many of the PLO's own officials were eager to disprove accusations of moderation. The PLO needed Egyptian or Jordanian support to counter Syria's menace, but its fear that Cairo or Amman might dominate the organization and force it to abandon traditional demands made it pull back and veto promising diplomatic initiatives. In short, in 1984 the PLO found itself plagued by its classical problems: Arafat's indecisiveness, internal politics blocking a clear choice to compromise, inability to stand up to radical Arab states' pressure, and fear of falling under moderate regimes' control.

But in 1984, when Israeli Prime Minister Shimon Peres's eagerness to negotiate with Jordan raised again the possibility of a diplomatic settlement without the PLO, Arafat was left with no choice but to turn toward King Husayn. Neither Jordan nor the PLO had forgotten their bloody 1970 war and subsequent estrangement. King Husayn had imprisoned or expelled the PLO's officials and gunmen, banned its propaganda, and barred its organizers from Palestinian refugee camps in Jordan. Both Arafat and Husayn understood that they were locked in fierce competition for Palestinian loyalty in Jordan and the West Bank, and Jordan knew that a PLO-ruled neighboring state could drag it into war with Israel, might ally with other Arab states against it, and could seek the loyalty of its own Palestinian majority.

Nonetheless, their common interests and Asad's antagonism still pushed the PLO and Jordan together. When Algeria and Kuwait refused to risk Syrian anger by hosting the 1984 PNC meeting, Arafat agreed to hold it in Amman, with King Husayn as a featured speaker and host. The pro-Syrian rebels denounced Arafat as a traitor; the PFLP and DFLP refused to attend.[1]

From King Husayn's standpoint, he was being squeezed out of the West Bank from two sides: Israel's occupation seemed to be becoming permanent; and the PLO appeared to be achieving a near-monopoly among Palestinians there. Husayn could not regain the territory without PLO support. Thus, he proposed an alliance to Arafat. While the two men were ready to throw their arms around each other's shoulders in an embrace, each was on guard to ensure that his brother's fingers did not stray around his throat.

Arafat and Abu Jihad slouched nervously in their seats while Husayn lectured them at the November 1984 PNC meeting in Amman on the need to work together. The king's speech was brilliant, perhaps the greatest in his long career. He urged the PLO to cooperate with Jordan as "a natural return to the normal state of affairs." Given its location, Jordan could do more for the PLO than any other Arab state. Husayn recalled his own presence at the first PLO meeting, held in Jordanian-ruled East Jerusalem in 1964. It was not his fault, the king insisted, that good relations had broken down.

Next, he hinted that Jordan had not abandoned its claim to the West Bank. His country had already rescued the West Bank from Israel once, Husayn reminded the audience, by annexing it in January 1950. If the Palestinians wanted Jordan to save them again, they need only ask. In other words, the PLO's inability to deliver the West Bank/Gaza Palestinians from Israeli rule, Husayn guessed, would eventually drive local people back to supporting him.

Husayn then belittled the PLO by suggesting that it had underestimated the task of defeating Israel all by itself, deluded "that the restoration of the territory was around the corner." The king reminded the PNC meeting that he had accepted the Arab League's 1974 anointment of the PLO as the Palestinians' sole, legitimate representative. But he regarded this step as having transferred the burden of the Palestinian cause to the PLO. By demanding sole responsibility, the PLO was also fully responsible for the lack of progress on the issue.

After seventeen years, Husayn continued, the West Bank and Gaza Strip were still under occupation. Time, he added, in sharp contrast to the usual Arab optimism, was on Israel's side. Israel was becoming stronger and the Arabs more divided. The hegemony of conservative forces in Israel and its tightening control over the territory made quick diplomatic progress a necessity. In contrast, the PLO believed that time was on the Arab side and that worsening conditions on the West Bank would make it riper for revolution.

Confronting directly the PLO's rationale for intransigence, Husayn asked, "How long shall we heed those among us who say: 'Leave it for future generations.'" They did not know that future generations would be better able to achieve victory, especially with the enemy becoming ever stronger.

Instead of useless boasting and being the prisoner of slogans, then, the Palestinians and Arab states should be flexible and moderate enough to win international support and even to produce a proposal which Israel might accept. That initiative was a "Jordanian–Palestinian formula" providing "certain commitments" the world deemed essential for a peace settlement. Although Husayn would not have dared to spell these out, he implied that they included a readiness to recognize Israel.

Husayn's solution was a Jordan–PLO partnership. "If the future seems too dark," he said, it was because this relationship had been neglected. If the PLO wanted to work with Jordan, Husayn was ready. "However, if you believe that the PLO can proceed alone, we will tell you to go ahead, with God's blessing."[2]

In the following months, the king continued his campaign to change PLO policy. He called in West Bank members of Jordan's parliament and urged them to advocate a pragmatic strategy. The Palestinians had a "natural right" to all the land, but the best they could do in practice was "land in exchange for peace," to make peace with Israel in exchange for the territories captured in 1967. Husayn hoped that two deported West Bank mayors newly added to the PLO Executive Committee, Fahd Qawasma and Muhammad Milhim, might tilt the PLO in a more pro-Jordan direction. A West Bank delegation, inspired by Jordan, met Arafat to urge him to act quickly in forming a Jordan–PLO partnership to negotiate.[3]

Many of Arafat's closest comrades, however, preferred to rebuild the alliance with Syria rather than follow King Husayn's advice. Even after hearing the king's speech—and despite the absence of the PLO's most hardline factions—the 1984 PNC meeting took the traditional extreme positions. Its political resolution referred to Israel as the "1948 occupied territories" and "occupied homeland" and called Arab citizens of Israel "an integral element of the Palestinian people." Qaddumi, the PLO's director of foreign affairs, alluded to Israel as "the part of Palestine occupied in 1948." The PNC voted to permit Palestinian contacts only with anti-Zionist Israelis, a renunciation of Sartawi's efforts.[4]

The meeting's main theme was that Habash and Hawatmah and the PLO's other radical critics would be given no excuse to accuse Arafat of excessive moderation. Three PLO Executive Committee seats were reserved in hopes of enticing back these defectors. "National unity," said Qaddumi, "continues to be the Palestinian revolution's main preoccupation."[5]

Arafat granted that the lack of Arab unity harmed his cause and that circumstances were unfavorable. He told the PNC meeting that he favored both an independent Palestinian state with Jerusalem as its capital and a Jordan–PLO alliance. Ruling out any major policy shift, Arafat quoted to the PNC meeting an appropriate passage from the Qur'an: "True to their covenant with God . . . some still wait: But they have never changed their determination in the least."[6]

The PLO's leaders defined its strategy along the lines of the policy set in 1974 and 1977. The organization, said Abu Iyad, might accept a "temporary settlement [as] the initial—and not the final—stage of liberation." In the words of Shafiq al-Hut, the veteran director of the PLO's Beirut office, "The establishment of a Palestinian state over part of the Palestinian soil does not amount to a renunciation of the strategic aim. It is a pity that Israel realizes that . . . and knows that the establishment of such a state constitutes the reassertion of Palestinian identity and the beginning of the end for Israel."[7]

Thus, Arafat's policy was a complex mix of motives and goals in which he was once again more a prisoner of constraints than the master of the forces he led. Any effort to obtain a West Bank/Gaza Palestinian state without changing the PLO's premises was doomed by internal opposition as well as by U.S. and Israeli suspicions. If he wanted to maintain the PLO's traditional program, progress was impossible. The same dichotomy faced him in regard to Jordan: the radicals opposed a rapprochement; a successful partnership could lead to Amman's domination. From Arafat's standpoint, as long as he could pursue all paths simultaneously, there was no need to choose.

But Arafat first had to deal with King Husayn's more focused political initiative. Jordan's king saw 1985 as a window of diplomatic opportunity. The PLO, split and weakened by defeats in Lebanon, was easier for Jordan to influence and perhaps even manage as a junior partner. Israel's government was headed by Prime Minister Shimon Peres, who favored a land-for-peace deal with Jordan on the West Bank. But Yitzhak Shamir, who was due to replace him in October 1986, doubted any Arab willingness to make peace and wanted to keep the occupied territories.

Husayn thus moved quickly. On February 11, 1985, the king and Arafat signed a historic agreement, drafted by Jordan, proposing to exchange land for peace and accept conditions "cited in UN resolutions" in order to obtain Israel's total withdrawal from the West Bank and Gaza, and Palestinian self-determination there in a Jordan--Palestinian federation. Several key issues—their joint delegation's composition, interlocutor, and the two Arab parties' relationship in the proposed federation—were left vague and contradictory.

Husayn tried to play down real conflicts between the partners' views, putting the most moderate interpretation on the PLO's stand. Sometimes his regime defined the future West Bank as being under Jordan's total control. At other times, it spoke of a Jordan-dominated federation, a looser equal partnership, or a Palestinian state. The PLO preferred the last option, said Hani al-Hasan, but he was willing to consider a "confederation" defined as "two states, bound by a treaty."[8]

To avoid a last-minute PLO reversal of the deal, as had happened in 1983, Amman publicly announced the agreement before Arafat submitted it to his Executive Committee. Jordan's clever timing threw the PLO into confusion. Since the organization needed Jordan's help, it was reluctant to disavow the accord altogether. But the virulently negative reactions from the anti-American, anti-Husayn forces—the USSR, Habash, Hawatmah, and even many in Fatah—made PLO leaders decide to kill the agreement by interpreting the terms in the narrowest way.

"I do not conclude agreements to please the United States or to win Israel's acceptance," Arafat assured critics. "I conclude agreements with the aim of mobilizing all the Arab resources, including . . . Jordan and the Palestinians, in order to create a solid base for continuing the struggle." Impassioned debates at the PLO's Tunis headquarters considered complaints raised by Abu Iyad and Qaddumi. The PLO Executive Committee emptied the accord of content by adding amendments and reservations.[9]

Husayn and the original agreement implied that the PLO would accept UN Resolution 242, which had become a code word for willingness to recognize Israel. Hani al-Hasan explained, "Frankly and clearly, I say that we reject Resolution 242. We rejected it in the past and will reject it in the future."

The accord urged a Jordan–Palestine federation; the PLO demanded an independent Palestinian state, with perhaps a loose confederation later. The agreement proposed a joint Jordan–Palestinian delegation whose Palestinian members would be acceptable to the PLO, Israel, and the United States; the PLO insisted on a PLO deputation. Abu Jihad affirmed, "Nobody [will] negotiate on our behalf [or] share our representation . . . There is no compromise on this whatsoever."[10]

King Husayn portrayed the use of the phrase "peace for land" as constituting recognition of Israel. The PLO explicitly rejected that idea. "We reply to the slogan, 'Land for Peace,'" explained Abu

Iyad, "by saying, 'The Palestinian land and Palestinian national rights for peace.'"[11]

Qaddumi explained, "The plan's form and spirit do not meet the national legitimate rights of the Palestinian people [and] asks us to cede representation to others." Abu Iyad added that by accepting Jordan's offer, "We lose our representation of our Palestinian people." Habash charged that Amman wanted "to detach [the Palestinians] from the PLO"; Hawatmah opposed cooperating with a monarchy he wanted to overthrow.[12]

The PLO presented this rewriting operation on a take-it-or-leave-it basis. "If Jordan sees any contradiction in its view of the draft formula with our understanding and point of view," Qaddumi said, "then it is better to call a halt." This demand totally negated Jordan's effort for an innovative new approach. The PLO position thus met its internal needs but was also a formula for continued deadlock and revolutionary posturing. "No solution can be found," commented the *Jordan Times*, "when there is nothing but inaction on our side."[13]

Yet the PLO saw no need to change its historic policy. In speaking of UN resolutions, explained Hani al-Hasan, the Jordan–PLO agreement "means including 150 of them" and was designed to avoid endorsing 242. "In the PLO view peace means the establishment of a democratic state on all the Palestinian territory in which everybody, both Arabs and Jews, will live free of religious or racial discrimination." Arafat admitted that twenty years of struggle had not brought victory, but attributed this to the Arab regimes. If only the Iran–Iraq war ended, Arab unity increased, Egypt abandoned the Camp David treaty, and Syria again supported him, Arafat implied, the PLO could still reconquer Palestine.[14]

Arafat's dilemma arose from several factors. He could not afford to stand completely outside the diplomatic maneuvering lest Jordan make a unilateral deal with Israel and the United States that excluded the PLO. But having barely escaped Syrian domination, Arafat was not about to accept Jordan's hegemony, especially since many of his followers preferred Damascus to Amman. Rather than freeing him from a need to appease hardline colleagues, the pro-Syrian rebellion added credibility to the threats of other militants still inside the PLO.

In addition to the PLO's own problems, Syria was the main factor foiling King Husayn's effort. Damascus held a number of cards, including control over Lebanon, its own Palestinian clients, and Soviet support. While Asad's commitment to the anti-Arafat rebels drove Arafat into Husayn's arms, this new alignment made Damascus all the more determined to block any peace process that would bring together its enemies—Israel and the United States—and rivals—Egypt, Jordan, and Arafat's PLO.

Terrorism was already being used by Syria to discourage Jordan or the PLO from pursuing negotiations. In April 1983 the PLO moderate Isam Sartawi was murdered in Portugal by the then Syrian-backed Abu Nidal who, as a reward, was permitted to move his headquarters to Damascus. In October Jordan's ambassadors to India and Italy were wounded. The next month a Jordanian security man in Athens was killed and another embassy employee wounded; in December a Jordanian diplomat was killed and another wounded in Spain. In December 1984 PLO Executive Committee member Qawasma, considered to be friendly toward Jordan, was killed in Amman to show that Husayn could not protect allies even in his own capital. In April 1985 a rocket was fired at a Jordanian airliner taking off from Athens. In July the Jordanian airline's office in Madrid was attacked and a diplomat was killed in Ankara. In September a Jordanian publisher was murdered in Athens.

Damascus also struck directly at the PLO by encouraging one of its own allies in Lebanon, the Shi'a Muslim militia Amal, to attack Palestinian camps. Amal's southern commander said, "Under no circumstances will Arafat's people, and those who have perpetrated military chaos, be allowed to accelerate their military activity and reestablish their headquarters amongst the peaceful villages of the south . . . We say to the Arab countries: 'Why do you want us to cooperate with the PLO, while you yourselves act in contradiction to that request?'"[15]

By the beginning of 1985 the PLO had been largely eliminated as an independent variable in Lebanese politics. Israel and Syria opposed a return of Arafat's forces. The PLO's former Lebanese Druze and Shi'a allies, as well as its Christian enemies, took a similar stand. In May 1985 Amal's assaults on Palestinian refugee camps in Beirut killed 600 Palestinian civilians and guerrillas, while 1,500 others were missing, more casualties than in the 1982 massacre. Nor could Arafat necessarily depend on other Arabs if he followed a moderate policy. In July 1985 Kuwait National Assembly speaker Ahmad al-Saʿdun called for ending his country's economic support to Jordan and the PLO because they were "capitulating" by considering negotiations.[16]

Arafat was thus constrained by radical forces both inside and outside the PLO, as well as by his own mistrust of U.S. and Israeli intentions. But the PLO's weakness also made it necessary to gain time to rebuild the organization. Deprived of any base in Lebanon, an alignment with Jordan was the only way "to be directly on the borders" of Palestine. The agreement with Jordan, said Khalid al-Hasan, was a public relations gesture "aimed at preserving the PLO." Abu Iyad noted, "I know that this agreement is basically aimed at marketing the PLO, as some Jordanians and Palestinians say, to the Americans." Qaddumi added, "We shall never recognize Israel's right to exist."[17]

Both the United States and Israel, however, saw the February accord as promising, at least if Jordan's interpretation prevailed. On a May 1985 visit to Washington, King Husayn outlined a step-by-step plan. First, the United States would meet a joint delegation including non-PLO Palestinians; then, Arafat would say he was willing to recognize Israel; the United States would respond by talking to a delegation including PLO officials to plan an international peace conference. The PLO never confirmed, however, that it accepted this arrangement, and its top leaders repeatedly contradicted Husayn's offer.

Still, the United States wanted to encourage the formation of a joint Jordan–Palestinian delegation that might move toward recognizing Israel and create the basis for direct Arab–Israeli negotiations. Mistrusting the PLO and aware of Israel's refusal to negotiate with it, U.S. policymakers' also preferred—as in their earlier Camp David and Reagan plan initiatives—self-government by West Bank/Gaza Palestinians in association with Jordan as the best chance for peace.

There were also procedural differences between the United States and the Arab partners. Husayn and Arafat insisted on an international conference attended by the UN Security Council's permanent members and Arab states. Washington and Jerusalem wanted direct negotiations, arguing that an international forum would inevitably fail: Syria would wreck the meeting by pushing the Arab side toward intransigence; Moscow would make propaganda and undermine the moderates by raising maximum demands. U.S. policy's main goal had been to reduce Soviet influence, not surrender the major American advantage in the superpower competition of holding a monopoly on mediation.

The United States proceeded to explore whether the PLO was really willing to accept UN Resolution 242, recognize and negotiate seriously with Israel, and abandon terrorism. It was unsure that King Husayn could really deliver the PLO for talks in an acceptable framework but was willing to investigate this possibility. In Assistant Secretary of State Richard Murphy's words, "If 1985 is the year of opportunity, as Arab leaders say, then the Arabs themselves are going to have to make some hard decisions."

The results, however, were disappointing. Arafat's list of potential Palestinian negotiators, even after Jordan's editing, consisted almost entirely of PLO officials. Washington found that this proposal contradicted U.S policy and even Husayn's own formula. And when Israeli Prime Minister Peres accepted two of the proposed delegates who were not PLO members—Hanna Siniora from the West Bank and Fa'iz Abu Rahme from Gaza—the PLO withdrew their names. Abu Iyad commented that Peres's choice of the two men from the occupied territories "is logical. All the Israelis want is to establish a distinction between [Palestinians inside and outside the occupied territories] . . . whereas we form a single people."[18]

U.S. policy gave the PLO a choice: it could indicate a readiness to recognize Israel or designate pro-PLO but independent West Bank/Gaza Palestinians to stand in for it. The PLO was unable to accept either alternative. Internal conflicts and the leaders' aversion to concessions made the U.S. conditions for its direct participation unacceptable. Equally, the PLO would not allow those living in the territories to act, fearing they would abandon it or be manipulated by Israel, Jordan, and the United States.

While these diplomatic problems were already leading to a breakdown of the Jordanian initiative, an ensuing crisis over terrorism and reprisal did the rest. Throughout 1985 the PLO's member groups continued terrorism in the mistaken belief that more armed struggle would bring Israeli and U.S. concessions. Actually, these assaults had the exact opposite effect, making them unwilling to recognize or negotiate with the PLO. In April Israel intercepted a ship, the *Atavarius*, carrying a terrorist force sent from Algeria by Arafat's right-hand man, Abu Jihad, on a mission planned in Fatah's reactivated offices in Amman. More boats were intercepted on similar missions for Fatah's secret commando unit, Force-17. Fatah members with explosives were arrested in Frankfurt, Rome, and Madrid.

In May 1985, while Secretary of State George Shultz was visiting Jerusalem, a Fatah squad planted four bombs in the area. The secretary of state warned, "Those who perpetrate violence deal themselves out of the peace process." This wave of attacks culminated in a brutal September 25 murder of three Israeli tourists in Cyprus by Fatah's Force-17. The killers were a British neo-Nazi skinhead working for the PLO, a former member of Arafat's bodyguard who had been in the PLO's Athens office, and a Fatah man evacuated from Lebanon. PLO denials of involvement thus rang rather hollow.

Israel's air force retaliated by bombing PLO offices in Tunisia on October 1. Among those killed were the deputy director of Force-17, the deputy commander of Force-17 in Tunisia, and others involved in similar pursuits, as well as a number of Tunisian bystanders. Arafat accused the United States of being behind the attack. President Reagan said that Israel and other nations had the right to strike back at terrorism, "If they can pick out the people responsible." Shultz's response stressed regret for Tunisian casualties, though, and the United States abstained on a UN resolution which condemned Israel for the raid without mentioning the terrorist attacks that had motivated it.

Six days later, on October 7, four gunmen from the Palestinian Liberation Front, which was led by PLO Executive Committee member Abu al-Abbas, hijacked the 23,000-ton Italian cruise ship *Achille Lauro* off Egypt's coast and made hostage its 545 crew members and passengers. The liner was on an eleven-day trip with stops including Israel, where the terrorists planned to take it over, but they were discovered and forced to seize the ship sooner. One of the gunmen had led a 1979 attack on Israel, murdering a man and his four-year-old daughter.

They shot a 69-year-old, wheelchair-bound American and threw his body overboard. Rather than denounce this murder, the PLO first claimed the man had died of natural causes. Qaddumi suggested his wife pushed him overboard to collect insurance money.

The PLO denied any knowledge of the hijackers but sent Khalid al-Hasan and Abu al-Abbas to Cairo, where they negotiated a surrender, with an alacrity perhaps due to an Egyptian warning that U.S. forces might soon launch a rescue attempt. U.S. intelligence also intercepted radio communications between the PLO's "mediators" and hijackers showing that the two sides were working hand in glove.

The PLO told Egypt that it would try the men in Tunis if they were spirited out of the country. Egyptian President Mubarak then falsely announced that the gunmen had left Egypt when they were actually still at a military base there. But when Abu al-Abbas and his men flew out on an Egyptian military transport, four U.S. Navy fighter planes forced it to land at an air base in Sicily, where Italian authorities seized the terrorists.

Italy, however, wanted no political conflict with Arafat. Its prime minister ignored a U.S. request to arrest Abu al-Abbas, who was given refuge in an Egyptian building in Rome. Italian prosecutors were not even permitted to question him. Abu al-Abbas was allowed to leave and an arrest warrant was issued only afterward. A court ultimately sentenced the other men to from four to nine years in prison.[19]

The behavior of both Egypt and Italy revealed a basic principle about the attitude of many Arab and non-Arab countries toward the PLO: they did not want to help the organization but were also reluctant to act against it out of fear of offending the Arabs or triggering terrorist attacks against themselves. Mubarak did, however, pressure Arafat to issue a November 1985 declaration promising to confine future attacks solely to Israel and the occupied territories. This was no abandonment of terrorism, merely a more careful choice of victims. Arafat pledged to punish wayward PLO members, starting with the *Achille Lauro* perpetrators. But the PLO chief did nothing. Abu al-Abbas merely kept a low profile for a few months, followed by a warm personal welcome by Arafat back to active participation on the PLO Executive Committee.[20]

The U.S. government rejected Arafat's Cairo declaration altogether. It would not, Shultz commented, approve Arafat's renouncing "all terrorism except in Israel or the West Bank." "The U.S government," said Ambassador for Counterterrorism L. Paul Bremer III, "has always considered politically motivated attacks against noncombatants anywhere (including Israel and the occupied territories) to be terrorism."[21]

The PLO's prevarications over the *Achille Lauro* affair made it less attractive as a negotiating partner and less credible as a moderate force. Whether or not Arafat knew of Abu al-Abbas's plan in advance, he neither criticized nor disciplined its organizers. Abu Iyad, sitting next to Arafat at a Baghdad press conference, said that the PLO would not abandon Abu al-Abbas, adding, "The capitulationist is the one who merely talks and does not confront his enemy." Arafat needed the support of men like Abu al-Abbas to prove that he was not—as Syria and others charged—a "capitulationist."

These considerations also led to another lost opportunity. A planned meeting between a Jordan–PLO delegation and Britain—which seemed a dress rehearsal for the long-awaited U.S.–PLO meeting—fell through in November after the PLO refused to allow two PLO Executive Committee members to sign a carefully worded statement implying their willingness to recognize Israel. Amman sided with London to criticize the PLO for mishandling the affair. The PLO Central Council, meeting that same month, again failed to endorse UN Resolution 242 or Resolution 338, of October 1973, which called for implementation of Resolution 242.

"The PLO has been involved, in recent weeks, as in the past," said Shultz, "in acts of terror and violence . . . Those who are ready to sit down with Israel and try to work out peace, those who accept Resolutions 242 and 338, and those who are prepared to stop the so-called 'armed struggle' deserve a place at the peace table, whatever their label may be—and those who aren't willing to do that don't deserve a place."[22]

If PLO leaders wanted to be the Palestinians' sole legitimate representative, King Husayn complained, they must "live up to their great responsibilities in that regard." Husayn gave his frustration free rein at the August 1985 Arab summit with a devastating critique of the unwillingness of the Arab states and PLO to support his efforts: "How can we make progress when there is disintegration instead of congregation, regionalism instead of Pan-Arab solidarity, plotting instead of harmony, hegemony instead of fraternization, destruction instead of construction, and the placing of obstacles instead of their removal?" Logic had been replaced with anarchy "and dialogue with terrorism." Husayn warned that his peace initiative was "the last opportunity to save the land, the kinfolk, and the holy places. If it succeeds, it would be a blessing and for the general good; and if it fails, then may God help Palestine and its people and everyone in the region in facing the results."[23]

But the Jordanian initiative had failed. King Husayn formally abandoned it in February 1986 and blamed Arafat for the debacle. "We opened all the doors for [the PLO] but they continued to move in empty circles," he said. Jordan again closed PLO offices in July 1986 and expelled its officials. "We are unable to continue to coordinate politically with the PLO leadership," noted the king, "until such time as their word becomes their bond, characterized by commitment, credibility and constancy."[24]

"Jordan will not be a trustee for the Palestinian people or a substitute for the PLO, the sole legitimate representative of the Palestinian people," Husayn promised. "Nevertheless, in view of its direct link to the occupied Palestinian territory and Pan-Arab responsibility, Jordan will continue to play the role of helper and supporter for the Palestinian people in the occupied territories." In fact, he was already trying to reestablish waning Jordanian influence in the West Bank. He increased the size of Jordan's parliament to 130 members, including 56 from the West Bank and 9 from Palestinian refugee camps on the east bank. This legislature passed a law reaffirming Jordan's responsibility for the West Bank and for Palestinians, in effect defying the PLO's claim to be "sole, legitimate representative." Jordan established its own Palestinian group under Atalla Muhammad Atalla (Abu Za'im), head of PLO military intelligence and ex-commander of Fatah's military forces in Lebanon. It also proposed a five-year development plan for the West Bank and persuaded four Palestinians to accept office as mayors there.[25]

One of these mayors was Zafir al-Masri, scion of Nablus's most powerful family and a man on good terms with both Husayn and Arafat. Determined to block any moderation, a hit team from the pro-Syrian PFLP murdered Masri in March 1986. Arafat and Abu Jihad swore to avenge the mayor's death, and his funeral turned into a major pro-PLO demonstration. But they promptly forgot that pledge, and soon thereafter reestablished good relations with the PFLP.

A number of other events added to the PLO's discomfiture. In October 1986 King Hasan of Morocco invited Israeli Prime Minister

Shimon Peres for a meeting. While Hasan urged Israel to deal with the PLO, the visit seemed a sign that the Arab consensus was crumbling further. Tunisia–PLO relations deteriorated after one of Arafat's top aides, Colonel Hawari, was caught preparing a retaliatory bombing campaign against Morocco from its territory.

Once again this cycle of diplomacy and violence revealed the limits on Arafat's political strength and will power. On the inter-Arab level, the frictions in Jordan–PLO relations and the enmity between Syria and the PLO showed the delicate balance on which Arafat's independence rested. On the internal political level, Arafat could not control and would not criticize terrorism lest other groups prove themselves more militant or militarily successful.

Even Arafat was frustrated by his inability to escape the vicious circle of PLO politics. "I don't think he has ever been so demoralized," said a friend in 1985, or "ever in such a corner." A pro-PLO journalist added, "Arafat, his whole raison d'etre now at stake, finds himself face to face with a simple but almost impossible choice: either to accept 242, and thereby betray most of what his 'revolution' once stood for, or to persist in spurning it, thereby denying himself even the chance of respectability in American eyes and a recognized place in the peace-seeking." Khalid al-Hasan commented cynically in 1985, "If we were in the Israelis' shoes, we would ask ourselves whether we should make any concessions whatever, in view of the circumstances in which the Arabs are operating today." Another friendly journalist wrote in 1986, "As so often in the past, guerrillas of all PLO factions seem more interested in keeping their increasingly rickety organization together than in achieving some form of national homeland for their long-suffering fellow Palestinians." A sympathetic writer noted, "The PLO has its back against the wall, and any waiting for external initiatives may be fatal for it."[26]

In 1987, while the Iran–Iraq war was preoccupying Arab leaders, Kuwait, in a remarkable turnaround unthinkable a few years earlier, reregistered its tankers as American ships and requested Washington's protection. Arab states had accepted having U.S. warships in the Gulf. The 1987 Arab summit in Amman focused on the war, largely ignoring the Palestine question. "It seems that the Palestinian people [are] now far away from reaching any target [they] set, even more than . . . in the past," wrote a PLO intellectual.[27] King

Husayn showed his contempt for Arafat by not even bothering to come to the airport to greet the PLO leader.

Isolated and battered, Arafat moved in a militant rather than a moderate direction by patching up relations with the radical PFLP and DFLP. Habash and Hawatmah had been shocked by the Syrian-backed offensive against Palestinians in Lebanon, while the failure of Jordan–PLO cooperation removed their main objection to Arafat's policy. Soviet–Algerian mediation brought the PFLP and DFLP back into the PLO. Arafat sidestepped their demand for reforms to reduce his authority but did formally cancel the 1985 Jordan–PLO accord and criticized Egypt.

Making a dramatic entrance with Habash and Hawatmah at the April 1987 PNC session, Arafat declared, "We now all stand together, united until the final liberation of Palestine." Abu al-Abbas was reelected to the PLO Executive Committee, ending his brief sabbatical after the *Achille Lauro* affair. Fatah began to cooperate with some factions in the Palestinian fundamentalist Islamic Jihad, and even the anti-PLO Palestinian terrorist Abu Nidal showed up for a secret, though unproductive, meeting with Arafat. These events were an impressive demonstration of the deep Palestinian attachment to unity, but also showed how the high priority put on solidarity made it hard to modify the PLO's radical strategy and aims.[28]

Nor did the hardline orientation endanger the support of moderate Arab states. On the contrary, once the danger of negotiations passed, Kuwait and Saudi Arabia gave money and Abu Jihad even returned to Amman to discuss ways of easing tensions. After Israel's withdrawal from Lebanon in 1985, the PLO was able to stage some cross-border operations, though Lebanese Shi'a fundamentalists and Syrian-controlled Palestinian groups were more effective in such attacks.[29]

By far the most important development was the increasing activism of Palestinians in the West Bank and Gaza. The PLO had began stepping up organizing there since the late 1970s, but its stress on armed struggle over political action limited that effort. PLO supporters had swept the 1976 elections held by Israel, but the fact that the new mayors now held an independent mandate reinforced the PLO's mistrust of them.

Once the disasters in Lebanon left it no other place from which

to operate, however, the PLO had to reassess its strategy in the occupied territories. At the time of the 1983 split, violent demonstrations in the territories protested the internecine fighting. Khalid al-
Hasan commented, "I think now that the people inside . . . have
more weight than we have. Their support to us gives us the international legality . . . They are the only source left to resist."[30]

Living in close contact with Israel, Palestinians on the West Bank
better grasped that state's reality and strength while also feeling
more keenly the urgency of ending the occupation. Thus, they were
willing both to struggle and to compromise. The West Bank's Palestinian middle class, realizing that the PLO's prospects for destroying
Israel were poor, was more concerned about freeing Nablus and
Hebron than about regaining Tel Aviv or Haifa. Fahd Qawasma, a
West Bank mayor who had later become a PLO Executive Committee member, commented in 1981 that he originally believed the
Arabs could conquer Israel. "Later, I understood that the Israelis
wanted their own flag, they wanted their own state." Perhaps, in
fifty or sixty years, he averred, there would be a merger.[31]

The Palestinians inside the territories also gained confidence that
they knew what needed to be done. The exiles who ran the PLO,
Qawasma commented, "do not understand the Israeli mentality in
the same way as those living in the occupied territories. We have
to deal with the Israelis day and night, and we come to understand
what is the best way to tackle the problem of relations between the
Arabs and the Israelis."[32]

Facing practical issues pushed part of the West Bank/Gaza elite
toward pragmatism. "If a newly born Palestinian state has a chance
to emerge in the West Bank and the Gaza Strip, we must think
about . . . power, water, schools, hospitals, roads . . . The first duty
of any elected official should be to develop his country, not to develop his arsenal."[33] Yet Qawasma's murder by the PFLP showed
why those Palestinians were constrained.

Still, those living in the territories were also dismayed by the
PLO's incompetence, infighting, and corruption. There seemed no
reason to believe that the occupation would ever end, or certainly
that the PLO would be able to end it. "The PLO Must Not Forget
the Palestinians" was the appropriate title of an article by the West
Bank journalist Daoud Kuttab: "The PLO's greatest asset is the Palestinian people themselves. Their support for the PLO is the main
reason for its survival."[34]

One manifestation of impatience with the PLO among people of the West Bank and Gaza was the growth there of Islamic fundamentalism. Reflecting this trend, a top PLO official said, "The leaders can come to any solution they want about a mini-state in confederation with Jordan. The real war will be won when the Islamic people rule all of Palestine with Jerusalem as the undivided capital." This ideology was a reaffirmation of Palestinian society's strong religious strand. Although influenced by Iran's revolution, the trend owed more to contacts between Gazans and fundamentalists at Egypt's universities. At first Israeli authorities tolerated Islamic groups to counter the PLO until they became even more active in violent activities. While middle-class elements advocated greater moderation, fundamentalists urged more militancy.[35]

A balance sheet for the mid-1980s would show that the PLO had succeeded in inspiring a strong Palestinian identity, a yearning for nationhood, and support for the PLO. Up to a point, it was able to obtain help from Arab states, the Soviet bloc, the Third World, and even Western Europe. But the PLO was nonetheless largely a political and military failure. Israel was not seriously threatened, and the PLO's terrorism made it abhorrent to many people and governments. The efforts to mobilize Arab support or to launch a peoples' war did not work. Funding from oil-producing states was drying up, and financial pledges were going unfulfilled. The occupied territories were still occupied.

The PLO had been especially ineffective in taking advantage of diplomatic opportunities. Within its grasp in the 1980s had been a partnership with Jordan, U.S. recognition, and rule of the West Bank and Gaza. But the same political genie that promised Arafat these three wishes also threatened him with four curses: bloody retribution from Syria, organizational disintegration, Jordan's domination, and loss of personal power. Such conflicting pressures sabotaged the PLO's efforts. Palestine National Fund Chairman Jawid al-Ghusayn said with disgust in 1986, "What is the harvest of twenty years of struggle? We have managed to create a Palestinian identity and bring our cause to the world's attention. Otherwise, it has been a total failure."[36]

The PLO was being pulled in different directions. Syria, Iraq, and Libya sought to take it over; The United States and Israel wanted to circumvent it by negotiating with a joint delegation of Jordanians and non-PLO Palestinians; Jordan and Egypt wanted to moderate it and push it into peace talks as their clients. Trying to maintain Palestinian unity and stay on good terms with—but independent from—all Arab forces, Arafat refused to choose. This strategy had its advantages, but it also prevented progress, limited outside backing for the PLO, and encouraged all parties in continued efforts to manipulate or subvert him.

By the late 1980s, then, the PLO's options were to moderate its aims, cooperating with the United States and Jordan and compromising with Israel; to organize and mobilize the Palestinian people; to wage war against Israel's army; or to pursue a course of political intransigence and terrorism. Typically, the PLO would try all four approaches simultaneously.

5 >> The Intifada and the Diplomatic Option, 1987–1988

Nothing is more common on the West Bank than stones. Many of them are flint, as valuable a raw material in human prehistory as oil is today, because it was the best substance for making tools in an era before people learned to refine metals. Having so much high-quality flint in convenient, hand-sized rocks was a key factor in the early development of civilization in that part of the world.

Beginning in December 1987, however, these stones had a new function. They became the weapons used by thousands of young Palestinians as projectiles against both Israeli soldiers and civilian cars, buses, and their passengers. The result was a new set of tactics for revolutionary movements and a dramatic turning point in the history of the Arab–Israeli struggle.

The PLO called this uprising in the West Bank and Gaza "the greatest event" in the Palestinian revolution's history. After over twenty years of Israeli occupation, Palestinians—through a continuous rebellion that began in December 1987—quickly made the occupied territories impossible for Israel to govern.

Yet this revolt—called the *intifada* in Arabic—was incapable, by itself, of ending Israel's rule or creating a Palestinian state. Only a diplomatic agreement between the Palestinians and Israel could achieve this goal. Since the intifada had no structured, independent leadership or power to force Israel's withdrawal, it was the task of Arafat and the PLO to reach a negotiated solution. If he was unable to do so, local activists might look elsewhere for leadership; or, deprived of hope, the uprising could collapse.

The intifada put the Palestinian issue back on the world agenda, winning it considerable international sympathy. It strengthened the PLO's hand vis-à-vis Jordan, polarized Israeli opinion, and isolated Israel. The uprising, a West Bank journalist wrote, shifted "the focus of the Palestinian–Israeli struggle from the question of the PLO and terrorism to the question of Israel's occupation of Palestinian land."[1] In short, the revolt changed the Palestinians' image from being terrorists to being victims.

At the same time, the intifada caught the PLO by surprise, and the organization was uncertain about what to do with it. Who in the world could have believed or predicted, asked Arafat with some astonishment, that the intifada would continue and escalate, letting Palestinians touch the world's conscience so effectively, reaching every house throughout the globe?[2] Once the inhabitants of the occupied territories seized control of their own fate, while still identifying with the PLO, their importance in Palestinian politics drastically increased.

The people of the West Bank and Gaza had come to understand that the occupation was able to exist so easily because they accepted it so passively in exchange for certain benefits such as the income from working inside Israel and a rising living standard. There had been far more mass collaboration than active resistance for many years. But now Palestinians undercut Israel's ability to govern the occupied territories by boycotting the Israeli authorities and products, resigning from jobs for the civil government, and going on strike. Once fear and respect for the rulers was undermined by these activities, those sentiments could not be rekindled.

This breakthrough was not made effortlessly. Palestinians deemed to be collaborators with Israeli intelligence—often anyone violating an intifada order, criminals, or those unfortunate enough to have a feud with someone better connected to the street gangs— were intimidated or slain.[3] Israel's army, confronted by demonstrations or by rock-throwing teenagers, responded with tear-gas, beatings, arrests, rubber bullets, and gunfire, along with the destruction of some houses and the deportation of a few leaders.

Hundreds of Palestinians were killed by Israeli forces or by other Palestinians. Ricocheting bullets often killed young children. Those who died at Israeli hands were made into martyrs, and their funerals became occasions for new demonstrations. The territories' economy collapsed and living standards were cut in half. Israel closed schools because they had become recruiting grounds for demonstrations. When Israel reopened them, after a period of international pressure and quiet, the cycle began again.

A PLO leader claimed hyperbolically, "Our people suffer murder, expulsion, deportation, detention, torture, and terrorism unprecedented even in the days of the Nazis."[4] But if the situation was so terrible, the PLO would have to find some way to alter it.

The PLO's strategy for regaining Palestine had always depended primarily on armed struggle and outside Arab support. In contrast, the intifada depended on mass participation and largely on the local Palestinians' own resources. Despite the impressive unity demonstrated by the uprising, however, there was a real conflict underneath the surface. The simplest, most moderate goal was to win sympathy from Western news media, public opinion, and governments, which, presumably, would pressure Israel into withdrawal from the occupied territories. The more moderate Palestinians in the West Bank and Gaza knew, however, that this would happen only if they made a peace with Israel that would require some concessions from themselves. Yet others, more radical, saw the uprising as capable of physically forcing Israel to withdraw without diplomatically compromising the goal of struggle toward total victory. Many individuals held both these moderate and radical ideas simultaneously.

While PLO leaders and local activists were successful in preventing this dichotomy of vision from splitting the intifada along factional lines, these two divergent strategies made it difficult to transform events into political gains. After years of increasing suffering, coupled with a lack of progress, the intifada's leadership became frustrated and exhausted. Though activists were generally able to maintain ardor by example, encouragement, and intimidation, mass participation tended to decline over time.

Israel, too, faced strategic and tactical paradoxes. The central issue was whether one believed that the Palestinians and Arab states were willing to make a lasting peace or merely sought to improve their position in the next round of conflict. Israelis in the former camp were willing, even eager, to give up most of the territories; those accepting the latter view thought future security necessitated holding onto them.

Even the two parties in Israel's governing coalition were split along these lines: the Labor party and left were ready to negotiate with the local Palestinian leadership or even with the PLO if given proof of their willingness to end the conflict by compromise. By contrast, the Likud party and the right—supporting the Jewish settlers in the territories—hoped to put down the uprising, perhaps with a grant of very limited autonomy, and to retain the territory. As power and perceptions shifted, the Israeli government alternately arrested or released key Palestinians, unable to decide whether the first priority should be to negotiate with them or try to put down the revolt.

On the tactical level, Israel faced an unpalatable choice. When the army reacted by breaking up demonstrations, there were violence and headlines around the world; if it did nothing, local Palestinians took control and escalated the confrontation. As a democracy, Israel was unwilling to employ the overwhelming force that might have crushed the rebellion. But no matter what level of repression Israel used, the result was the existence of two rulers in the West Bank and Gaza—Israel and the Palestinian intifada. This political and military deadlock let the uprising continue but also meant that the occupation continued.

Certainly, there had been previous waves of demonstrations and rioting in earlier years, but these had involved only a few people for brief periods of time. Israel had always seen the PLO as mainly a military threat. The occupation government had cracked down on armed groups while permitting some political activity as a safety valve. The PLO rightly suspected that this technique was intended to produce passivity or even to generate a group of local leaders willing to make a deal. When Israel held free elections in the territories in 1972, the PLO called them "part of a Zionist-colonialist plan" to liquidate the Palestine problem by stabilizing the status quo. Those who participated were denigrated as "traitors."[5]

Some of these men participated in the Communist-organized Palestine National Front in 1973. More pro-PLO candidates, including Fatah supporters, won the 1976 elections and created the National Guidance Committee in 1978 to oppose the Camp David agreements. Israel deposed the most activist mayors in 1982 and deported some of them.

With the PLO in such peril after the 1982 war and 1983 split,

Palestinians felt even more need to rally to the cause. Gradually, the PLO realized that those leaders elected to replace older, pro-Jordan mayors were its supporters. But Fatah was slow to promote these local initiatives because it did not securely control them. The PFLP and DFLP as well as the Communists were the pioneers in political organizing there. The latter began such efforts on the West Bank around 1974–1975. The DFLP started its efforts in the 1975–1977 period, and the PFLP followed suit between 1977 and 1979. Fatah was a latecomer, commencing serious work about 1979 and not really gaining momentum until as late as 1983.

Even after the intifada began, Arafat clung to his traditional methods, both ideologically and militarily. At first he simply demanded Israel's withdrawal without giving it any incentive to do so. When that did not work, he argued to the Palestinians that their key instrument in combatting the Israeli presence was what the PLO did best, if not well—military operations and rallying Arab states. As an Arab proverb says, when the only tool you have at hand is a hammer, every problem looks like a nail.

To encourage the rebellion in the occupied territories, the PLO tried another of its traditional tactics: stepping up terrorist attacks on Israel, mainly across Lebanon's border. Ironically, the one assault that helped spark the intifada had come not from the PLO but from the anti-PLO, pro-Syrian PFLP-GC, when one of its men killed six Israeli soldiers in November 1987. The PLO responded with praise and exaggeration: "Heroic operations [are] taking place throughout our occupied territories from Gaza, from the Negev, Jerusalem, Nablus, Jenin to Tel Aviv, Haifa, the Galilee and southern Lebanon." Although the PFLP-GC opposed him, Arafat claimed, "They are also fighting under the command of the PLO . . . What matters is that the one who carried it out was a Palestinian or an Arab fighter." He had not repeated such assertions when the PLO or Fatah wanted to dissociate itself from terrorism. Still, when a PLO group hijacked a bus and murdered three Israeli workers in December 1987, he said, "What matters is that operations have not stopped and will not stop as long as Israel persists in its position."[6]

But the terrorist option was politically counterproductive and ineffective even in narrow military terms. Arafat's attempts to create a West Bank underground army through Force-17 went nowhere because Israel could break up any institution that became too structured. In April 1988 Israeli commandos even infiltrated the very headquarters of the PLO in Tunis and assassinated Abu Jihad, Arafat's closest lieutenant, head of his Military Council, and main coordinator of the intifada. The operation eliminated the PLO's best strategist and displayed its inability to protect its leaders or secrets.

If terrorism was proving counterproductive by the end of the decade, the PLO also lacked a conventional military option. Gone were the days when Arab armies might march to war for the Palestinian cause. If anything, they went into battle *against* the PLO. Syria arrested several thousand Arafat supporters among Palestinians in that country while killing others in Lebanon. Egypt urged the PLO toward a diplomatic settlement. Arab oil-producing states had less money to contribute and little inclination to give it. The USSR, undergoing its own political transformation, could no longer be depended on to counter the United States; on the contrary, Moscow, too, was pressing the PLO to recognize Israel. No wonder Arafat expressed such heartfelt gratitude to Algeria and Tunisia for merely allowing the PLO to hold meetings or to maintain its headquarters on their soil.[7]

Rather than use the intifada as leverage in trying to build a bridge to the United States, Arafat at first increased tension with the Americans. After Abu Jihad's death, Arafat claimed that the U.S. government was planning to kill more PLO leaders. He ordered attacks on U.S. citizens and facilities, a threat which could only have increased the PLO's isolation.[8] In short, Arafat saw the intifada within his traditional political framework, as a mass revolutionary upsurge—a sort of peoples' war without guns—that would force Israel to withdraw from the occupied territories and the United States to surrender to his demands, without any compromise of his long-term goals.

Despite Arafat's inability to take full advantage of the intifada, over the following months the PLO did make some significant strategic moves as events forced it to heed Palestinians in the West Bank and Gaza. Although caught by surprise at the intifada's outbreak, the PLO quickly acted to establish a national command of its supporters to direct the uprising. Since activists were affiliated with individual groups—and not with the PLO as a whole—the intifada's leadership mirrored the PLO's fragmented structure. This National Unified Command (dubbing itself "the PLO's fighting arm in the occupied territory") was a coalition of delegates from Fatah, the Communists, the PFLP, and DFLP. Each PLO faction had its own youth group: Fatah, the Shabiba; the PFLP, the Volunteers; the DFLP, the Democratic Youth.

Islamic fundamentalists were arising as still another competitor for power. In August 1988 the Muslim Brotherhood's Hamas also declared itself a separate group, outside the National Unified Command. It criticized the PLO nationalists, issued its own leaflets, declared and enforced its own strike days, and pressured against any moderation in the struggle or its goals.

Twenty years of contact had taught many—though by no means all—of the Palestinian elite in the West Bank and Gaza not to underestimate Israel's staying power or to overestimate terrorism's potential achievements. By the same token, twenty years of occupation had also made them eager to bring it to an end as quickly as possible, even if this entailed concessions and a change in strategy. As it became clear that the uprising would not drive Israel out, Palestinians in the West Bank and Gaza began begging and then demanding that the PLO take political and diplomatic steps to end the occupation.

The PLO had long subordinated these "inside" Palestinians to the simple role of remaining steadfast while it made the decisions and acted. The uprising challenged this relationship. People in the territories assumed a leading role in the struggle, and their views became central for the first time in the Palestinian power balance. They remained deferential to the PLO—unwilling to disavow it or make independent political choices—but were less afraid to say what it should do. Leading local figures from the West Bank and Gaza pressed the case for urgency and diplomacy on the PLO leaders. The PLO had to consider changing course or risk losing its standing among them.

At a February 1988 dinner hosted by Hani al-Hasan at his home in Saudi Arabia, for example, Palestinian guests told PLO leaders present to leave the rioting youths alone, since they were achieving more than its well-dressed diplomats or well-armed fighters. "Palestinians inside the territories will never take a public stand denouncing a symbol of the Palestinian movement," said a businessman from Jordan. "But the people inside have sent a clear message that the uprising isn't the PLO's revolution, but their revolution."[9]

Abu Iyad agreed up to a point: "Seeing children risking their lives imposed on us the need to achieve a realistic peace. They faced us with a *fait accompli.*" If the PLO was still in Beirut, "there would have been no intifada" because people in the territories would still be awaiting salvation from the outside. "If they had not requested that political initiative," he explained, "it would not have happened." Another PLO leader called the intifada "the real mother of the peace process."[10]

But could the PLO finally undergo the transformation to moderation so often wrongly predicted or even mistakenly proclaimed as fact after such events as the 1979 Camp David treaties, the 1982 defeat and flight from Lebanon, the 1983 Syrian-sponsored split, and the 1985 Jordanian initiative? In each case, there may have been some incremental development toward greater realism or moderation but no dramatic revision of PLO strategy and goals. The uprising, however, was unlike anything that had happened before.

Although prompted in the short-run by an economic recession and in the medium-run by the PLO's failure to liberate the occupied territories, the intifada's foundation rested on the transformation of the West Bank and Gaza in a typical pattern of Third World social development. Peasants had become workers and town-dwellers. A growing consumer culture, based on earnings from Israel and contact with that Western society, opened new ideas and expectations while weakening traditional society and its patronage system. Relations among family and clan members changed as a young generation with Western-style education questioned elders and institutions.

New ideologies, and the very notion of political ideology, spread. Improved transport and communication quickened the pace. Lower classes challenged an elite whose right to lead had hitherto been taken for granted; new institutions redistributed power and prestige. When Gaza's traditionalist strongman Rashad al-Shawwa died, for example, pro-PLO activists including his own son seized that political empire for themselves.

Up to then, West Bank and Gaza politics had been dominated by long-established town families. A private account given to an American diplomat in 1957 by a powerful West Bank figure, Ihsan Hashim, explained the system. The area's leadership, said Hashim, would always come from the great families: the Nusayba, Alami, Khalidi, and Husayni clans from Jerusalem; the Tuqan, Hashim,

Abd al-Hadi, and al-Masri of the Nablus area. He was convinced that no leaders would ever arise from the misery of the refugee camps—whose residents were 20 percent of those living in the West Bank, 65 percent in Gaza—or from the peasants. The masses "have always followed us and they will follow us in the future. We understand politics and leadership. With us it is a profession."[11]

In this system, age dominated over youth because experience denoted wisdom. Respect for authority—particularly within the family—was paramount. But by the 1980s young people, having attained a formal and political education, often felt superior to their elders, viewing the experience of the previous generation not with reverence but with scorn, as a long story of defeat and subservience to foreigners.

Just as Palestinian national identity arose in reaction to the Zionist challenge in the 1920s and 1930s, it intensified in the West Bank and Gaza in response to the Israeli occupation. Partly cut off from the rest of the Arab world, Palestinians became communally and individually more self-reliant. They had "largely lost hope in salvation from the Arab world or in the ideology of Pan-Arabism," the West Bank journalist Daoud Kuttab wrote in 1987. "Gone are the days when Palestinians could be fooled by Arab rhetoric . . . Young Palestinians today make up their own minds independently of parents or community leaders." If they believed the PLO was "producing no results, they will force the PLO into a more radical posture or else they will go looking for a more radical leadership within the PLO."[12]

The top level of these new young activists often came from the great families, but most of them did not. Their identities were shaped by three, often overlapping, experiences: as students in high schools and colleges; as members of youth groups formed by PLO and Islamic fundamentalist fronts; and as terrorists. These cadres also met and mixed, developing their ideas and relationships, while imprisoned by the Israelis.

The new intelligentsia arose from among a growing number of students and teachers, like those forming the vanguard of revolutionary movements elsewhere in the Third World. Colleges that had been established or greatly expanded with Israel's permission after 1967—Al-Najah, Bir Zayt, Bethlehem, and Hebron Polytechnic—mass-produced activists.

In this way, the constituency for nationalist groups grew from dozens to thousands in the 1970s and 1980s. Teachers saw political indoctrination as their duty; pupils spent more time on political activities than on studies. Demonstrations and stone-throwing were "virtually part of the curriculum," explained Kuttab. Students came to see their own society in a more critical manner. They were now part of an alternative leadership defined by formal training rather than inherited status. Student council elections pitted the Marxist and nationalist PLO groups against Islamic fundamentalists in sometimes violent confrontations.[13]

While the intifada was largely spontaneous in origin, its street leaders were also products of PLO and Islamic fundamentalist youth clubs, founded in the 1970s and early 1980s, which indoctrinated them while providing practical political skills and experience. Many of the key senior activists deepened their own commitment while in Israeli jails; some were among 1,500 Palestinian prisoners released in 1985 in exchange for the PFLP-GC's freeing of three Israeli soldiers it held prisoner in Lebanon. Allowed to remain in the territories, many of them quickly returned to political organizing.[14]

Luyis Abdu, born in Hebron in 1956, was an interesting though atypical example of this career path. As a terrorist, he tried to set off a bomb in Israel's Lod airport in the late 1970s. In prison he learned Hebrew. After his release in the prisoner exchange, Abdu began translating Israeli books on Zionism and politics into Arabic and distributing them in the West Bank. The purpose was to learn from the enemy's successes. He wrote for the PLO-backed East Jerusalem newspaper *al-Fajr* and established a small publishing and research center. Jailed for six months in 1986 and in 1987, Abdu was finally expelled and went to Cyprus.

His idea about building the infrastructure for a Palestinian state within the occupied territories—imitating historic Zionist practice—was important for leaders in the occupied territories. But ultimately Abdu's contact with Israeli thinking and his friendships with journalists and intellectuals there had a limited effect. On Cyprus, he became editor of a PLO magazine, *al-Istiqlal,* which published extremist material, including an article in March 1990 denying that the Holocaust ever happened.[15]

Other Palestinians were involved in more violent activity. An example of the senior generation was Ata Muhammad Husayn abu Qirsh, born in 1944, first apprehended by Israeli forces in 1964 after infiltrating from Egyptian-ruled Gaza, and imprisoned for three years. In 1969 he was arrested for leading a Fatah terrorist cell and sentenced to twelve years' imprisonment. Released in 1976, abu Qirsh was again taken into custody in 1981, charged with establishing Fatah cells, and sentenced to seven years. Released in April 1988, he became an intifada leader in Gaza until his expulsion by Israel in June 1989.

Others in the movement who had been toddlers when abu Qirsh began his activity included Adil Hamad, born in 1960, and Husayn Uthman Muhammad Khadr, a year younger, both of whom led Fatah youth groups in their home areas. Throughout the 1980s they organized students, led demonstrations, and attacked alleged collaborators' houses. Periodically, they were detained for several months or given short prison sentences. Khadr, for example, served eighteen months of a five-year prison term from 1985 to 1987. Israel expelled them both in January 1988.

The end of the Persian Gulf oil boom and lack of their own state bureaucracy—the usual source of jobs for educated Arabs—limited employment opportunities for young West Bank Palestinians in the 1980s. The PLO and its constituent groups subsidized newspapers, trade unions, and other institutions which hired these graduates, ostensibly as journalists or labor organizers but actually as full-time political cadre. These pro-PLO West Bank/Gaza leaders lacked the inclination or power to challenge the Tunis headquarters. Local leaders might select tactics, but the PLO set strategy and communicated its decisions from Abu Jihad through an Amman-based supervisory committee and its European—especially Paris—offices. The recruitment of terrorists and money smuggling was centered in Amman.

Orders to the intifada arrived through the fax machines of PLO-subsidized, activist-staffed East Jerusalem newspapers and tiny trade unions. Money was laundered through banks, black market currency exchanges, and visiting delegations. The PLO, trying to prevent any single powerful West Bank figure from emerging, put few of the deportees from the territories in top posts. When Abu Jihad was assassinated, the PLO chose him—not someone killed in the territories—as the martyr symbolizing the uprising.

Among the activists in the territories who managed to develop some of their own ideas, a key figure was Faysal al-Husayni, who held authority by his combination of toughness and charm, family prestige and money. His credentials were reinforced by a revolutionary past. He had worked with Arafat in the late 1960s, during Arafat's secret visit to the West Bank, had undergone Syrian military training, and had been involved in terrorist efforts. In more recent years, he had become a mediator of inter-Palestinian conflicts and tried to convince Israelis of the movement's moderation. He was as much the West Bank's delegate to Fatah as he was Fatah's agent.

Secretly, Husayni and others were proposing a Palestinian strategy to make a unilateral declaration of independence and establish a provisional government in which leaders from the territories would—in equality with Tunis—hold half the posts and PNC seats. In January 1988 they made fourteen demands, including calls for municipal elections, the release of all prisoners, an end to deportations, lifting the state of siege, a stop to Jewish settlement in the territories, and a just and lasting peace agreement.[16]

These "inside" leaders urged the PLO to capitalize on the uprising to free them from Israeli control as quickly as possible. Publicly loyal to the PLO as the symbol of Palestinian nationalism, local Palestinians criticized it privately for reacting so slowly and uncertainly. In 1988 al-Fajr, the pro-Fatah West Bank newspaper, asked the PLO for "clear, specific and straightforward [decisions]. There is no room left for confusing rhetoric." The National Unified Command's leaflet 27 urged the PLO to act so as to be able to participate in peace talks "on an equal footing."[17]

Powerful outside forces pushed in the same direction. Trying to revitalize Soviet foreign policy, Mikhail Gorbachev, the PLO's most powerful patron, encouraged it to adopt more moderate positions and recognize Israel.[18] Britain and France also urged the PLO to abandon terrorism and to accept Israel's right to exist.

The amazing lack of support from Arab states was another factor which the PLO had to take into consideration. With the West Bank and Gaza in full-scale revolt and hundreds of Palestinians being shot, Arab rulers sat back and did virtually nothing. The 1988 Arab summit promised little, and delivered even less, financial aid. The struggle could not be escalated, Abu Iyad claimed, because there was no way to support families when their breadwinners were on strike much of the time. Arafat sighed, "I am tired of asking for these commitments to be honored." Nor was there any Arab political initiative. Egypt kept its peace with Israel and urged PLO concessions to gain Western recognition. Even President Mubarak asked Palestinians to stop the violence so that negotiations could proceed. The PLO's "responsibility," he said, "is no longer restricted to adopting protesting or objecting stances. It must take the daring and positive steps which are required for the sake of the Palestinians' future." The PLO felt abandoned. "We are alone in the struggle," said Abu Iyad. Khalid al-Hasan lamented, "The Arab stand no longer exists . . . It is now less than zero."[19]

But the intifada and all this pressure alone did not suffice to make the PLO move. Ironically, the key ingredient was provided by Jordan, the Arab state that had always competed with the PLO for control of the West Bank and leadership of the Palestinians. King Husayn had kept his border to the West Bank—whose residents still used Jordanian passports—open while subsidizing almost 20,000 civil servants there. As late as April 1987 he was still seeking a deal with Israel to get the territory back. But given the lack of diplomatic progress and the potential danger of trying to absorb a restive, pro-PLO populace, Jordan had good reason for at least temporarily giving up trying to regain the territory. King Husayn also miscalculated in thinking that by walking away he would make the PLO seek his help.

On July 31, 1988, he cut Jordan's administrative and legal links to the West Bank, in effect undoing the 1950 annexation and apparently renouncing any attempt to renew it. Arafat was stunned. Husayn's action ostensibly fulfilled the PLO's dream of eliminating Jordan's influence, but it also posed a serious problem.

For twenty years the PLO had feared a deal between Jordan and Israel; now Jordan was out of the picture and the PLO had to assert its own claim. A PLO official recalled, "We felt we had to move fast, in case the Israelis decided to step in and fill the vacuum . . . We realized we had to take crucial decisions." The need to respond was the immediate cause that would lead the PLO to declare an independent state, just as competition with Jordan had driven previous innovations in its policy. Arafat's advisor Abu Sharif crowed, "The Jordanian option . . . is over. Now there is the PLO, and only the PLO." But how could the PLO meet the challenge?[20]

Other diplomatic developments suggested an answer. In April

Sweden's foreign minister had visited the United States to offer himself as a conduit for U.S.–PLO contacts. A few weeks later William Quandt, an American Middle East specialist, and Muhammad Rabie, a Palestinian-American economist with strong PLO contacts, gave a paper to the U.S. government suggesting ways the PLO might meet U.S. conditions for a dialogue. In June the State Department's Bureau of Near East Affairs, long champion of a more pro-PLO policy, suggested a U.S. initiative along these lines. Secretary of State George Shultz rejected that idea, but Khalid al-Hasan, acting as Arafat's emissary, conveyed his organization's interest in reaching an understanding.

Since the mid-1970s, U.S. policy had been to deal with the PLO only if and when that organization accepted UN resolution 242, recognized Israel's right to exist, and abandoned the use of terrorism. Now the United States reminded the PLO that diplomatic exchanges could begin once those conditions were met. Assistant Secretary of State Richard Murphy asked Palestinians "to turn away from the dead-end path of violence and rejectionism and to forge an effective, forward-looking political program. Israel's existence and security are non-negotiable. But the shape and content of a future settlement are exactly what negotiations are about."[21]

During the summer of 1988 a lively debate took place in the PLO and among Palestinians on how to respond to Jordan's move. Officials flew into Tunis to participate, saying, "We're here to witness history."[22] The most dramatic statement was Bassam Abu Sharif's position paper distributed at the June 1988 Arab summit. Both sides in the conflict, it said, want peace, security, and the right to run their own affairs. "The key to a Palestinian–Israeli settlement lies in talks between the Palestinians and the Israelis. The Palestinians would be deluding themselves if they thought that their problems with the Israelis can be solved in negotiations with non-Israelis, including the United States." Progress could occur, he insisted, only through talks between Israel and the PLO which would lead to the creation of a Palestinian state with international security guarantees for Israel. The PLO's purpose, Abu Sharif claimed, was "not the undoing of Israel, but the salvation of the Palestinian people and their rights." Israel need not fear a Palestinian state that would inevitably be weaker than itself and whose stability would be preserved by the PLO's "democratic nature." "We are ready for peace now, and we can deliver it."[23]

Such words had been so long delayed, so difficult to utter, that merely saying them—at an Arab summit, no less—took on remarkable significance. The key question was whether this was going to be official PLO policy or just a public relations' effort to impress the West. His paper was written only in English, not Arabic. Some West Bank Palestinians praised the statement; Abu Iyad and Habash strongly criticized it. A radical Kuwaiti newspaper expressed the hopes of many Palestinians and Arabs that the document "is only a political tactic." Why, it asked, had the PLO cheered the murder of Sadat because he made peace with Israel only to commit treason itself? Publicly, Arafat defended neither the document nor its author. Conflicts within the PLO, and Arafat's fear of exacerbating them, seemed paralyzing. Mubarak complained: "The Palestinians cannot agree among themselves. They trampled the Abu Sharif initiative . . . Without agreement among the PLO's various factions, how will the process go on?"[24]

In August the PLO Executive Committee finally responded to King Husayn's bombshell by calling for a PNC meeting within one month. Rabie traveled to Tunis and confirmed Arafat's interest in entering a dialogue with the United States. A high-ranking Soviet diplomat met Arafat in Tunis and urged flexibility. Yet the PNC meeting was repeatedly rescheduled as the PLO struggled to reach an internal consensus that might somehow meet the U.S. conditions.[25]

In contrast, declaring an independent Palestinian state achieved wide support, especially if it could be done without recognizing Israel. The juridical basis was to be UN Resolution 181, proposing separate Jewish and Arab regimes in Palestine, which U.S. and Zionist leaders had supported when it was passed in 1947. At the time, the Palestinians and the Arab states rejected the plan and went to war to prevent its implementation. Twenty years later, the PLO Charter had called Resolution 181 "entirely illegal, regardless of the passage of time," because it was "contrary to the will of the Palestinian people and to their natural right in their homeland and . . . to self-determination." Arafat attacked it as "this ill-omened resolution adopted (unjustly and wrongly) by a majority of one vote."[26]

Now PLO leaders wanted to use the resolution as the sole international accord recognizing a right to establish a Palestinian state. They knew that previous programs, in Abu Iyad's words, had not "taken us one step forward." Something new was needed. "We must admit we do not have all the time in the world," he warned. To be passive meant giving up responsibility and leadership. There were few options. "We are not capable of war," and Arab regimes would not fight. "We need an initiative to prove to our people that we exist on the political map, so that there will be a goal for the continuation of revolution and struggle."[27]

The best way to fight on for a full victory, he continued, was to accept a West Bank/Gaza state for the time being, even though it did "not represent all our historic ambition." Reconquest of all Palestine might be left "for future generations." The question was not "Should we accept Israel or remove it?" but, rather, "Do we want to establish a state or not?" Action must be taken immediately, "otherwise we will lose the opportunity."[28]

Thus, Abu Iyad justified putting top priority on establishing a West Bank/Gaza state without recognizing Israel or foreclosing future options. He could not accept Israel's right to hold "any part of the land of Palestine," stating that the PLO's future "does not include any concessions." The existence of two states was only a "short-term solution." Similarly, the relatively moderate Nabil Sha'th said the PLO was following "an interim working plan for establishing a Palestinian state on a part . . . and not on all the national soil. Thus, the Charter still stands." The PLO would try to fulfill this entire program by replacing Israel with a PLO-ruled Palestinian state.[29]

Such statements could be interpreted as a verbal smoke screen, covering a moderate turn in PLO strategy while preserving unity with the radicals and the masses' support. Yet as long as a barrage of such statements continued, neither Israel nor the United States would be convinced that the organization had altered course. It was not clear whether PLO leaders were willing or able to impose a historic change.[30]

A few PLO leaders and more West Bank activists argued openly that Israel could not be destroyed, that revolutionary and extremist rhetoric had brought little gain, and that Palestinians must achieve something now to better their lives. They wanted a Palestinian state on the West Bank and Gaza and were willing to pay for it with a clear acceptance of peace with Israel. In other words, they argued for an explicit change in PLO objectives.

On the other end of the political spectrum, most of the smaller PLO groups, and the pro-Syrian and Islamic fundamentalist forces outside the organization, argued that a major policy shift would sell out the revolution. Their solution was an intensified military, not diplomatic, campaign.

Fatah's mainstream had a more complex, nuanced response, believing that the time had come to achieve tangible gains for Palestinians, mobilize support in the territories, and eliminate forever any direct role for Jordan. To obtain U.S. recognition required the PLO to appear flexible and moderate. "The days of indirect contacts with the United States are over," said Khalid al-Hasan. "They took us nowhere in the past twenty years."[31]

Thus, the PLO tried to straddle the line between a new aim— a peace settlement giving Palestinians a West Bank/Gaza state in exchange for dropping their claim on Israel—and updating the old strategy of gaining a state without foreclosing further struggle. One of the most astute journalistic observers of the organization concluded, "Inside the PLO, opinions vary from the view in favor of putting the clock back to 1947, before the partition of Palestine, to that of a small minority prepared to recognize Israel now and settle for just the West Bank and Gaza Strip."[32]

By being so ambiguous, a new program could serve both aims. Moreover, the PLO had finally learned that launching its own initiative might put on its enemies the onus for a continuing stalemate. By appealing to world opinion, the PLO could also, in Abu Iyad's words, force the United States and Israel into a corner. Since the United States was quicker than Israel to believe that the PLO was being more moderate, this gap might split the two allies, also a major gain for the PLO.[33]

Thus, the PLO's leaders sought simultaneously to do two opposite things: persuade their most militant factions and their own consciences that they were not retreating from traditional positions— thus keeping the organization united—while convincing the United States and Israel that the PLO had turned over a new leaf. This was, to say the least, a hard task since each audience had access to the statements made to appease the other. Still, one useful technique was to make harder-line statements in Arabic, almost always ignored by the Western news media, and more temperate ones in English. Another method was to employ such ambiguous language that it could be interpreted differently for disparate audiences and occasions.

Thus, the intifada shook up PLO policy and thinking, especially when the local residents spearheading it demanded the PLO act effectively to end the occupation. The crucial question remained whether the PLO had genuinely accepted a two-state solution— Israel and a West Bank/Gaza Palestinian state living side by side— or still sought a two-stage solution, to use any territory gained as a springboard for trying to destroy Israel.

Why did the PLO change so slowly and grudgingly and why was it changing at all? It was loath to abandon the heart-felt, long-held claim to all historic Palestine and an ideology equating concessions with treason. Radical Arab rulers, smaller PLO groups, Islamic fundamentalists, and many in Fatah wanted even more militancy. Arab states' inactivity largely narrowed the conflict to an Israeli– Palestinian one, but this did not necessarily mean the struggle was now only over the West Bank and Gaza. The intifada generated unrealistic euphoria that total Palestinian victory was possible; the PLO's rhetoric often insisted on gaining all Israel as well as the territories occupied in 1967.

In contrast was the opportunity, perceived by Egypt and some Palestinians, to become truly committed to a moderate peace initiative and change the conflict's whole direction. Israel had always held the diplomatic initiative and for four decades had usually enjoyed Western sympathy; the Arab states and Palestinians had only reacted to events and acted to please themselves rather than to win broader international support. The intifada uprising gave the Arabs a chance to take the other role. PLO officials in Tunis might still indulge in hot rhetoric, indecisiveness, and oversized ambitions; Palestinians in the territories wanted results.[34]

All these issues would come together in November 1988 at the long-awaited Nineteenth PNC meeting in Algiers, which seemed poised between being a turning point in the PLO's history and another example of the constraints that had so often bedeviled that organization.

6 >> Rehearsals for a Moment of Truth, 1988–1990

"Bonne Chance"—good luck—said the sugar-coated message atop a chocolate cake on the delegates' buffet at the November 1988 PNC meeting in Algiers. By luncheon's end, the cake was still untouched, an apt metaphor for a group needing much luck but still trying to have its cake and eat it, too.

During huge riots a few days earlier, Algeria's army had killed several hundred civilians protesting shortages of goods and poor living conditions. Demonstrators had even set fire to some cabinet ministers' homes. Downtown Algiers was dotted with burned and looted buildings, symbolizing the failure of the revolution on which the PLO had modeled its own struggle. Also mirroring the PLO's dilemma was the growing challenge to Algeria's radical nationalist regime from Islamic fundamentalist groups.

The PNC members gathered at the national conference center near the golf club, just beyond Algiers' suburbs. These Palestinians, mostly conservative, successful businessmen and professionals, favored expensive suits. In America, the intifada had made Palestinian *kaffiya* scarves a trendy item of clothing. But there were more of them on Washington streets than at the meeting, where Arafat was the only delegate wearing one. Here the older generation and people from outside the occupied territories were very much in control.

After Arafat's fiery opening speech, PLO leaders emerged from the plenary to tell reporters how forthcoming the meeting's outcome would be. Starved for information and assured of a straightforward endorsement for UN Resolution 242, journalists optimistically reported that the PNC was about to recognize Israel. Indeed, the debate was over the paragraph in the political resolution mentioning UN Resolution 242, but matters were not so simple. Delegates joked that no PLO leader even wanted to stay in hotel room 242, because the PLO was torn between developing a new policy and preserving unity. Arafat charged like a football quarterback, with a phalanx of guards blocking for him, in and out of caucuses to promote a compromise. In the end, he succeeded: 338 out of 447 members present—excluding the PFLP delegates and some others—voted for the key clause. The PNC's final resolution was then adopted unanimously.

While Arafat had dedicated the meeting to the intifada, it was equally aimed at changing U.S. policy. In sharp contrast with the past, anti-Americanism was largely absent. But the effort to meet U.S. preconditions for dealing with the PLO came up against the leaders' own hesitancy to change their policy and risk splitting the organization. Thus, the PNC tried to give the impression that it was recognizing Israel, while not recognizing Israel; accepting UN Resolution 242, albeit with major qualifications; condemning terrorism, but with loopholes; and seeking a Palestinian state on just the West Bank and Gaza, though never actually saying so.[1]

The last session continued long past midnight as final compromises were made. Finally, Arafat stood on stage looking out at the audience of delegates and waiting for the applause to die down. It was about 2 A.M. on November 15, 1988. In his trademark combination of khaki military uniform and kaffiya scarf, he read a declaration of independence for the state of Palestine in his high-pitched voice.

As soon as he finished, an Algerian military band played the Palestinian anthem, "Biladi, biladi," while a Palestine Liberation Army officer slowly raised the tricolored Palestinian flag. Everyone was exhausted from the last-minute bickering and bargaining over the resolution's wording. A few delegates made short festive speeches and one recited a little spontaneous poetry as the PNC's nineteenth session ended.

It seemed more like an anticlimax than the culmination of many years of struggle. The language of the PNC's political resolution was highly ambiguous. Arafat's lavish praise for his host and declaration of Palestine's independence under the protection of Algerian guns were reminders of the PLO's dependence on Arab regimes. Such help from Arab rulers could not be taken for granted: there were few other Arab capitals where that session could have been held.

Moreover, the land whose sovereignty was being proclaimed lay four borders and 2,000 miles away. Although Arab nations quickly recognized the new "state," its territory and many of the citizens claimed by the PLO were still under Israeli occupation, while most of the remainder were refugees. And although the meeting purportedly indicated willingness to make peace with Israel, the declaration of independence implied the PLO's claim to rule all of Israel and its Jewish inhabitants as well.

Arafat's reading of the Palestinian declaration of independence was followed by a virtual journalists' riot as they scrambled to grab copies of the accompanying political resolution which defined PLO policy. What they read sobered them considerably: it was carefully written to minimize any hint of recognizing Israel. The *New York Times* called the PLO position "the same old fudge that Yasir Arafat has offered up for years" and "another wasted opportunity."[2]

The only part of the PNC resolution about Israel spoke in the following terms: "The occupation's crimes and its savage practices destroyed the Zionist claim that the Zionist entity was democratic. This lie misled world opinion for 48 years; Israel now appears in a true light: A fascist, racist, colonialist state based on the usurpation of the Palestinian land and on the annihilation of the Palestinian people. A state that threatens, launches attacks, and expands onto neighboring Arab lands." This characterization seemed designed to delegitimize Israel's right to exist. After all, if "the Zionist entity" was so evil, its continuation was intolerable and it could not be trusted as a negotiating partner.[3]

The declaration of independence, too, avoided recognizing Israel. While noting that UN Resolution 181 "partitioned Palestine into two states, one Arab, one Jewish," the PLO called that decision, in language close to the PLO Charter, a "historical injustice" depriving Palestinians "of their right to self-determination." This right could only have been fulfilled by control over all Palestine. The declaration continued, "Yet it is this resolution that still provides those conditions of international legitimacy that ensure the right of the Palestinian Arab people to sovereignty and national independence."

Thus, the PLO accepted Resolution 181 inasmuch as it provided for a Palestinian Arab state but not as a juridical basis for a Jewish state. Again, PLO officials gave conflicting interpretations, but this formula fulfilled Abu Iyad's view, "I did not say that the [Palestinian] state would be on the basis of partition" of the Palestine mandate into Israel and a Palestinian Arab state. "I only spoke about the part [of the UN Resolution] that gave us legitimacy."[4]

Similarly, the PLO's alleged approval of Resolution 242 vanished on a close reading of the PNC's documents. The resolution was approved only in the context of all UN resolutions, a formula Arafat had used for years and one which the United States and West European countries had never deemed meaningful. Arafat conditioned even this "on three basic principles: a Palestinian state, self-determination and the right of return." It was more accurate to say, as did one PLO spokesman, that this was "the first time we did not reject 242."[5]

The PNC's specific proposal was also designed to avoid having to recognize or make peace with Israel. It demanded Israel's withdrawal from all territories occupied since 1967 and removal of the Jewish settlements established there. These territories would then be placed under the UN's supervision for a short period after which they would be handed to the PLO. Only later would there be an international peace conference to produce a comprehensive solution, achieving security and peace for all. Qaddumi summarized the plan as "similar to the [Israel–Egypt and Israel–Syria] disengagement in 1973. Israeli withdrawal first, after that negotiations start."[6]

The condemnation of terrorism was equally tortuous, based on earlier PLO promises which had never stopped it from committing terrorism before. The resolution endorsed "the right of peoples to resist foreign occupation, colonialism, and racial discrimination and their right to struggle for their independence," and declared "its rejection of terror in all its forms, including state terror." Yet the PLO had always claimed that its attacks on Israel were, by definition, legitimate military operations though aimed at civilians. Thus, even Abu al-Abbas, under U.S. indictment for the 1985 *Achille Lauro* hijacking and the murder of an American passenger, voted to condemn terrorism.

At the meeting, PLO spokesman Ahmad Abd al-Rahman claimed

it was unfair to label the organization as terrorist since it had so often issued resolutions condemning terrorism. But the U.S. State Department easily identified twenty-two PLO terrorist acts between its 1985 declaration promising to stop international terrorism and March 1988. Arafat defined as legitimate "any operation against any Israeli occupying my country," explicitly referring to Israel within its pre-1967 borders as "occupied Palestine." Thus, the PLO's acts and statements contradicted its assertions. Just three weeks before the PNC meeting, seven Fatah terrorists were captured en route to an Israeli kibbutz where, their commander said, they planned to take hostages. A few days before the session started, Fatah claimed credit for a grenade attack in Haifa where an Israeli boy standing outside a toy store lost a leg.[7]

Indifferent to these nuances, Arab and many Third World regimes quickly recognized the Palestinian state. In contrast, Western states did not acknowledge the claim, and Moscow's response was especially disappointing for the PLO, only taking note of the declaration of independence.

"The Israeli reaction is not our concern," commented one delegate. But this was the PLO's main error. No Israeli government would give up territory, even under U.S. pressure, at the very least unless the PLO persuaded Israelis that it had really changed its strategy and goals. Palestinians in the occupied territories understood that fact far better than did the PLO leaders in Tunis. It was all very well to proclaim an independent state but, no matter how pleasing this might be to Palestinians emotionally, this mere announcement changed nothing in their lives.

The deliberate ambiguities and careful wording of the PNC resolution and of PLO leaders' speeches in the following months did not resolve these issues. The PLO obfuscated whether "Palestinian territory" only meant the West Bank and Gaza or all Israel as well. Arafat could still say in one breath that he wanted mutual recognition "between two states" and was "ready to sit in an international conference with the Israelis, no matter whom they send," while a moment later reiterating, "We are opposed to a Zionist state; Zionism is a racist movement, according to a UN resolution. We don't want a racist state in this area."[8]

PLO officials interpreted the PNC resolution as they liked, rarely expressing willingness to accept Israel's existence. The resolution, in Abu al-Abbas's words, "does not mean recognition of Israel's right to exist. It means nothing more than Palestinian readiness to fight the political battle." PNC chairman Abd al-Hamid al-Sa'ih said the PLO, like the fundamentalists, would struggle "until all of Palestine is liberated." Those reading the PNC political statement carefully, he added, would find that it neither accepted the UN resolutions nor "the Zionist entity." On one day in December 1988, Qaddumi denied that the PNC resolution recognized Israel while the PLO's UN observer asserted that it did.[9]

How could these contradictions be reconciled? The answer lay in the nature of the PLO's politics. First, the November 1988 declaration used deliberately tricky, ambiguous language designed to bridge internal differences and to avoid foreclosing future options. Yet this very approach prevented progress, since it left continued suspicions about whether the apparent evolution was real and irreversible. For the first time, the PLO was seriously entertaining the idea of a compromise settlement with Israel, but it was also tempted to believe that a public relations campaign might yield as much political benefit at a far smaller cost.

One view of this thinking came from the Palestinian writer Nimr Sirhan. Given the overall political situation and international balance of power, Sirhan argued, "The establishment of a Palestinian state is impossible without the recognition of Israel." True, those demanding all of Palestine "do indeed represent our people's conscience and strategy," but the most that was possible now was to accept an Israel somewhat smaller than the one created in 1948. Even accepting the pre-1967 borders seemed too radical to Sirhan.[10]

"Let us learn a lesson from what Salah al-Din did during the era of the Crusades," Sirhan continued, "when he accepted a liberated part of Palestine and recognized a Crusader state on another part of Palestine," until his successors "unleashed their swords and wiped out the Crusaders' invasion."[11]

Many Palestinians criticized even this view as too moderate, though accepting the need to pursue the two-stage strategy developed in the 1970s. Qaddumi's comparison of the PLO's proposal to that era's disengagement agreements, the ambiguous messages over recognizing Israel, the demand for the return of all Palestinian refugees to Israel, and the desire to preserve terrorism as an option for the next stage all showed how short a distance PLO leaders had moved in their own thinking.

The question, of course, was whether such ambitions would merely remain a dream or would shape a future Palestinian state's behavior. Much of the initiative's Palestinian support did seem based on a belief that it was intended to win U.S. concessions in exchange for superficial changes in PLO policy. No one could be sure whether Arafat was trying to fool his own extremists or his perspective interlocutors. Thus, the PLO's hints had to become clear policies before being rewarded. The U.S. government was not convinced by the PNC meeting's results, calling its resolution a step forward that was not yet satisfactory. While Arafat had seriously entered the diplomatic playing field for the first time, the ball was still in his court.

Diplomatic efforts continued behind the scenes. President Reagan's National Security Advisor Colin Powell sent Arafat a message through some American Jewish peace activists meeting the PLO leader in Stockholm, Sweden, on November 21. The letter gave Reagan's pledge to start a dialogue with the PLO if it met the U.S. conditions of recognizing Israel, accepting UN Resolution 242, and rejecting terrorism.

At the Stockholm meeting Arafat privately went farther than the PNC resolution, saying he would accept a West Bank/Gaza Palestinian state living peacefully alongside Israel and commenting that, by doing so, he had "abrogated" and "nullified" provisions of the Charter. On November 25 the Swedish Foreign Ministry passed the text of Arafat's statement to Secretary of State Shultz.[12]

But this informal statement was in no way binding on the PLO. Shultz decided to keep up the pressure. The next day the U.S. government denied Arafat a visa to address the UN in New York on the grounds that he was responsible for continuing terrorism against Americans and others. The UN General Assembly then voted to convene a special session in Geneva, Switzerland, to hear him speak. On December 12 the State Department secretly told Arafat that it would open a dialogue if he met the U.S. conditions in his Geneva speech; Arafat pledged to do so.

Thus, as Arafat mounted the podium on December 13, 1988, the U.S. government expected a breakthrough. Shultz scheduled a press conference to announce a U.S.–PLO dialogue; State Department officials settled down in front of a television, copies of the agreed language in hand, to watch the performance. But Arafat again broke his promise, making a polemical speech instead of a conciliatory one. The State Department noted "some positive developments" but was actually quite discouraged. Shultz canceled his press conference. One more long diplomatic effort was on the brink of failure.[13]

To avoid forfeiting this opportunity, Arafat went further at a press conference the next day. Finally, resentfully, he said the magic words, speaking in English: "Our desire for peace is strategic and not a temporary tactic . . . Our state provides salvation for the Palestinians and peace for both the Palestinians and Israelis."

He accepted the "right of all parties concerned with the Middle East conflict to exist in peace and security, including—as I said—the State of Palestine, Israel, and other neighbors in accordance with Resolutions 242 and 338." He added, "We totally and categorically reject all forms of terrorism, including individual, group, and state terrorism." Clearly under great personal stress he concluded, "Enough is enough. Enough is enough. Enough is enough . . . We want peace . . . we are committed to peace, and we want to live in our Palestinian state and let others live."[14]

A few hours later, Shultz announced the U.S. conditions were met. For the first time since the PLO's creation almost a quarter-century before, it would be formally engaged in talks with the United States.

But the PLO's leaders did not take full advantage of this opportunity. Arab and Palestinian factors pressured them against concessions. Moreover, PLO leaders assumed that Israel was a U.S. puppet which would do what Washington ordered. They seized on the dialogue as a triumph to show constituents that the intifada was forcing a change in U.S. policy. Since the United States was being forced to give the PLO a state, they did not have to convince Israel to do so. The Palestinian uprising, Iraq's victory over Iran, and other factors, Nabil Sha'th claimed, "changed the balance in favor of the Palestinian cause." PLO broadcasts to the territories boasted, "The U.S. Administration has . . . been forced to cooperate with the PLO as the Palestinian people's sole representative."[15]

Rather than explaining to its followers that mutual concessions were necessary to reach a compromise peace settlement, the PLO told Palestinians that total success would soon come if they only stood firm. Rather than prepare its supporters for a major change in policy, the PLO assured them that no real alteration was necessary. Even Arafat's personal stationery as president of Palestine bore a map showing all Israel as part of that state.[16]

While the PLO now expected that the United States would meet its demands, the U.S. government defined this step not as negotiations but as constructive dialogue, only the start of a diplomatic process in which the PLO would have to prove its moderation and convince Israel that a solution with Arafat was possible. And the U.S. government added that even this opening stage would endure only if the PLO was seen to live up to Arafat's pledge in Geneva.

Egyptian President Mubarak, trying to be the PLO's mentor in diplomacy, advised Arafat to change the PLO's policy to take advantage of the situation's opportunities. Only by being more moderate could it appeal to those who could "influence Israel, such as the United States and European countries." Otherwise, these states would continue to support Israel's policy.[17]

Arafat disagreed, claiming that the PLO had great leverage over the United States and that the Arabs held "99 percent" of the cards. This was a carefully chosen image. A decade earlier, Anwar Sadat had justified making peace with Israel through U.S. mediation by commenting that the United States held "99 percent" of the cards.[18]

Rather than try to persuade Israelis that they could achieve peace and security by dealing with the PLO, Arafat argued that only Washington counted. Israel's decisions, he insisted, were made "in Washington and not in Tel Aviv." He recalled the 1956 Suez crisis, when Britain, France, and Israel invaded Egypt but pulled back at President Dwight Eisenhower's insistence. "What happened when he ordered them to withdraw? They immediately withdrew." He expected Israel to do the same now, quickly and simply, from the West Bank and Gaza. Arafat had reasons for feeding false hope to the Palestinian masses. As a politician, he knew that encouragement was needed to maintain the rebellion and to outbid his Islamic fundamentalist competitors. "Victory," he said in a broadcast to the occupied territories, "requires no more than an hour of patience . . . We are in the last quarter-hour of our suffering."[19]

Indeed, the intifada, the November 1988 PNC session, and the December 1988 Geneva press conference had given the Palestinian question a higher profile and the PLO a better image. Arafat was received by the Pope in December 1988 and by the European Community leadership in January 1989, and was invited by President

François Mitterand to Paris in January 1989. Basking in these successes, though, PLO's leaders in Tunis were prisoners of their own
optimistic assessment. In fact, Israel would not quickly crumble under the intifada's assault. Dealing with it only cost four percent of
Israel's defense budget, said Israel's Defense Minister Yitzhak Rabin
in 1989. Israeli society "has adjusted itself . . . What is the choice?"[20]

The PLO thus needed to offer Israel an attractive enough alternative, in addition to pressure from the rebellion and international
criticism of Israel's policy. "What is required from the PLO now is
not concessions, but clarity in reaching out to the peace-oriented
side of Israel," said Professor Rashid Khalidi. "The organization
must make it clear that the Palestinians are offering something the
Israelis can live with." But this did not happen. Meanwhile, the
Palestinians were running into problems.[21]

The intifada's first year had been marked by big demonstrations,
but there was less mass participation in 1989 and 1990 and far more
internecine killings of alleged collaborators. Israel could not stop
the uprising, but neither had months of constant rebellion made
any progress toward ending the occupation, establishing a new
state, or materially improving the lot of the Palestinians.

Ironically, the real historic "collaborators" with Israel had been
the West Bank and Gaza elite, now on good terms with the PLO.
Their families had bought and sold Israeli products; even the most
vocal nationalists among them had enjoyed good relations with Israel's administration in the occupied territories. These middle-class
people—called, contemptuously, "the princes" by intifada street
leaders—were the Palestinians most eager for a compromise settlement and often acted as go-betweens to the Israeli peace movement
or government. The radicals and Islamic fundamentalists attacked
them for their moderation. One widely publicized leaflet accused
pro-Fatah activists Sari Nusayba and Radwan Abu Ayyash, the Arab
Journalists Association's leader, of embezzling intifada funds. In
July 1989 the PFLP threatened to kill Jamil al-Tarifi, a lawyer and
former vice-mayor of al-Bira, who met Israeli leaders with Fatah's
permission.

The PLO portrayed the internal disputes among factions and individuals, or between fundamentalists and nationalists, as creations
of Israel. Quoting the Qur'an, Arafat urged followers to be "strong
against unbelievers, [but] compassionate among each other." He

explained, "Otherwise we will fall in the trap that our enemy is making for us, as happened to the revolution of 1936." Palestinians remembered how factional bloodshed had helped destroy that revolt. Criticizing internal conflict in the Gaza Bar Association, Arafat proclaimed, "We will not allow the Zionist enemy . . . to infiltrate through our passing disputes to fragment our strong national unity."[22]

In thousands of rock-throwing demonstrations against Israeli patrols, almost a thousand Palestinians were killed between December 1987 and the end of 1990. But these casualties were nearly equaled by the growing number of murders of Palestinians by one another. Unwilling to admit that even random killings happened outside his control, Arafat took responsibility for them, as "a president of a republic delegates his powers to the field commander to execute this soldier or that officer." Victims whom the PLO later decided to be innocent would be declared "martyrs of the Palestinian revolution."[23]

Yet Arafat's influence was often quite limited. A more realistic assessment of the division of power was made by a teenage leader of the Nablus "Red Eagles," captured after that gang killed five women (including a female cousin he personally murdered in a matter of family honor), two elderly men, and others. Arafat "is not aware of everything that happens in the territories or in all of Palestine. [Arafat] is abroad, we are here." Arafat worried about ordering a more moderate policy in part because he did not know if his commands would be obeyed.[24]

The PLO's sense of nervousness was increased as the months passed in 1989 and diplomatic exchanges made no progress. The international media and foreign governments became less interested in the intifada. "Every event that becomes monotonous and routine dies," said Khalid al-Hasan. The turmoil in the USSR and the collapse of Communist rule in East Europe upstaged it.

The PLO feared that U.S., Israeli, or even Egyptian plans might split people in the territories from the PLO. PLO leaders now began complaining, "The Americans haven't done anything for us" and Washington was merely "stalling while waiting for the intifada to die." Occasional U.S.–PLO meetings in Tunis between U.S. Ambassador Robert Pelletreau and a PLO delegation, however, were far less important than the efforts being made in Washington itself.

President George Bush's new administration took office in January 1989. "We are concerned," explained Secretary of State James Baker, "that if we act too precipitously we might preempt promising possibilities." He wanted to find a way to address both "Israel's legitimate security needs and . . . the legitimate political rights of the Palestinian people." This involved a delicate balancing act to avoid losing either side's cooperation.[25]

On April 14 Israel's coalition government—between the liberal Labor party and conservative Likud bloc, led by Prime Minister Yitzhak Shamir of the Likud—produced its own plan to negotiate with elected Palestinian leaders from the territories. While these people could not openly be PLO members, they almost certainly would be its supporters. Moreover, the election idea had been first proposed by local pro-PLO Palestinian leaders in January 1988 and was later taken up by Israeli Defense Minister Yitzhak Rabin.[26]

Rabin's Labor party was enthusiastic about elections. It believed that the local inhabitants, though considering themselves part of the PLO, would be more interested in securing Palestinian rule over the territories than in claiming the land within Israel's borders. The Likud, however, worried that Israel might be pressed or maneuvered into dealing with the PLO and accepting a Palestinian state ruled by it. Shamir endorsed the plan to keep good relations with the United States and maintain his coalition while hoping the PLO would say no. A Shamir supporter warned, however, "Every plan has its own dynamic." Just as Prime Minister Begin went to the Camp David meeting without intending to destroy Jewish settlements in the Sinai, "the election plan is also liable to lead to the conversion of Judea, Samaria and Gaza into a sovereign Arab region."[27]

The PLO was not so confident of using the plan to its own advantage. It wanted to represent directly the Palestinians in any talks and to be guaranteed a state as quickly as possible, without compromises. Actually, some West Bank leaders were so eager to negotiate an end to the occupation that they suggested elections might be acceptable. Faysal al-Husayni explained, "We do not oppose any solution or method that could lead us to a genuine Palestinian state." He urged the PLO to bargain rather than reject the proposal. "We must not fear discussion. To the contrary, we can push the Israelis further and further into a corner."[28]

PLO leaders, however, were adamantly opposed to elections, which Abu Iyad said would divert people's attention from the intifada and "divide Palestinian support among different candidates." The PLO Central Council rejected elections, and the local activists had to accept the decision.[29]

The PLO had three basic objections to the U.S. and Israeli proposals. First, empowering local West Bank and Gaza leaders seemed a dangerous gamble that might lead to loss of the PLO's control over events. Local leaders might make concessions to Israel, and they could eventually challenge or displace the PLO. The growing Islamic fundamentalist movements in the territories in particular posed a radical alternative to the PLO's role. The organization understandably worried that a more democratic arrangement or more local influence via elections could undermine it altogether.

Second, the PLO rejected the proposal as dealing only with the needs of Palestinians whose homes were in the West Bank and Gaza, not with those displaced in 1948 and dispersed in other lands.

Third, the PLO leaders had half persuaded themselves that the intifada was winning and that there was no reason to negotiate when a few more months of struggle would hand them a victory.[30]

In this case as with earlier proposals for a transitional process in the territories, the PLO did not try to adapt the plan to its own advantage. After all, the PLO's supporters would certainly win any elections. Those daring to oppose its nominees would face dishonor—because the PLO had so much popular support—or death, since the PLO would use intimidation. Once it controlled the Palestinian delegation and the institutions of self-rule, as Husayni hinted, the PLO would be in an excellent position to obtain an end to the occupation and gain independence.

Moreover, the West Bank and Gaza, once they were under Palestinian control, could provide a home for refugees living in Lebanon, Jordan, or elsewhere. But of course to free this land, the PLO would have to make real concessions. Most of the refugees who had lived in what was now Israel, as well as Marxist groups and Islamic fundamentalists, did not want to settle for just the West Bank and Gaza. The PFLP and DFLP, for example, denied that the 1988 PNC meeting had recognized Israel. They held Arafat's promises in Geneva merely to be his individual opinion, and "a flagrant violation" of the PNC's resolutions, "not binding on the PLO or on its institutions."[31]

Arafat himself did not consolidate or extend the positions set down in 1988. For example, in May 1989 he made world headlines by declaring the PLO Charter "caduque" during a visit to Paris. PLO officials variously interpreted this French word as meaning anything from "null and void," to "superseded" but not abrogated, to no change at all.

Moreover, extremist reactions were not limited to the smaller groups. At Fatah's August 1989 congress in Tunis there was a strong reaction against any moderate line. The 1,200 delegates passed a resolution full of hardline language, calling creation of the "Zionist entity," that is, Israel, a crime and demanding intensified armed struggle. There was no word of endorsement for the Geneva statements that formed the basis of the U.S.–PLO dialogue. After the United States criticized the meeting's statement for its "tone of confrontation and violence and its preference for unrealistic principles and solutions," Arafat simply issued a new one without some of the offending phrases.[32]

This total lack of change in the PLO's main group, which was under Arafat's direct leadership, should not have been a surprise. Arafat and his colleagues had done nothing to spread the new Geneva principles among the rank and file. On the contrary, they acted as if there had been no recognition of Israel or rejection of terrorism. Instead, Khalid al-Hasan was saying, "Whoever historically concedes the rest of Palestine is a traitor." Abu Sharif suggested that the August 1989 Fatah statement "should not be scrutinized linguistically and grammatically, but should be seen from its general tendency." But that general tendency showed only limited change or progress. At best, the PLO was being guided by the 1988 PNC resolution, which the United States had deemed inadequate at the time. Nor were PLO leaders interpreting that document in an especially moderate way.[33]

By maintaining its ambiguity, the PLO gave the United States less of an incentive to support its direct or immediate involvement in negotiations. Since the PLO had not convinced most Israeli voters or even the Labor party—much less the Likud—that it was ready to make real peace, no conceivable Israeli government would negotiate with the organization. Only an indirect process might work, unless or until the PLO was more forthcoming, mutual confidence was built, or local Palestinian leaders were able to bridge the gap.

The U.S. government agreed that Israel's May 1989 offer was a serious one that could break the deadlock in the peace process. U.S. officials lobbied for the plan with the PLO and West Bank/Gaza Palestinians. But to balance this position, the United States made gestures toward Palestinian political rights and indicated support for an eventual Israeli withdrawal from the occupied territories. To respond to one of the PLO's criticisms, Baker called on Israel to help find a "creative solution . . . to enable the participation of Palestinians who do not currently reside in the West Bank and Gaza Strip" and urged that country to give up "the unrealistic vision of a greater Israel."[34]

With the PLO still unable to respond to Israel's plan, Egyptian President Mubarak produced a ten-point blueprint of his own in July and August. Egypt's role in the peace process was pivotal since it was the most important single Arab state, the sole Arab country at peace with Israel, a U.S. ally, and the PLO's patron. Mubarak had ample incentive to help mediate a peace accord, for success would strengthen all these assets, guaranteeing his preeminence in the Arab world. Thus, Mubarak was determined to find an offer the Israelis might accept and one that the PLO could be persuaded to endorse.

Taking the Israeli proposal as a framework, Mubarak's proposition suggested ways to ensure elections were conducted without Israeli interference and to establish a clearer link between the balloting and an ultimate Israeli withdrawal from the territories. The election rules would include the presence of international observers, free speech for candidates, removal of Israeli troops from polling areas, participation of East Jerusalem residents, and a freeze on Jewish settlements in the territories. Israel would commit itself to accept the results. As for linkage, the postelection negotiating process would be governed by four principles: UN Resolutions 242 and 338, Israel's willingness to trade land for peace, security guarantees for all states, and recognition of Palestinian political rights.[35]

But despite Egypt's urging, the PLO was not persuaded.[36] Ironically, Israel's Likud party opposed Mubarak's plan because it, too, expected the proposal would inevitably mean PLO control of the territories. The Labor party part of Israel's coalition government endorsed Egypt's proposal, partly because it concurred with the PLO view that the local residents would take over. But in October, the

Likud members of Israel's inner cabinet voted down Mubarak's plan.

Almost immediately, Baker came up with a new offer built on the original Israeli and Egyptian ideas and designed to win PLO support without alienating Israel. The Egyptians would assemble a Palestinian delegation—implicitly chosen by the PLO—including East Jerusalem residents and deportees representing Palestinians outside the territories. After the United States and Israel approved the list, an Israel–Palestinian meeting would prepare for elections. Baker implied that the PLO would surely direct the delegation from behind the scenes and agreed that the Palestinians could raise issues other than the election itself.[37]

Given these concessions, Israel's Likud ministers sought added assurances that the PLO would be excluded from direct participation. The United States refused to make further changes and applied some pressure, linking U.S. aid for resettling the hundreds of thousands of Soviet Jewish immigrants to Israel with an Israeli freeze on building or expanding Jewish settlements in the territories.[38] On November 5 Israel's cabinet voted to accept Baker's points, but only with reservations over the participation of East Jerusalem residents and deportees.[39]

Offered the opportunity to exacerbate divisions among Israel's leaders and widen a U.S.–Israel split, the PLO nonetheless rejected Baker's proposal as giving it too small a role. Instead, the PLO demanded an international conference with its own direct participation. Mubarak dealt with the rebuff by ignoring it. He simply told the United States in early December that the PLO agreed to Baker's plan. Washington overlooked both sides' reservations, interpreting each Israeli or PLO "Yes, but . . ." as a "Yes." Nonetheless, both the PLO and Israel preferred to say no.[40]

Terrorism also posed a problem for the peace process. The State Department's secret message to Arafat defining the dialogue specified that the PLO "publicly disassociate" itself "from terrorism by any Palestinian group operating anywhere." If a PLO group or its members committed terrorism, "We expect that you not only condemn this action publicly but also discipline those responsible for it, at least by expelling them from the PLO."[41]

But after Bethlehem mayor Elias Freij suggested a one-year truce to facilitate negotiations, Arafat warned that anyone calling for the uprising's end "exposes himself to the bullets of his own people." The State Department complained that this threat fit "very badly" with Arafat's rejection of terrorism.[42]

Although Fatah refrained from openly attacking Israel, its Western Sector and Force-17 sections did so with molotov cocktails, grenades, and bombs. Smaller PLO member groups publicly announced their attacks. PFLP men crossed into Jordan from Syria to fire rockets at Israel; the PFLP, DFLP, and PLF tried to send squads across the Lebanese border. But the State Department bent over backwards to avoid acknowledging any terrorism in order to maintain the U.S.–PLO dialogue: minimizing the PLO membership of the smaller groups, ignoring evidence of continued terrorism by Fatah, and refusing to define attempted attacks across the Lebanon–Israel border as terrorist on the grounds that their targets "were unclear" since Israel killed or captured the terrorists before they were able to carry out their mission.

Abu Iyad explained that while the PLO rejected the idea that the intifada itself use arms, it wanted to escalate "the armed struggle away from the intifada's areas but in interaction with it." In other words, the PLO could continue cross-border attacks. "We did not promise the Americans or others that we would stop the armed struggle," he claimed, totally denying the basis of the U.S.–PLO dialogue. Terrorism meant only international operations; armed operations inside the territories or against Israel were permitted, even if they "affect civilians by mistake."[43]

This was different from the commitment the United States thought Arafat made at Geneva where he stated that any group engaging in terror "shall be expelled from the PLO ranks." The PLO used the loophole of claiming every attack to be a legitimate strike at military targets. It also endorsed raids by member groups against civilian targets, as when the DFLP openly declared that one of its raids from Lebanon was intended to hit the Israeli agricultural village of Zar'it.[44]

To argue about defining "armed struggle" and "terrorism," however, was beside the point. PLO armed attacks jeopardized the peace process, hardened Israeli positions, and ultimately subverted the U.S.–PLO dialogue. Arafat's unwillingness or inability to control, expel, or punish those sabotaging the peace process through terrorism undermined his diplomatic option.[45]

The PLO, for example, praised and justified the act of a Gaza man who seized the steering wheel of an Israeli bus on the main intercity line and forced it into a ravine in July 1989. Sixteen passengers were killed and twenty-five injured. The PLO also cheered a February 1990 Palestinian fundamentalist attack on an Israeli tourist bus in Egypt which killed nine and injured seventeen passengers. Cairo was angry at the PLO for supporting this deed. The magazine *Mayo* complained, "Why don't you say it loudly once and for all, that you don't want peace, and you don't want stability in Egypt." This was a "stab in the back" after Egypt had done so much for the Palestinians.[46]

By the start of 1990 the peace process had become so entangled—as the United States tried to keep the PLO or Israel from walking out—as to seem hopeless. Shamir rejected including East Jerusalem residents in the Palestinian delegation, saying that this jeopardized Israel's claim on the city. The United States and Israel's Labor party suggested that these people might simply register from their residences in other West Bank towns. Shamir opposed including Palestinians from outside the territories to represent their compatriots living in Arab states. The United States and the Labor party proposed that Israel let some Palestinians previously deported from the territories return and then join the delegation.

On the other side, the PLO demanded that it openly choose the Palestinian delegation; Israel demanded that Egypt formally select it. The PLO wanted an open agenda for the Cairo meeting; Israel insisted on talking about elections. The United States provided for opening statements in which the Palestinians could mention their desire for a state and ultimate PLO participation, and then focus on elections. Both Shamir and Arafat disliked these compromises and looked for a way out of the process.

The Peres–Shamir national unity government could not reconcile the contradictory objectives it faced. To put down the intifada would require harsher measures; to convince local Palestinian leaders to join negotiations meant offering them more. By refusing to deal with the PLO, Israel encouraged it to block progress; by failing to convince Israel that it had abandoned its traditional goals, the PLO lost any opportunity to change Israeli policy. The deadlock would not be broken by grudging, ambiguous hints about recognizing Israel accompanied with frequent references to long-term plans to destroy it, or promises to abandon terrorism amidst continuing terrorist attacks.

"Don't you understand," an American Jewish peace activist wrote Arafat, "that words of moderation must be translated into deeds before they can be believed? It is true that the PLO has moved, but it has not moved nearly far enough." If the PLO went further, Israel's policy would follow suit. While an overwhelming majority of Israelis opposed talks with the PLO, half were already willing to exchange territory for peace. Far more would favor bilateral negotiations if the PLO moderated its behavior and demands.[47]

Pressed by his Labor party partners to accept Baker's plan, Shamir finally refused to do so in March 1990. The government coalition fell, and Shamir reconstituted the cabinet as a rightist one with himself still as prime minister. Since Israel, not the PLO, had publicly and officially rejected the peace process, the Bush administration put most of the blame on it for the failure.

This U.S.–Israel tension presented the PLO with another golden opportunity to divide Washington and Jerusalem further. Washington was ready to support a UN resolution condemning Israeli settlements in the occupied territories in April 1990, but the PLO and some Arab states kept demanding tougher language and the deal fell through. Similarly, the State Department promised Arafat to raise the level of the U.S.–PLO dialogue if he gave a temperate speech to the May 1990 UN session in Geneva. Instead, he made a hardline statement which included his flourishing of an Israeli coin which, he claimed, contained a secret map showing Israel's intention to conquer most of the Arab world.[48]

On May 30 a large terrorist force of sixteen men left Libya by sea on their way to attack Israel's coast. They were former Fatah fighters the PLF had recruited with Iraq's assistance and trained with Libya's help. It was a major Jewish holiday and the beaches were packed with families. The force's orders were to kill civilians in Tel Aviv. Instead, Israeli forces sank some of the terrorists' boats, killed four of the men, and captured the other twelve on the beach moments after they landed.[49] Here was a major and highly visible terrorist attack, launched by a PLO member group. The U.S. government could not avoid holding Arafat to his word, but the PLO refused to criticize or punish the act. Despite U.S. efforts to salvage the dialogue, the Bush administration felt compelled to suspend it on June 20.

The round of peace efforts begun in 1988 was at an end. The PLO had largely squandered the political capital from three years of costly struggle by the intifada and its own policy reevaluation. Arafat implied recognition of Israel in Geneva, but the PNC's contradictory and ambiguous language, PLO leaders' hardline statements, and the organization's failure to confirm or firmly adopt Arafat's words there as a new strategy left serious doubts about its beliefs, intentions, and ability to deliver. Arafat did not crack down on terrorism and extremism in its ranks, and the PLO made little effort to persuade Israel that a West Bank/Gaza Palestinian state was the best way to achieve a stable peace.[50]

The PLO's structure and ideology had once again taken precedence. No matter how blame is apportioned for the collapse of the 1988–1990 peace efforts, the PLO was the big loser. The lack of practical gains demoralized Palestinians, who now turned once again to an external savior. If the PLO could not help them, perhaps Iraqi dictator Saddam Husayn could. When Iraq invaded Kuwait in August 1990, the PLO supported it. The resulting crisis again pushed the intifada and the Palestinian issue onto the back burner while seriously weakening the PLO's position.

7 >> The PLO and the Arab States

Yasir Arafat unintentionally revealed the essence of the PLO's relations with the Arab states when he said in 1973 that the PLO would fight on like the Spartan troops at the ancient battle of Thermopylae, who defended Greece "until at last the rest of the Greek forces arrived."[1] True, the Spartans battled courageously, but the other Greek cities never sent their armies to help. The Spartans were wiped out.

To judge only from the Arab states' propaganda, they have been totally devoted to the Palestinian cause and the PLO. In fact, however, they have always pursued their own interests, refusing to fight Israel or the West on the PLO's behalf and often treating the Palestinians and the PLO with contempt. A history of bitter experiences might have taught the PLO that it could not rely on any Arab regime, "that virtually every Arab state has stabbed them in the back at one point or another," as a veteran Palestinian nationalist has written. Yet the Palestinians and PLO could not break their wishful expectation that an Arab ruler would be their savior in 1990, when President Saddam Husayn of Iraq became their great Arab hope.[2]

The major Arab powers—especially Egypt, Syria, and Iraq—are far stronger than the PLO or a Palestinian state could ever be. They control large territories, huge economic resources, well-equipped armies, and populations far exceeding the total number of Palestinians, even if that dispersed people were to be gathered together. Arafat had some assets, mainly the prestige and popularity of the Palestinian cause, but while such symbols have been potent at some times, at other moments they motivated far more Arab talk than action.

Instead, Arab states often saw the PLO as a useful tool to manipulate but never considered it an equal partner, neither consulting it nor respecting its interests when setting their policy toward Israel or the United States. When not ignoring the PLO, they interfered with it. A PLO intelligence chief estimated that the Arab states were responsible for three-quarters of Palestinians killed in the struggle.[3] Only in exceptional cases—Jordan for a few months in 1969 and 1970, and the weak divided state of Lebanon from the mid-1970s to 1982—did Arafat briefly gain the upper hand over a state.

The Arab states limited their assistance to Arafat and attached strings to any help they did provide. For almost two decades following 1948, the Palestinians accepted subordination to the Arab states, believing that Arab unity would bring them liberation. But when Fatah took over the PLO and claimed itself to be the vanguard for the anti-Israel struggle, the liberation of Palestine, and Pan-Arab unity, the PLO became a potential threat to the sovereignty of the Arab states.[4]

The Arab–Israel conflict was no typical international dispute over land or power, easily settled by compromise or some ingenious formula. To outsiders, wrote one scholar, failure to resolve the issue was "as puzzling as the solutions are obvious." It seemed simple for Israelis and Palestinians to recognize each other and divide the territory to give a national homeland to both peoples. Arab governments could recognize Israel, security guarantees could be worked out, and a golden age of peace and prosperity begun.[5]

This conflict's logic, however, was that of an existential struggle. Basic principles within Arab nationalism and Islam rejected Israel's existence and consequently negotiations with it, even aside from the issue of who is to hold which piece of ground. There could be no compromise with an entity which was allegedly blocking achievement of a united Arab state or a true Islamic society. To abandon the battle against Israel was to betray the most basic of Arab and Islamic political goals, a step no Arab state could easily contemplate.

In turn, the Israelis, seeing the Arab goal of their state's destruction and, in practice, their personal elimination, became intensely wary of making compromises with Arab states, a defensiveness that reinforced Arab misperceptions of Israel's own motivations and behavior. To take some drastic examples of the skewed thinking of Arab leaders, Syria's Defense Minister Mustafa Tlas wrote a book claiming that Jews murdered children to obtain blood for Passover matzo. Saudi Arabia distributed the notorious Czarist antisemitic forgery, *The Protocols of the Elders of Zion*, which claimed that Jews were plotting to rule the world. Kuwait's UN ambassador, a Palestinian, spoke of a "cabal which controls and manipulates and exploits the rest of humanity by controlling the money and wealth of the world . . . It is a well-known fact that the Zionists are the richest people in the world and control much of its destiny." Even sophisticated Arab intellectuals repeated amazing conspiracy theories and spoke of Israel's "hegemonic design" to rule the whole region.[6] Many Arabs believed that Israel must expand or disappear and so posed an inevitable threat to their own countries.

But the Arabs' difficulty in accepting Israel arose not only because they psychologically and philosophically rejected the permanence of a non-Arab, non-Muslim state in the region or because they misunderstood Israeli motivations, but also because of their leaders' pragmatic assessment of the political benefits of intransigence and the dangers of compromise. Opposition to Israel, for example, was often the only subject on which Arab leaders could agree.

Ironically, this consensus quickly became divisive. Each regime tried to use the conflict as a tool to curry domestic support and as a weapon against rival Arab states. Rulers competed with one another to prove themselves the most righteously militant. Those in confrontation with Israel demanded and received large-scale aid from wealthy oil-producing states. Consequently, lost wars and territory only increased Arab determination to erase the stain of failure from their reputations. While those overcome in war usually sue for peace, the Arab states opposed any compromise after the 1948 and 1967 defeats.

The continuing existence of Israel, one Arab writer noted, "is a memorial to Arab weakness and division." Its survival was a living, humiliating reminder of the painful hollowness of Arab and Islamic ideology which could neither be wished away with words nor crushed by force of arms.[7] In short, practical political considerations—domestic, foreign, and economic—meant that Arab regimes benefited by exploiting, not by peacefully resolving, the Palestinian issue.

The Arab–Israeli problem often seemed so salient to Western observers precisely because it was the one topic most easily discussed among the Arabs. Blaming the region's shortcomings on Israel was safe and popular among Arab intellectuals and journalists, who were not permitted to criticize their own government. Indeed, there was something for everyone in maintaining the fiction that the Palestine question was the region's central, overwhelming issue, rather than internal conflicts and rivalries among and within Arab states. Each Arab government mobilized its subjects and diverted internal criticism by using the Palestinian issue to prove that it was fulfilling its nationalist and Islamic duty. Every Arab ruler could accuse rival countries or local dissidents of being allies of Zionism who weakened the unity needed to confront Israel. Opposition groups could claim power by decrying the incumbents' ineffectiveness in combating the Zionist threat.

Radical rulers insisted that rival regimes were not energetic enough in combatting Israel and thus should be overthrown. Leftist or Islamic fundamentalist movements called for insurrections at home as a precondition for fighting and defeating Israel. Revolutionaries portrayed Israel's existence as proof of the West's inevitable perfidy and enmity; moderate Arab leaders countered that the West was only deluded by Zionist propaganda and could be won over.

Similarly, conservative Western experts claimed that the Arab–Israeli conflict was the sole source of Arab hostility to the West, denying that past or present conflicts with their own countries gave rise to Arab grievances. Hence, they suggested, bilateral relations might be preserved and regional problems resolved at Israel's expense and at little cost to themselves. Western radicals, on the other hand, portrayed the PLO as an idealistic revolutionary cause seeking to create a just society. For them, caricaturing Israel as a Western creation was one more way to condemn their own countries.

Yet while the Arab regimes acted pragmatically in attacking Israel and pledging support for the PLO, they also learned to be practical in their caution, by simultaneously being militant in word and timorous in deed. Supporting resolutions at the United Nations, donating money, or even aiding terrorism behind the scenes were relatively low-risk propositions for Arab states. But a PLO trying to drag them into another losing war with Israel became a nuisance; when the PLO supported their foes it became their enemy. Thus, Arab states watched impassively as PLO headquarters was chased from Amman to Beirut, and from Beirut to Tunis.

Arab politicians coupled a hardline, tough-minded strategy with an ingenuous pose. In practice, they acted as if they might endlessly reiterate their intention to fight and destroy Israel through every possible channel yet suffer no consequences in the form of Israeli retaliation. When Israel did strike back, its actions were portrayed as proof of its inherently aggressive, expansionist nature.

Arab governments themselves understood better than Westerners how politics, particularly Middle East politics, worked. "Aggressors thrive on appeasement," Iraqi Ambassador Nizar Hamdoun explained. "The world learned that at tremendous cost from the Munich agreement of 1938 . . . How could the German generals oppose Hitler once he had proven himself successful? Indeed, aggressors are usually clever at putting their demands in a way that seems reasonable. Hitler first pretended that he had limited goals, which Europe might accept."[8]

But since Israel could defend itself, its threat or use of force deterred Arab states from a conventional military assault. Once frustrated at their inability to destroy Israel, Arab states reduced their role in the Arab–Israeli conflict. The high costs and disappointing outcomes of the 1967, 1973, and 1982 wars, widening inter-Arab disputes, the Iran–Iraq war, and political quarrels with the PLO generally accelerated this trend.

Once Egypt, exhausted from wasting its limited resources, broke the Arab consensus and made peace with Israel, Syria had more reason to avoid a conflict. Preoccupied with the Iranian threat in their front yards, Saudi Arabia and Kuwait had even less time for the PLO's cause. Jordan periodically closed PLO offices and blocked it from attacking across the border into Israel. Lebanese Druze, Christian, and Shi'a groups limited PLO presence in their jurisdictions, and the latter two even fought it.[9]

Thus, Arafat walked a tightrope in trying to maximize Arab support, balancing every favor by leaning in the opposite direction, preserving his independence by using it only sparingly. No matter what any Arab ruler did against him, Arafat always remembered that the Arab leader who shot at him one day might become the one he kissed another, and the reverse as well. This extraordinarily difficult task showed Arafat's greatest skill but also damaged the PLO's ability to adjust to conditions and opportunities. A sympathetic historian wrote, "Few independence movements have been so heavily dependent on external assistance," and the PLO's survival was conditioned on maintaining "unity at any price." [10]

By avoiding domination by a single patron or conflicts with Arab states that might cause them to revoke his license as the Palestinian leader, Arafat won a considerable degree of autonomy for the PLO. He understood that having some Arab rulers as enemies would necessitate having others as masters, and vice versa.

Arafat traveled in perpetual motion among Arab capitals, preserving his connections and making deals. Conflicts between Arab states gave him maneuvering room. When Jordan attacked the PLO, Arafat took refuge with Syria; when Syria assaulted the PLO, he turned to Jordan and Egypt. Falling out with the moderates, Arafat accepted the patronage of Iraqi dictator Saddam Husayn.

Like the PLO's terrorist strategy, which was also a beneficiary of this approach, its Arab policy promoted the organization's survival while blocking its success. The PLO's ability to continue fighting depended on Arab states providing bases, supplies, training, money, arms, political backing, and protection against retaliation. Terrorists were far more prolific and deadly when they had genuine passports, weapons shipped through Arab diplomatic pouches, and lavish funding. Concerned that jailing PLO agents would damage their relations with Arab states, West European governments were reluctant to punish the PLO.

Giving or denying patronage, however, also allowed the Arab regimes tremendous leverage over the PLO. Syria and Egypt refused to let the PLO to attack Israel across their borders in the 1960s; Jordan expelled it in 1970; Syria attacked it in Lebanon in 1976; Iraqi gunmen shot down its officials in 1977; Egypt abandoned it by making peace in 1978 and 1979; Syria split it in 1983; Lebanese Christians and Shi'a Muslims massacred its people in 1982 and 1985; Iraq pushed it aside by invading Iran in 1980 and Kuwait in 1990; and after 1983, Syria-controlled parts of Lebanon were also off limits to Arafat.

In contrast to Arafat's strategy, smaller PLO groups, out of weakness and ideology, often became clients of Arab regimes. At worst, these groups often became mercenaries, striking targets approved by their state sponsors, including the contract murders of PLO officials. Abu Nidal was the best example of this relationship. After leaving the PLO in 1974, he attacked it in league with his first host, Iraq. In 1982 his attempted assassination of Israel's ambassador to London was the immediate cause of Israel's advance into Lebanon. When Iraq expelled him in 1983, in order to court Western support for its war with Iran, Abu Nidal went on to Damascus and carried out an anti-Jordan terrorist campaign for Syria. Fearful of Western retaliation, Syria cast him out in 1986. Next he moved to Libya, mounting the massacres at Istanbul's synagogue in September 1986 and on the Greek ferry *City of Poras* in July 1988. Qadhafi closed down his operation in 1989 when the Libyan leader decided to seek respectability. Abu Nidal also worked closely with Poland and East Germany, selling arms and perhaps doing operations for them. Nonetheless, Arafat negotiated with him between 1986 and 1988 over readmission to the PLO, and Fatah gladly took over his defecting supporters in 1989 as well as recruiting active international terrorists from other groups.[11]

In the wake of their military defeats and in the light of their other priorities, the Arab states went from an unwillingness to wage war for the Palestinians' sake to waging war on the PLO or even refusing to contribute money to it. While a 1978 inter-Arab agreement promised $250 million a year to the PLO and $150 million to a Jordan–PLO committee, only Saudi Arabia paid its share. Highly publicized financial pledges often went unfulfilled. Nor did Arab states give much to UNRWA, the humanitarian relief effort for Palestinians refugees, over 40 percent of whose budget was provided by the United States. One researcher called the PLO "the richest and most powerful terrorist group in the world."[12] Still, it was poor compared with the needs of the state-in-the-making it was trying to be.

In contrast, when Egypt announced plans to rebuild the ancient Alexandria library in early 1990, the United Arab Emirates, Iraq, and Saudi Arabia offered $20 million each. A pro-PLO newspaper commented, "We only wish that these Arab leaders would demonstrate equal generosity in supporting the intifada." Arafat pointed out the contrast between the rich Arab states' generosity to Afghan guerrillas and their tightfisted attitude toward the Palestinians. After the PLO supported Iraq's occupation of Kuwait in 1990, the wealthy Arab states stopped donations altogether.[13]

The gap between the Arab states' rhetorical enthusiasm and stingy support provoked Arafat's growing ire. "Honestly," he said in 1985, "the problems we face in our relations with some of our Arab brothers are much worse than those we face vis-à-vis Israel." He declared that mountain snows were warmer and more hospitable than the Arab rulers' hearts.[14]

Sabri Jiryis, director-general of the PLO's research center, concluded at the same time that the Palestinian experience disproved the whole concept of Pan-Arabism. Rather than help the PLO, the Arab states had "either abstained from fulfilling that role, or even acted against it." In reality, there was no single Arab nation, but rather many Arab "peoples with different regimes with very frequently conflicting interests."[15]

As Jiryis hinted, the Arab–Israel conflict was not the cause but merely the most visible manifestation of the search for Arab identity, internecine strife, and anti-Western resentments that made the region's politics so tumultuous. "It may come as a surprise to many Arabs and foreigners," wrote an Arab intellectual in 1979, "to know that the Palestinians are not always the fundamental cause of a military clash in the Middle East, nor are they the reason why Arab governments fight their wars against Israel." Rather, the "Palestinian cause is, and has been, a pawn of inter-Arab rivalry."[16]

Part of the problem for the PLO was that while Arabs often had an abstract sympathy for the Palestinians' cause and plight, they disdained them for having lost their country or envied them for their education, wealth, or good jobs in Arab countries. In the tiny Gulf emirate of Qatar, for example, 20,000 Palestinians formed the largest expatriate Arab group, holding high posts in the government, professions, and business. They included the most powerful Finance Ministry official, the national bank's head, and the ruler's chief advisor on engineering and contracting. But their loyalty was always suspect and their tenure insecure. When the PLO supported Iraq's invasion of Kuwait, Qatar expelled many of the most prominent Palestinians.[17]

Over 300,000 Palestinians lived and worked in Kuwait for decades without ever gaining equal rights there. Saudi Arabia tried to keep Palestinians out of the country altogether. If Palestinians had become, as they liked to say, the "Jews of the Middle East" in their dispersion, they also filled that group's historic role as a target of antipathy. "In the Gulf," claimed a Palestinian intellectual, they were "treated like third-rate human beings."[18]

But there was also a major political divergence between the PLO and Arab states. The former was preoccupied by the "Palestine issue," demanding that all Arabs make the destruction of the "Zionist entity" and the liberation of the Palestinian homeland their top priority. Arab regimes were more concerned with the "Israel issue"—having a conflict with a strong, unfriendly neighboring state which they were unable to eliminate and which could hurt them. Fighting against Israel was not the same thing as helping the PLO, and helping the PLO was a low priority for the Arab states.

The PLO's problem in gaining support from Arab regimes deepened as these countries developed more distinctive, divergent characters and were willing to express their own interests openly. Undoubtedly, it meant far more to be an Iraqi, Egyptian, Jordanian, or Syrian in the 1980s or 1990s than it did in earlier years when citizens of these infant states remembered a time before these boundaries existed. There was no charismatic leader who even had a popular following outside his own borders. Arab governments put their own goals, problems, and grudges first, and Pan-Arab nationalism declined because of such failures as Nasir's inability to unite the Arab world, the quarrel between ruling Syrian and Iraqi Ba'th party branches, and Lebanon's civil war. Rather than expel foreign influences, rulers sought help from Washington or Moscow in these quarrels, dividing the Arab world into two camps. Syria and Libya pursued their own interests—in total disregards for Arab solidarity—by supporting non-Arab Iran in its war with Iraq.

As Arab states lowered the Arab–Israeli conflict's priority, Western sympathizers failed to note this change, insisting that "the entire Arab world feels a sense of solidarity" with the Palestinians. The conflict was said to be the root of anti-Americanism, Islamic fundamentalism, and all other regional ills.[19] The Arabs themselves had no such illusions and were well aware of their rising neglect, disunity, and passivity on the Arab–Israeli conflict issue. "Since the oil embargo of 1973," wrote Hisham Sharabi, a leading Arab intellectual, a decade afterward, "there has not been any credible Arab pressure to influence American policy toward the Arab world."[20] Literature professor Edward Said pointed to the way in which Arab rhetoric maintained "an enthusiasm for distant generality [which] covers up particular experiences and with them immediate failure." The struggle to obtain the unattainable left the Arabs "embittered or apathetic."[21]

While unwilling to make war, Arab leaders were equally aware of the risks of making peace. Tougher rhetoric was often used to conceal their passivity toward Israel. Thus, Arab rulers whipped up public opinion by heated rhetoric and then became the prisoners— or even victims—of their own demagoguery, intimidated by pressures they had helped create. Nasir once told a U.S. envoy in the 1950s, "I don't want to happen to me what happened to [Jordan's] King Abdallah," assassinated by Palestinian nationalists. "That is why I cannot risk an agreement with Israel."[22] The murders of Presidents Sadat and Bashir Jumayyil, in 1981 and 1982, though also motivated by other issues, seemed to validate this fear.

Despite their rhetorical consistency, the Arab states were more often divided than united by the Arab–Israeli conflict. Each country had some interests conflicting with the PLO. Jordan wanted the West Bank for itself and feared PLO competition for the loyalty of its Palestinian citizens. Egypt made peace with Israel to regain the Sinai peninsula. Lebanese Christians allied with Israel in trying to win the civil war there. Syria made war on the PLO in Lebanon and split the organization; Libya and Iraq used terrorism in trying to control it. Baghdad subordinated the issue, first, to its war against Iran and then to its ambition over Kuwait. Saudi Arabia preferred to invest in the West and to obtain U.S. protection rather than to press Western countries on the PLO's behalf. The PLO was painfully aware of the states' growing lethargy on the issue.

Iraqi dictator Saddam Husayn illustrates this pattern. For two decades, he trampled on the PLO's interests. Yet Arafat, who had unsuccessfully tried Syrian, Jordanian, and Egyptian patronage in the 1980s, turned toward Iraq in the 1990s. Iraq stood in the wings as an alternate, more radical, patron. So extreme was its historic policy that Iraq was the sole Arab country preferring to withdraw its troops from the front in the 1948 war rather than sign a ceasefire with Israel. But rhetorical militancy was often a substitute for direct engagement. In 1970, for example, Iraqi troops stationed in Jordan did nothing while King Husayn crushed the PLO.

Although Baghdad talked of sacrificing itself on the altar of Palestine, Saddam was soon openly proclaiming that Iraq and its concerns came first. He played rough with the PLO, maintaining puppet Palestinian groups inside and outside of the organization. Palestinian refugees resident in Iraq were restricted and mistrusted. Even members of pro-Iraq PLO groups were closely watched by the secret police, and Iraqi citizens feared to make friends with them. In the late 1970s Fatah and Iraq fought a covert war, attacking each other's officials in Britain, France, Pakistan, and Lebanon.

Just after Iran's 1979 revolution, Arafat had predicted that Islamic Iran and the Arabs would unite against Israel. A year later, Iraq attacked Iran and the two sides became blood enemies. As long as Iraq was fighting Iran, between 1980 and 1988, its needs conflicted with those of the PLO. In a bid for U.S. support in the mid-1980s, Iraq's Ambassador to Washington, Nizar Hamdoun sent American journalists and policymakers full-color copies of a captured Iranian map which showed Tehran's eventual goal to be the capture of Jerusalem and the destruction of Israel. His motive was to invite U.S. support for Iraq as *de facto* protector of Israel.

At a small dinner party in Washington during a 1985 visit, Iraq's Foreign Minister Tariq Aziz explained that the Iran–Iraq war was his country's principal problem. A drunken American columnist was outraged. "You must tell Secretary of State Shultz," he shouted, "that the Arab–Israeli conflict is your main concern!" The somewhat shaken diplomat tried to calm his guest. "Of course, the Arab–Israeli issue is important but that is not my mission's purpose." But the enraged American went on chastising the startled Iraqi leader for failing to live up to his expectations of proper Arab behavior.[23]

Arafat, too, had expectations of what Iraq should do. He claimed that the war's end would make Baghdad and other Arab states devote themselves to supporting the Palestinian people's cause.[24] Saddam seemed a valuable ally, victor over Iran and master of ample oil wealth and a one-million-man army. Having already developed missiles and chemical weapons able to hit Israel, Iraq was busily building nuclear and biological arms as well. With the USSR no longer giving the Arabs a nuclear umbrella and superpower alternative to the United States, the PLO and other Arabs sought a local replacement.

Pessimistic about the peace process, suspicious of U.S. intentions, and weary of Egyptian demands for more moderation, Arafat moved closer to Iraq in 1989. The PLO shifted some offices from Tunis to Baghdad and began holding many top-level meetings there. Arafat came monthly to Iraq's capital to be greeted with all the pomp reserved for a head of state. Iraq gave him a big Palestinian embassy building and his own private jet.

When Saddam Husayn threatened to destroy half of Israel with chemical weapons in April 1990, Palestinians, frustrated at the intifada's inability to make political gains through militancy or negotiations, began seeing him as a liberator, as they had done with Nasir in the 1950s and 1960s. Iraq, the PLF's patron, may have sponsored that group's May 1990 terrorist attack on Israel's coast in order to destroy the peace process.

Arafat also saw Saddam as the region's new strongman. At the May 1990 Arab summit in Baghdad, the PLO leader helped Iraq's ruler claim Arab leadership. Calling Saddam a "noble knight," Arafat said that Baghdad's missiles and chemical weapons provided the Arabs the strength "to achieve liberation from Baghdad to Jerusalem and from al-Faw [southern Iraq] to Gaza." Yet despite this lavish praise, Saddam Husayn neither pressed for increased aid to the PLO nor even insisted on mentioning the Palestinian issue in the meeting's final communique.

Egypt was livid about Iraq's "stealing" the PLO away from it and upset about Arafat's lack of cooperation in the peace process. In the summer of 1990 Cairo's government-controlled press attacked Arafat's "betrayal." A PLO leaflet issued on August 1, 1990, called Egypt an American "puppet" and "an obedient tool in the hands of the American administration."

The next day, Saddam Husayn invaded Kuwait, and Arafat backed what he thought was the winning side. An East Jerusalem Palestinian newspaper suggested that Iraq should have sent its troops to the West Bank, "where they would be welcome." But an Arab journalist sighed, "God save this nation from its heroes!" For Iraq's invasion and annexation of Kuwait again divided the Arab world and diverted attention from the Palestinian struggle. Kuwait had once been Arafat's home and the place where he founded Fatah. Now he was siding against the country that had given him refuge and riches. The PLO's policy antagonized its financial backers in Saudi Arabia and Kuwait, its political patrons in Egypt, the United States, and USSR, and its potential negotiating partners in Israel.[25]

Iraq mustered relatively little Arab support because most other regimes thought it was acting out of selfish interests and would target them next. In response, Saudi Arabia requested U.S. help to protect its independence. Egypt and Syria acted in their own national interests to oppose Baghdad's aggression and bid for regional domination.

In contrast, Arafat claimed the United States was the threat, "aspiring to take control of the world's sources of oil." When the Gulf War began, the PLO accused the United States of "cowardly aggression" against Iraq, warning that "blood, catastrophe and destruction" will sweep the world.[26]

In supporting Saddam, Arafat and the PLO were echoing their constituents' genuine adulation for Iraq's ruler. Frustrated by the failure of the intifada or PLO to end the occupation, Palestinians repeated the old mistake of subordinating their future to Arab leaders and betting on a military rather than a diplomatic option. Once again, Palestinians seemed to be a radical, anti-American, and destabilizing force. At first, only Abu Iyad warned of this policy's dangers: "We are opposed to the invasion and annexation of Kuwait," he said. "We cannot revolve in Iraq's or any other state's orbit."[27] But he loyally supported Arafat's stand.

The PLO's stance tore up all its promises from the previous two years. The organization's moderation was shown to be fragile as Arafat reverted, almost with an audible sigh of relief, to his traditional, radical stance. The PLO acted partly out of disappointment with the results of the 1988 peace initiative: Israel refused to negotiate with it, Shamir and his party did not want to give up any territory, and the PLO disapproved of the whole proposed procedure for negotiations.

Yet the PLO's new policy, though popular among Palestinians, hurt the Palestinians even more than the previous deadlock. If, as Arafat often said, the PLO's peace initiative was strategic, not tactical—permanent, not temporary—how could he abandon it so easily? And if the PLO really understood the necessity of a historic diplomatic compromise solution entailing acceptance of Israel, it should have realized that depending on Iraq to destroy Israel with chemical weapons would never bring a Palestinian homeland.

The PLO's alignment with Iraq unleashed an unprecedented storm of criticism from Saudi Arabia, Kuwait, and Egypt. *Al-Ahram*, Egypt's leading newspaper, called Arafat's embrace of Saddam "prostration" before the man who had plunged "his poisoned dagger in the Arabs' back." A high Saudi official wrote that Arafat "not only abandoned Kuwait but also lauded its butcher!" The PLO needs new leaders, said a Saudi writer, who "can speak to the world in more civilized way and who oppose any kind of aggression and occupation, if it is by Israel, Iraqi, Palestinian terrorists or others."[28]

An Egyptian journalist asked, "How can one blame the Gulf states now for not sympathizing with the organization and with the Palestinian intifada, some of whose leaders sent a cable to Saddam Husayn saying that his invasion of Kuwait is the first step to Jerusalem and the liberation of Palestine?" A leading Kuwaiti intellectual wrote, "The day will come . . . when you will see with your own eyes that there is no longer any need for you or your organization."[29]

But the Arab states' expression of dismay at the PLO was more than verbal. They pulled the financial rug from under the intifada. Kuwait's government-in-exile, Saudi Arabia, and other Arab oil-producing states insisted they would give the PLO no money. Their direct donations to West Bank schools and hospitals, $35 to $50 million a year, were also cut off. Palestinians in Kuwait, thrown out of work, were unable to pay their five percent tax to the PLO— $120 to $125 million annually—nor could they send remittances—about $80 million a year—to their own families on the West Bank. The sharp fall in the value of Jordan's currency impoverished Palestinians in Jordan and the West Bank. Tens of thousands of Palestinians in the Persian Gulf were fired as a potential fifth column.[31]

Arafat's policy also damaged the PLO's international standing and diplomatic prospects. Iraq was neither able nor interested in mediating between the PLO and the United States or Israel. Indeed, Baghdad had no stake in furthering the peace process and a good reason to block it. On matters of principle, too, the PLO's actions weakened its case. Arafat had, in effect, supported one country's seizure by force of another people's land and contested the right of Kuwaitis to self-determination, exactly the way he described Israeli behavior in the West Bank and Gaza.

Whatever attempt Saddam made to link the Gulf and Arab–Israeli conflicts in order to buy time, the Kuwait crisis still made the intifada a sideshow. Obviously, he had not annexed Kuwait in order to free Palestine. By switching patrons from America's best friend in the Arab world—Egypt—to its worst enemy—Iraq—Arafat forfeited whatever diplomatic gains he had made earlier in Washington, erasing any U.S. incentive to bring him into a peace process.

As the disastrous consequences of supporting Iraq's conquest of Kuwait became clear, Jawad al-Ghusayn, who as chairman of the PLO's Palestine National Fund saw Arab states' contributions vanish, called Iraq's occupation "illegal" and claimed the PLO supported Kuwait. But virtually all the small PLO groups—the PFLP, DFLP, and the Iraq-sponsored ALF and PLF—backed Saddam Husayn even more vocally, publicly offering to commit anti-American terrorism on his behalf.

After four days of crisis meetings, the PLO leadership came up with a new, confusing position on August 19. It proposed an "Arab solution" to the crisis, which seemed an approach certain to result in Iraq keeping Kuwait. Gulf Arabs were unimpressed with this new "neutral" stance. A Saudi diplomat said the PLO was doing nothing while "a giant is murdering a little child." Exiled Kuwaitis asked Arafat in an open letter, "Don't you remember how many years you spent in Kuwait and the continuous Kuwaiti contributions and support to the Palestinian revolution?"

There was also disillusionment among Israelis who had advocated talks with the PLO. Seeing Arafat urging Iraq to attack Israel with missiles and chemical weapons did not seem to presage moderation, nor did the prospect of a Palestinian state some day inviting in Iraqi troops. Yossi Sarid, a leading Israeli politician urging talks with the PLO, strongly criticized PLO leaders for having made "every possible mistake." "Over the past two years," he noted, "the PLO had been trying to convince [Israeli public opinion] that it is a different PLO, 'accepting Israel's existence and renouncing terror.' Now the PLO has kicked the pail and all the moderation has spilled out." While moving "from bed to bed—and there is no Arab ruler who did not share his couch with them—they have learned nothing. Won't Saddam, who is prepared to sell his own mother, sell them?"[32]

By following Iraq rather than Egypt at that critical juncture, Arafat was making a fundamental choice. Egypt was the Arab world's most important country and the patron most likely to guide the PLO toward a West Bank/Gaza state. Cairo's triple status as a U.S.

ally, leader in the Arab world, and the sole Arab state at peace with Israel gave it tremendous advantages as a mediator.

Egypt's strength, self-confidence, military power, geopolitical position, and large population had already made it the only Arab country able to stand alone against the censure of all the other Arab regimes. Past sacrifices on the Palestinians' behalf had made Egyptians resent them and other "ungrateful" Arabs for demanding so much from Egypt while helping it so little. After Sadat made peace with Israel, the Arab world boycotted Egypt as a traitor colluding with Zionism and imperialism. But Egypt gained peace, the Sinai, a reopened Suez Canal and oilfields, and $2 billion a year in U.S. aid.[33]

Egypt was ultimately successful in preserving the treaties with Israel while winning reintegration into the Arab world. The other Arab states found, as Sadat had predicted, that they could not do without Egypt; and in 1989 it was readmitted to the Arab League. Even Syria reestablished formal diplomatic relations. Now there was a leader in the Arab world with an incentive for promoting peace and a more realistic assessment of the conflict.

Mubarak ridiculed the refusal of radical Arabs to recognize Israel. When Qadhafi urged Arab states to fight Israel in 1989, he replied, "God has granted us a mind with which to think. We fought for many years, but where did we get?" The Arabs had lost much money and many martyrs in the struggle, and their situation was still terrible. "I am therefore not ready to take more risks. Moreover, wars have generally not solved any problem. Regardless of the difficulties or obstacles surrounding the present peace process," it was the only way out.[34] Thus, by choosing Iraq over Egypt, Arafat was not only selecting a patron but picking the road of extremism and war over that of moderation and diplomacy.

Syria and Jordan, as other intermittent sponsors for the PLO, also represented options for that organization. Yet both of them in its own way had given the PLO many problems in their long, troubled relationships. Syria had been an alternative vanguard to the PLO, styling itself the "beating heart of Arabism" and Palestine's legitimate ruler. For Damascus, the Palestine problem was too important to be left to the Palestinians. Just as the USSR claimed to represent the international proletariat's interests, whether the workers liked it or not, Syria styled itself Arabism's guardian.

Syria's radical ideology was partly the result of a lack of national history, logical boundaries, and homogeneity sufficient to provide a secure identity without the tempting dream of a Pan-Arab empire. These factors were reinforced by the need to prove the legitimacy of the ruling Alawite minority, whose Arab and Islamic credentials were suspect to the majority Sunni Muslims. "Syria's main asset, in contrast to Egyptian power and Saudi wealth, is its capacity for mischief," explained the Arab scholar, Fouad Ajami.[35] For Syria, the Palestine issue provided an excuse for taking over Lebanon, isolating Egypt, intimidating Jordan from making peace with Israel, blackmailing Arab oil producers to finance itself, dominating the PLO, being the USSR's main local ally, and excluding Israel from a role in peaceful regional relationships. Damascus coveted Lebanon, Jordan, and Palestine (both Israel and the West Bank) as a future part of its own "Greater Syria" empire.

Since Syria claimed Palestine, it held that Arafat had no right to do as he pleased. The editor of the Syrian newspaper *Tishrin* complained that when Arafat claimed the PLO had a right to make its decisions independently, this was an excuse for "treasonous decisions . . . We will not tolerate freedom to commit treason or to sell out the cause. Palestine is southern Syria."[36]

Furthermore, Arab–Israeli peace would make Syria a second-rate power. No longer could it manipulate the conflict. A growing U.S. influence in the region would favor Egypt, Israel, and Jordan over Syria. Israeli and Syrian interests would still clash since the Jewish state would probably cooperate with Jordan, Egypt, and Lebanese Christians—all Syria's rivals. In short, Syria's obstructionism and hawkishness were quite logical.

This situation did not, however, make Syria a reliable ally for the PLO. As defense minister, Asad oversaw Arafat's arrest in 1966 and blocked aid to the PLO in its 1970 war with Jordan. As president, he made a 1974 disengagement agreement with Israel and closed the Golan Heights to PLO infiltrators, attacked the PLO in Lebanon in 1976, abandoned it when Israel invaded in 1982, and split it in 1983. Syria maintained its own puppet PLO groups—al-Sa'iqa, the PFLP-GC, and Abu Nidal, among others—and helped Habash and Hawatmah against Fatah. Even within Arafat's entourage, Qaddumi was pro-Syrian. Arafat was careful not to burn his bridge back to Damascus, but Asad continued their feud into the 1990s.

The PLO's mistrust and competition with Jordan was an even more central element in its history. While Syria was the only state challenging the PLO's ideological legitimacy, Jordan was the only country able to provide alternative representation for the Palestinians.

One can drive from Jerusalem to Amman in an hour, but the diplomatic journey between Israel and Jordan was still unfinished after many decades. The Jordan river is crossed by a rather unimpressive little bridge that would be considered insufficient for the purpose of spanning a barely named American creek. Israel calls it the Allenby, and Jordan the King Husayn I, bridge. To Jordanians, the river's narrowness symbolizes the close connection between Jordan and the West Bank, which Jordan ruled from 1948 to 1967 and hoped to regain. Thus, the 1974 Arab summit's decision to name the PLO as the Palestinian people's sole legitimate representative was a PLO victory over Jordan.

Yet the Palestinian issue was as vital for Jordan as for the PLO. "The cause of Palestine is the cornerstone of Jordan's domestic, Arab and foreign policy," said King Husayn in 1967. While important for all Arabs, to Jordan the question "is a matter of life and death." Even when the king cut his links to the West Bank in July 1988, he stressed that this would have no effect on Jordan's citizens of Palestinian origin on the east bank, "an integral part of the Jordanian state," and that "Jordan will not give up its commitment to take part in the peace process."[37]

Jordan, like Syria, was not eager to see an independent PLO-ruled state. The king at various times tried to outmaneuver and overcome Arafat through conflict, competition, and accommodation. At the same time, Amman feared permanent Israeli control might lead to an upsurge in antiregime sentiments among its own Palestinians, emigration of angry West Bankers to Jordan, or an Israeli campaign to make Jordan itself a Palestinian state as a substitute.

There were many ups and downs in the history of Jordan–PLO relations, and the PLO had good reason to distrust Jordan's intentions. Beginning in the 1920s, King Husayn's grandfather devised several schemes to obtain all or part of Palestine. He offered the Jews protection if they accepted his rule. To Palestine's British rulers, he gave loyalty in return for their backing. He also aided Palestinian Arabs opposed to the dominant Husayni faction. The first major plan to solve the conflict, the 1937 report by Britain's Peel Commission, proposed to give Jordan the Arab-populated portions of Palestine.

In 1947 Jordan spoke secretly to Zionist leaders about taking over the parts earmarked for the Palestinians but abandoned this idea after Palestinian Arabs and Arab states, insisting on going to war, rejected the UN partition plan. Instead, Jordan's Arab Legion invaded Palestine in May 1948, inflicting heavy losses on the Jews and seizing the West Bank, including East Jerusalem. In 1950 Jordan annexed the West Bank, with support from a Palestinian meeting held in Jericho. The next year supporters of Palestinian nationalist leader Amin al-Husayni (Faysal al-Husayni's cousin) assassinated Jordan's king on the steps of East Jerusalem's al-Aqsa mosque.

Between 1950 and 1967 Palestinian nationalism barely existed on the West Bank. Much of the local elite supported the monarchy; younger activists backed radical, antiregime, Pan-Arab parties. After Jordan lost the West Bank in the 1967 war, the PLO used Jordan as a base, subverting and openly challenging the monarchy. The king counterattacked and drove the PLO out of the country in the 1970.

In the following years, the king repeatedly tried to regain the West Bank. In 1972 he proposed a Jordan–West Bank federation; in 1974, he resisted the Arab League decision to make the PLO the sole Palestinian representative and sought a disengagement agreement with Israel. Husayn kept contacts and subsidies on the West Bank, creating a government Office for Occupied Territories Affairs in 1980. He promoted the 1982 Reagan plan to return the West Bank to Jordan. In 1984 Husayn asserted his claim by reconvening Jordan's parliament and appointing members to the vacant West Bank seats. With U.S. encouragement, pro-Amman West Bankers circulated a petition for federation with Jordan until stopped by PLO threats. Husayn persisted with the 1985 Jordan–PLO plan for a federation and held secret talks with Israeli Foreign Minister Peres in 1987.

A large number of Israelis also favored a return of the West Bank to Jordan. The Labor party advocated a "Jordanian option" for the territory's future, and Israeli leaders periodically met secretly with the king. Jordan, with Israel's encouragement, subsidized West Bank civil servants and teachers, backed an East Jerusalem newspaper, and kept close links to local politicians. Jordanian law and textbooks were still used in the West Bank. Many West Bank leaders were eager to work with the king to end the occupation.[38]

All these initiatives failed because of opposition in Israel, PLO rejection, the threats of other Arab states, and the king's own timidity. To step forward and negotiate with Israel, he would have to defy stronger Arab neighbors, the PLO, and many of his own people. He was also unsure whether the United States and Israel would offer enough to make participation worthwhile and safe. Jordan was unable to come to the peace table unilaterally. Too much support for negotiations could antagonize Arab neighbors. It would never be as strong as Israel, Egypt, Syria, or Iraq.[39]

Still, if any progress were to be made, King Husayn needed Arafat's cooperation, and the two men periodically sought to cooperate. They established a joint committee in 1978 to administer Arab aid for the West Bank residents. In 1979 Jordan allowed PLO offices in Amman to reopen under strict supervision. In 1983 and 1985 King Husayn tried to persuade Arafat to enter the peace process as his partner. After Arafat reneged, Jordan closed the PLO offices in 1986, encouraged a small split from the PLO, terminated the aid committee, appointed mayors for several West Bank towns, presented a West Bank development plan, and met with Peres to formulate a still-born peace plan. Finally, King Husayn sought to push the PLO into a corner in 1988 by severing ties with the West Bank. To his surprise, the PLO responded by declaring independence, trying to lay Jordan's claim to rest forever.

Yet whatever became of Jordan's direct claim to the West Bank, it would still have to consider the PLO as potentially threatening the loyalty of over half of its own citizens and many officials who were Palestinians. To cite just one example, Anwar Nusayba, former secretary of the Palestinian leader Amin al-Husayni, whose men murdered King Husayn's grandfather in 1951, later became Husayn's ambassador to London and defense minister. At a June 1990 dinner party, a Jordanian–Palestinian ambassador in the king's service boasted to an official of East Bank origin that Palestinian loyalty was beyond question. His interlocutor asked, "Really? In that case, who do you support, King Husayn or Arafat?" There was a long silence. "That answers the question," said the East Banker.[40]

Abu Iyad gave his view of the issue in a 1988 interview that must have chilled Jordan's leaders. "We refuse to accept [that Palestinians living in Jordan] should owe their principal loyalty to Jordan rather than Palestine . . . We have no objection that Palestinians in Jordan continue to live as Jordanian citizens until the establishment of the Palestinian state."[41] Thus, the fundamental conflict between PLO ambitions and Jordanian sovereignty seemed inescapable. The two sides called each other beloved friends and devoted allies while ferociously competing for Palestinian loyalty, the West Bank, and survival.

In Jordan itself, East Bankers controlled the army and intelligence, were united against Palestinian rule, and seemed able to maintain control. Yet Jordan's elite feared that a frustrated intifada and the economic impact of massive Soviet Jewish immigration to Israel would produce a destabilizing Palestinian exodus into Jordan. The specter of a strong Iraq or of an internal challenge from Jordanian Islamic fundamentalists allied to the PLO also worried Jordan's government.

Torn between fear of the PLO, Iraq, Syria, and Israel, King Husayn did a remarkable job of surviving at all. In theory, Jordan's rulers might have preferred to make peace with Israel but, as Crown Prince Hasan wrote, they were blocked "by our Arab brothers who were not asked to bear such a heavy burden." If these others had comprehended "irreversible political realities," they might have agreed to negotiate sooner and avoided much pain. Compromise was inescapable, Hasan continued. "No problem that has endured as long, has cost as many lives, and has engendered as much distrust, hatred, and discord as the Arab–Israeli conflict can have a cost-free solution."[42]

Yet the painful cost of a settlement was too high for Jordan, for whom the status quo seemed less dangerous than attempting to alter it. Palestinians and Islamic fundamentalists would not thank the king for regaining the West Bank by undercutting the PLO. Rather, they would excoriate him for making the necessary concessions. And the population he gained would be far less than loyal. Thus, Jordan and the PLO were locked together as unwilling brothers, albeit it never very far from fratricide.

Saudi Arabia was another key Arab state for the PLO, but because of its money rather than its strategic or military strength. As extreme in military weakness as it was wealthy, Saudi Arabia avoided trouble by combining radical rhetoric and subsidies for the PLO with practical restraint and good relations with the United States, the kingdom's protector. Whatever its rulers thought, they recognized the limits on their freedom of action.[43]

The gap between Saudi rhetoric and action was extreme. A Saudi-backed newspaper said, "We wish to exterminate Israel once and for all . . . Israel can never be a subject for communication with the Arabs, and can never justify its existence on our land . . . We do not exclude any action carried out against Israel, its subjects or its institutions." It called for heroes who would "sacrifice their own lives, on behalf of Arab history, while hitting Israeli targets deep in its own territory."[44]

Saudi Arabia, however, was not about to martyr itself for the PLO's cause. It might call Israel the main enemy, but it put priority on the Iranian, and later the Iraqi, threat. Saudi Arabia rejected repeated calls to use oil power against the West and bought growing amounts of American goods. Saudi officials would begin meetings by stating, "Of course, the Palestine issue is the most important question for us," then adding with a sigh of relief, "Now that we have that out of the way, our priority is to do something about the threat in the Gulf."[45] This kind of thinking became even stronger after Iraq's seizure of Kuwait. Fearing internal dissent and threats from radical neighbors, Saudi Arabia ignored Arafat's demands to put economic pressure on the West, distance itself from Washington, and give the PLO more money.

The PLO's problems with Arab states also undermined its alliance with the USSR. The PLO needed Moscow's aid, arms, and power to balance U.S. support for Israel. The Soviets long shared the PLO's opposition to U.S. mediation but never endorsed Arafat's goal of destroying Israel. Despite its enthusiastic pro-PLO propaganda, Moscow mistrusted Arafat, considering him a destabilizing troublemaker. Compared with the U.S.–Soviet or even Soviet–Syria relationship, the PLO was expendable. Abu Iyad, acknowledging the

PLO's handicap, regretted it did "not have any territory to give the Soviet Union a foothold" in the region. While the Soviets were neither eager nor able to "deliver" the PLO to a negotiating table, they urged it to make peace with Israel in exchange for a West Bank/Gaza state.[46]

Arafat could find no firm foothold in the quicksand of Arab politics. Egypt, Jordan, Iraq, Syria, and Libya had taken turns being his partner or enemy. They had alternated between interfering with the PLO and trying to free themselves of responsibility for the Palestinians.[47]

8 >> Contentious Unity

The PLO's structure was a central factor in shaping its destiny. On the one hand, its task was to unite Palestinians. Arafat proclaimed, "The PLO is not one of many Palestinian institutions, it is the all-embracing Palestinian institution that comprises all the institutions of the Palestinian people."[1] On the other hand, it had to bridge different Palestinian views and interests as well as play several roles, both populist and repressive, as simultaneously a national liberation and terrorist organization, a revolutionary group and a country in the making.

It was the only movement, Arafat claimed in 1990, that "simultaneously performs the functions of a state and a revolution—a state which has yet to be established, half of whose people are under occupation and the other half in the Diaspora," "with each community living in different circumstances," and facing a "difficult Arab environment."[2] The organization brought Palestinians pride and international recognition, transforming them "from a refugee people waiting in queues for charity and alms into a people fighting for freedom," said Arafat.

Yet these triumphs also had costs: the same characteristics that preserved the PLO also ossified it, inflicting as much or more self-injury as did adversaries' blows. The PLO lacked both the military strength to destroy Israel and, as long as it was locked in this pattern, the willpower to make the compromises necessary to negotiate successfully with it. Arafat acknowledged, "Our revolution is not a revolution of angels. It carries the illnesses of our people, their pluses and minuses; that's for sure." The PLO's configuration and ideology also meant, as Hani al-Hasan once candidly admitted, "that it took us a hell of a long time to come unambiguously to terms with reality."[3]

Observers often expected that Arafat would use his tremendous potential authority to discipline the PLO and bargain flexibly. After all, he seemed secure as the symbol of Palestinian nationalism, leader of Fatah and the PLO, and—by the grace of the PLO Central Committee in April 1989—president of the state of Palestine. Yet Arafat long deferred a bold initiative and accepted limits on his authority. As one PLO leader, Jamal al-Surani, put it, some might think that Arafat "issues the orders and must be obeyed." But he "is not the head. He and we are partners. We are not his employees . . . [Arafat] does not decide what is right and what is wrong on his own personal whim."[4]

Both the PLO's survival and its weakness was based on its being a loose coalition of autonomous groups which were often more attentive to Arab states than to Arafat. The Palestinian masses might identify with the PLO as a whole, but activists were loyal to its member groups, which held the real power. Fatah, by far the largest of them, furnished much of the PLO's staff and forces but was not highly centralized, and its domination over the organization was far from complete. Qaddumi commented, "Fatah is the backbone of the Palestinian revolution . . . but that does not mean that we are trying to take exclusive control. We have partners . . . and the independents. All of them together form a broad front."[5]

While the PLO tried to present a unified nationalist face, loyalty to family, clan, village, and region pervaded Palestinian social structure and politics. The dominant doctrine was Palestinian nationalism, yet the contending appeals of Islamic, pan-Arab, and Marxist ideologies further divided the PLO's member groups and the consciousness of the organization's leaders.

Although both the PLO and its member groups were largely secular, Islam was central to their identity, and thriving Islamic fundamentalist groups reinforced that factor, beginning in the 1980s. Some Islamic doctrines—that non-Muslims in historically Islamic lands must bow to Muslim rule, that Muslims cannot be rightfully governed by others, and that each Muslim has a duty to wage holy war—helped gain the PLO popular support for its goals and tactics.

A prevalent—though not the sole possible—Islamic view of Jews as inherently evil also struck a powerful chord among Palestinians. These ideas made it harder for the PLO to accept Israel's existence or believe that it would continue to exist.

Pan-Arab nationalism also sometimes subverted Palestinian nationalism. For a long time, Palestinians believed that the Arab states would liberate them, a doctrine revived by Saddam Husayn's popularity before and during his seizure of Kuwait. While the Arab public's passion on the Palestinian issue gave the PLO some moral and material leverage, it also let Arab rulers interfere in Palestinian affairs. Marxist influence was strongest among smaller PLO member groups—especially the PFLP, DFLP and, of course, the Communist party. While Marxism's appeal was circumscribed due to that ideology's conflict with Islam and traditional culture, it also had some affect on Fatah's thought, especially in regarding the United States as an imperialist enemy.

Given the many divisions among Palestinians and within the PLO, Arafat knew that his decisions might be hard to enforce. Maintaining unity took precedence over risky innovations. Only by accepting the "apparent chaos" of such a loose structure, Edward Said wrote, could the PLO bring together all shades of Palestinian opinion.[6] A more critical interpretation by Professor Fouad Moughrabi was that "the failure to set realizable objectives . . . that could help guide and focus peoples' energies was startling." Hatim Abu Ghazala, a leading Gaza activist, complained that the Palestinians were "the only nation in the world that has to govern itself by consensus and not majority rule. What is of paramount importance, the so-called unity of the PLO or Palestinian interests?"[7]

For many years Arafat and the PLO obsessively sought to have as close as possible to 100 percent support from Palestinians. Unable to impose unanimity, Arafat often bowed to preserve it, adopting the lowest common denominator as his strategy. He felt unable to use his judgment in making definitive decisions: "I am not at the Cannes Film Festival where I can choose the best movie."[8]

Palestinian history made him worry that splits among his people might be fatal. Thus, Arafat, reluctant to go much beyond the existing consensus or to impose a bold new policy, thought that he was protecting both himself and the movement by using his power minimally. Only Arafat could lead the PLO toward a compromise peace with Israel. This required him, however, to abandon the techniques and ideas that gave him authority in the first place, something his ideology, personality, and situation made him loath to do as long as he saw any other alternative.

The PLO's evolution was also retarded by its tendency to overestimate its successes and leverage, with Arafat often presenting the organization's weaknesses as strengths, exaggerating the movement's unity and his control. For example, he claimed that PLO military operations "are directed by one command and proceed according to one plan." Arafat bragged about the PLO's precarious circumstances as if this were a virtue: "We are the flying carpet revolution, we are treading on burning coals. Tonight I am seeing you in Baghdad. I don't know where I will see you tomorrow."[9]

Trying to reshape an unacceptable reality to his own design through words, Arafat transformed the 1982–83 defeats in Lebanon into a fantasy triumph in which "every child, every woman, every man fought to the end alongside the Palestine armed forces." Professor Hisham Sharabi's view of Arab political discourse applied well to Arafat's style: "Effect is created not so much by reasoning and explication as by repetition and intonation . . . in terminology that evoked emotional rather than rational responses."[10]

Equally, Arafat expressed pride in the struggle's duration as "the longest revolution in modern history." Yet this fact also implied that the PLO had an ineffective strategy and unreachable goal.[11] The Palestinians, of course, suffered most in the conflict. Losing their homeland brought great material deprivation and psychological trauma. It was not their fault they lived on the ground claimed by another nationalist movement, Zionism. But their own leaders and choices repeated earlier mistakes, thus contributing to lengthening and deepening their plight.

The consensus on which the PLO had been based was to destroy Israel through armed struggle and build a Palestinian Arab state incorporating Israel, the West Bank, and Gaza. Noted one student of the organization, "Fatah activists were only reflecting community feelings when they argued for the total 'liberation of Palestine' from its Israeli/Jewish colonists, as Algeria had been liberated from the colons, or China from the Japanese."[12] To retreat too explicitly from this goal, PLO leaders worried, would undermine unity and betray supporters.

Knowing the value of radical ideology and tactics in Palestinian or Arab politics, they largely set strategy on the belief that, in Abu Iyad's words, "our steadfastness and adherence to our land is our only card . . . We would rather be frozen for ten more years than move toward treason."[13] Such steadfastness—or extremism—reflected both sincere conviction and a practical grasp of Palestinian political realities, though less so of potentially productive alternative policies.

Since the PLO was seeking total victory for most of its history, it willingly sacrificed diplomatic success in order to protect its internal and inter-Arab flanks. Verbal attacks on the United States, calls for Israel's destruction, and terrorist operations were quite acceptable as serving a more vital political purpose of mobilizing Palestinian—and Arab—support while bolstering the PLO's unity and independence. What appeared to the West as opportunities were perceived by the PLO as threats.

This pattern manifested itself in regard to the PLO's attitude toward terrorism. There were no significant moral compunctions, doubts, or self-criticism expressed in its discussions on targeting Israeli civilians. The PLO knew that such attacks were popular among the masses of Palestinians and Arabs. A 1986 poll among West Bank Palestinians, the most moderate segment, showed that almost 88 percent justified seizing an Israeli bus and murdering a teenaged passenger; about 21 percent endorsed placing bombs on civilian airliners (60 percent if the target was an El Al plane), and nearly 37 percent backed the machine-gunning of travelers in the Vienna and Rome airports.[14]

Such attitudes and deeds affected the PLO's political culture. Those most adept at violence gained prestige, followers, and authority. Consequently, they denigrated diplomacy in favor of continuing the armed struggle that was their source of power. Since terrorism was most easily done by small groups, it encouraged internal fragmentation and fierce competition to stage the most spectacular acts. Violence also turned inward in fratricidal conflict and the murder of Palestinian, even PLO, moderates like Sa'id Hamami and Isam Sartawi.[15]

Criticizing another PLO group or an operation had political costs but accepting terrorism did not, at least among Palestinians or other Arabs. Using terrorism against Israel reduced the PLO's diplomatic

option, but Arafat argued that violence would force Israeli concessions through "the conscious and calculated linking of armed
struggle and political struggle." Even after the PLO's pledge to the
United States that it would not use terrorism, Qaddumi could declare in 1989, "The PLO is not prepared to condemn operations
which any Palestinian organization or faction undertakes."[16] Thus,
the PLO renounced terrorism in terms of reducing assaults on Western targets, while attacks on anything Israeli—including civilians—
were defined as legitimate armed struggle.

PLO leaders often argued that the ultimate goal of total victory
was more important than the time needed to attain it. All PLO symbols included a map showing all of Israel as part of Palestine, and
such words as "Palestine" or "occupied territories" could refer to
either all of Israel or just the land captured in 1967. By the late
1980s, PLO rhetoric gradually moved toward the latter definition
without ever abandoning the former one.

The historic shift toward moderation in 1988, for example, was
made in an ambiguous way typical of PLO politics. Some leaders
opposed Arafat's policy; others backed it out of readiness for a compromise peace; and most supported it as a way to continue armed
struggle and the aspiration to destroy Israel. While the PLO consensus was stretched to the limit, the result was still too inconclusive
to persuade the U.S. or Israeli governments that the organization
had really changed course.

During the same era the PLO's manner of relating to Palestinians
also led the organization in a vicious circle: it would not moderate
tactics or policy without first ensuring unity and popular support;
yet the leadership would not present to its people the stark choices
and firm direction needed to mobilize this support. Doing virtually
nothing to direct or organize the masses over the heads of the PLO
member groups—including his own—Arafat was unable to prepare
his public for a new orientation or use his popularity to centralize
authority in the PLO. Arafat himself admitted, "All Palestinian organizations without exception have failed to absorb and organize
the majority of the Palestinian people."[17] The PLO could not gain
Israeli or U.S. concessions as long as it continued terrorism and radicalism; yet it could not eliminate these features without being able
to show supporters some gains made by moderation.

Arafat's own ambivalence and his acquiescence to the PLO's anarchic internal politics made it hard to forge a consensus for a moderate, diplomacy-oriented policy. His personal indecisiveness repeatedly undercut the awesome potential power at his command. Arafat's style of locomotion manifested far more motion than movement: cautiously advancing, consolidating his position by retreating a bit, and finally dragging the PLO forward a tad. While sometimes stretching his mandate, Arafat hesitated to go too far or quickly retreated when challenged. A statement implying moderation would be soon matched by one restating intransigence; a step toward Egypt would be countered by a gesture to Iraq. This was often an effective technique for internal or inter-Arab politics but disastrous in handling diplomatic initiatives toward Israel or the United States. Arafat survived years of struggle and bloodshed to keep his cause, leadership, and organization alive. But surviving was not the same as succeeding, and he achieved much less than was possible, until he finally, dramatically, changed his approach in September 1993.

Up to that point, Arafat's hesitant, compromising approach was quite different from the dominating, centralizing technique of other Third World revolutionary leaders. Palestinians and Arab politicians who publicly accepted the cult of personal adulation surrounding him often spoke privately of their low regard for Arafat's ability. "Every hero has his flaw," a Palestinian journalist commented. "Arafat's is indecisiveness."[18] The style that served him so well in Palestinian and Arab politics—political timidity, ambiguity, and a premium on consensus—had to be abandoned if he was to make the bold decisions and impose the difficult choices necessary to lead his people to independence.

Those who know Arafat described him as shy and lonely; politics served as his mask.[19] Especially since colleagues were his surrogate family, Arafat often kept favored incompetents in high posts. The 1983 split in Fatah was partly provoked by this practice. As a PLO supporter lamented afterward, "We saw the corruption among some, we saw the stupidity and the mistakes, we forgave and we condoned in the name of exigencies and situations of stress. We knew that many people were chosen not for their skills, but for their loyalty. We knew that, ultimately, a good cause was at times misrepresented, distorted, and poorly served." Arafat, though not personally corrupt, surrounded himself with "an obese and comfortable elite" which sent its children to Europe, lived in big houses, and rode in chauffeured cars.[20]

Arafat's ability to hold Fatah and the PLO together, however, also rested largely on his personal bonds enduring for three decades with such key Fatah founders as Abu Jihad, Abu Iyad, and Qaddumi. Abu Iyad explained, "Had it not been for the cohesion of the historic leadership . . . the divisions and dissensions that plagued the movement in the wake of the Israeli invasion of 1982 would have torn Fatah apart and finished it off."[21] Nevertheless, by the 1990s this elite was aging and lacked apparent successors, while Arafat's two key supporters and potential heirs—Abu Jihad and Abu Iyad—had been assassinated. The danger of the PLO's high degree of dependence on Arafat was underlined in 1992 when he barely survived a plane crash in Libya and then required a major operation to remove resulting blood clots.

Abu Jihad was Arafat's personal favorite, reputed planner of many of the biggest terrorist attacks, and the PLO's political liaison to the intifada. His ability and terrorist activities made him an Israeli target. In April 1988 a nine-member hit team came to his seaside Tunis villa in two rented Volkswagen minibuses and a Peugeot, used silenced pistols to kill his driver and two guards, and shot him as he came out of his study carrying a revolver. Arafat showed his respect for his close confidante by making Abu Jihad the intifada's symbolic martyr.

Next to Arafat, Abu Iyad had the largest personal following in Fatah. Born in Jaffa in 1933, he went as a refugee to Gaza in 1948. He became a top official in PLO security and intelligence in the 1960s, and supervised the Black September terrorist group during the 1970s.[22] He often criticized Arafat's more flexible diplomatic moves—the 1983 visit to Egypt, 1985 agreement with Jordan, and 1988 peace initiative—but in the end backed him, as he did reluctantly in 1990 when Arafat supported Saddam Husayn. In January 1991, however, Abu Iyad was killed by a defector from Abu Nidal's group whom the PLO had made one of his bodyguards.

Faruq Qaddumi, the leading quartet's fourth member, headed the PLO's Political Department and took an even more hardline stand. Qaddumi was born in 1930 and grew up in Jaffa, but his family returned as refugees to his home town of Nablus in 1948. After meeting Arafat at Cairo University, Qaddumi worked at Kuwait's health ministry and for the U.S. oil company Aramco in Saudi Arabia in the 1950s. After joining the PLO, he rose to head the Political Department in 1973 after his predecessor was killed in an Israeli raid on Beirut. Qaddumi favored a close alliance with Syria and no compromise on the PLO's traditional goals. Although popular among the rank and file and regarded as the PLO's foreign minister, he was often bypassed by Arafat. Another Fatah founder, Abu Mazin, was put in charge of the PLO's negotiating strategy with Israel in 1991, and when Arafat recognized Israel in 1993, Qadummi did not support the deal.[23]

Khalid, born in 1928, and younger brother Hani al-Hasan were charter Fatah members who remained generally influential, though lacking direct power. In contrast to Qaddumi's links with a radical Arab state, they had lucrative ties to Saudi Arabia—which Saudi journalists called Khalid's "second country"—and Kuwait, where Khalid owned a construction company. Khalid urged Arafat to exert more control over the smaller PLO member groups, and left the Executive Committee in 1973 when this advice was ignored. His conservatism and Saudi contacts made him an ideal PLO liaison man with the United States in the 1970s and an advocate of cooperation with Jordan in the 1980s. Khalid's contact with Jews in pre-1948 Palestine made him think himself an expert on the Jewish question, and he was a key author of the 1988 policy shift, claiming that a two-state solution would bring Israel's collapse from within. Siding with the Saudis and Kuwaitis, the Hasan brothers were more openly and loudly critical of Arafat's leadership during and after the Gulf War.

While the PLO chiefs formed a shadow government, the organization embodied a society-in-exile. Its departments, each headed by an Executive Committee member, supervised cultural, educational, and social welfare activities, as well as mass organizations for workers, women, teachers, students, lawyers, and engineers. The Palestine Red Crescent, headed by Arafat's brother, ran hospitals and clinics. Such institutions spread PLO influence among Palestinians, building a sense of nationhood and community.[24]

The PLO and Fatah budget also funded the Palestine Liberation Army, military/terrorist units, diplomatic missions, schools, pensions, and secret funds to bribe countries and subsidize newspapers. The PLO invested money through its financial conduit, the Arab

Bank. Its Palestine Martyrs Works Society ran companies making clothes and furniture; other PLO business interests included farms and duty-free shops in Africa. Cash mainly came from Arab states and the income taxes of 5 to 7 percent paid by Palestinians working there. The organization's assets totaled several billion dollars and the official budget for fiscal year 1985–86 was $220 million. But income fell by as much as 50 percent when oil-producing states cut aid after the Kuwait crisis, forcing pay reductions or lay-offs and bringing more open criticism of Arafat's alleged fiscal mismanagement. This financial pressure would be a factor in Arafat's need to make peace with Israel in 1993.[25]

The PLO's military option was similarly reduced below that of earlier decades by its defeats and loss of Soviet support, and was limited to Lebanon, where Fatah had half of its 8,000 fighters. As Lebanon's government regained control of the country with Syrian help in the early 1990s, it disarmed and further restricted PLO forces. The PLO's and Fatah's military headquarters were in Tunisia, far away from the battlefront. Realizing that its involvement in terrorism was blocking efforts to achieve U.S. and Western recognition, Fatah—but not the smaller groups—reduced such operations internationally in 1974 and across the Lebanese border in 1981, while persisting with armed attacks into Israel and the occupied territories when possible.

Fatah tried to conceal such continuing activities by using secret elite forces led by some of Arafat's most trusted aides. The largest was Fatah's Force-17, established in the early 1970s as Arafat's bodyguard and internal discipline unit. Its founder was security chief Ali Hasan Salama, who led it until he was killed in Beirut in 1979 by Israel. Salama was replaced by Abu al-Tayyib, and Force-17 continued striking against Israel and individual Israelis overseas. It killed three Israeli civilians in Cyprus and two Israeli sailors in Spain in 1985 and staged numerous bombings in Israel, including an abortive March 1988 attack in Jerusalem during a visit by Secretary of State Shultz. In the mid-1980s Force-17 rebuilt Fatah's combat units in Lebanon and tried to set up a network among Israeli Arabs. But Abu al-Tayyib was not well-respected in Fatah. According to one joke, he would be willing to claim responsibility for the crash of the American spaceship Challenger.[26]

During the 1980s, Abu Jihad headed unconventional military operations through the Western Sector apparatus, which skillfully co-ordinated attacks in Israel and the territories. The PLO–Jordan detente in 1985 made it easier to supply guns and explosives in the West Bank. After Abu Jihad's assassination in 1988, Abu al-Hawl took over, but local cells became more autonomous from his weak leadership by the time he was assassinated by an Abu Nidal supporter in 1991.[27]

Fatah's remaining international terrorist operations were in the hands of Colonel Hawari, head of the Special Operations Group of Fatah's Central Security and Intelligence Apparatus. Hawari, formerly a Force-17 member and a bodyguard for Arafat, helped return some 5,000 Fatah fighters to Lebanon after their expulsion in 1982–83. His group was also involved in the 1986 bombing of a TWA plane in which four Americans (one an infant) died, and in attacks on U.S. facilities in Europe. That same year Hawari's operatives were arrested in Morocco while planning terrorist attacks to punish that country for hosting Israeli leader Shimon Peres. Hawari died on May 22, 1991, reportedly in an automobile accident in Iraq.[28]

The PLO's most important assets were Arafat's charisma, the Arab states' endorsement of the PLO as the Palestinians' sole legitimate representative, and popular support. But while Arafat tried to appease the member groups and other leaders, he also had to ensure his control over the institutions of the PLO and Fatah. The PLO's ruling body was the small Executive Committee, nominally selected by the PNC. Arafat, Qaddumi, and Abu Mazin represented Fatah on it.[29] The other member groups—the PFLP and the two warring factions of the DFLP, Abu al-Abbas's pro-Iraq PLF, the Iraq-controlled Arab Liberation Front, the tiny Palestine Popular Struggle Front, and pro-Moscow Palestine Communist Party (renamed the Palestinian People's Party)—had one each. Arafat's maintained his majority on the Executive Committee by choosing supporters who were then elected as independents.[30]

Similarly, Arafat controlled the PNC, which had about 450 active members, through a coalition of PLO officials, Fatah activists, and pro-Arafat independents—middle-class technocrats, bureaucrats, and businessmen—who far outnumbered sympathizers with other member groups. About 120 more seats were said to be held secretly by residents of the occupied territories, who Israel blocked from active participation.[31]

Ironically, Arafat sometimes found the PLO easier to rule than his own Fatah group. Fatah's Central Committee, for example, rejected his policy of cooperation with Jordan in 1983 and 1985.[32] Fatah leaders were politicians or warriors in their own right, and many of them, like Abu Iyad and Qaddumi, considered themselves to be guardians of the group's militancy. Tired of constant criticism that he was selling out, Arafat complained that he had to make certain moderate statements in order to counter U.S. and Israeli positions and urged his critics to distinguish between what was real and what was propaganda.

If his own Fatah colleagues sometimes gave Arafat problems, smaller groups were a constant source of trouble. They could not determine policy but were often able to influence it. These factions feared that the larger Fatah would overwhelm them organizationally and also betray the PLO's program. Their doctrines deemed revolution and violence as the necessary basis for success. They insisted on expanding terrorist attacks against Israel—which Arafat neither punished nor criticized—and condemned the United States as an imperialist, reactionary enemy inevitably opposing Palestinian goals.

Habash and Hawatmah, the PFLP and DFLP leaders, were Christians whose background opened them to the Western idea of Marxism as an alternative to an Arab–Islamic nationalism that excluded their religious community. Alliances with Syria and Moscow gave them leverage against Fatah. They championed Pan-Arab nationalism—Hawatmah was not even a Palestinian but a Jordanian—years before becoming Palestinian nationalists and retained an interest in promoting regionwide revolution. Thus, they quickly rallied to Iraq's side when it seized Kuwait. But no amount of militancy could negate the fact that their religious background and ideology made them less attractive than Arafat to the masses.

The PFLP and DFLP, both headquartered in Damascus and retaining their own independent military forces, saw their mission as preventing Arafat from betraying the revolution. The PFLP, the PLO's second-largest group, often opposed Arafat's policy and periodically—though temporarily—quit the PLO's institutions. Its resolve was always to be the most radical group in rhetoric and deed.[33] The DFLP saw itself as a Marxist–Leninist group. Its relatively well-educated activists generated ideas later adopted by the whole PLO: the "secular democratic state" to replace Israel (though secularism was too much for Fatah's social conservatives), the 1974 two-stage strategy to eliminate the Jewish state, the alliance with Moscow, and the need for grassroots' organizing in the occupied territories. Yet the DFLP's ideological sophistication also limited its popular appeal. Yasir Abd Rabbu, born in 1944 and the DFLP's member on the PLO Executive Committee since 1977, became such a close advisor to Arafat that his supporters split the group after the Kuwait war. Both the PFLP and Hawatmah's DFLP opposed recognition of Israel in 1993, boycotting the key Executive Committee meeting which endorsed Arafat's decision.[34]

Abu al-Abbas and his tiny PLF best illustrated Arafat's dilemma in dealing with a fragmented PLO.[35] This Iraqi-backed group had only a few hundred members yet was able to use terrorism to generate world headlines and disrupt Arafat's diplomatic initiatives—in 1985 by hijacking the *Achille Lauro*; in 1990 by attacking Israel's coast and destroying the U.S.–PLO dialogue when Arafat refused to criticize or punish Abu al-Abbas. Arafat could have saved the dialogue by removing him from the Executive Committee but did not do so at the time for the sake of unity and in deference to the PLF's Iraqi sponsor. By the time Abu al-Abbas left the Executive Committee in October 1991—in light of the PLO's weakened position after the Kuwait crisis—the gesture was too little, too late to benefit the PLO.

Another example of the complex interplay in PLO circles was a rivalry between Bassam Abu Sharif and Ahmad Abd al-Rahman for control of the public relations' apparatus during the 1980s. Most PLO statements explicitly advocating peace with Israel came from Abu Sharif, an ex-PFLP radical who seemed a sincere convert to his new view and influenced Arafat toward the concessions needed for making peace with Israel. But such a stance also fit his job of improving the PLO's image in the West and Western media, which he courted to give a dovish slant to its policy. An Executive Committee member called him "more a journalist than a PLO official," and the organization often denied his words. In contrast, the hardline Abd al-Rahman was the PLO spokesman and editor of its magazine, *Filastin al-Thawra*. Arafat thus had the militant Abd al-Rahman speaking to the Arab world and the moderate Abu Sharif giving a different impression to the West.[36]

Such policy differences arose not only from personal disputes but also from crosscurrents among Palestinian constituencies. The PLO had to represent a people divided among different states and conditions. About one third of Palestinians lived in the West Bank and Gaza, about one third in Jordan, and about one third evenly split between other Arab states and Israel.[37] The most important sector among them were those who had become refugees in 1948 now living outside the historic land of Palestine. For them to regain homes lost in 1948 required Israel's destruction. This group naturally tended to favor a harder line, having no special attachment to the West Bank and Gaza as the location of a Palestinian state.[38]

While the PLO evolved politically toward accepting a West Bank/ Gaza state in exchange for recognizing Israel, it had great difficulty in abandoning what most Palestinians saw as their right and hope to rule all of Palestine some day. Arafat worded every resolution and speech so he could interpret them to the radicals as consistent with the PLO's demand that all Palestinian refugees have a "right of return" to their original homes inside Israel. Palestinians were proud of having taught those born as refugees to identify with their pre-1948 "home" towns or villages, now in Israel. Yet this education also bred resistance to settling for less, making a West Bank/ Gaza state seem irrelevant for those originating in the lands that became Israel in 1948.

For most Palestinians, the Return was the struggle's whole purpose and essential outcome—the day when Palestinians would reclaim their homes and Israel would vanish as if it had never existed. To abandon one's vision of the Return, explained a Palestinian writer, "is to rip up the tree on which his history and raison d'etre grow [and] rush headlong on a trip to madness." If Palestinians had lost their entire country, then the only worthwhile goal was to have that whole country restored to them. How, asked Abu Iyad, could he tell someone originally from Nablus that he can go home but not someone from Jaffa or Haifa?[39] Almost all top and mid-level PLO leaders traced their origins back to places now incorporated into Israel. Abu Jihad was born in Ramle; Abu Iyad in Jaffa; the Hasan brothers in Haifa; Abu Mazin, Abu al-Hawl and Nabil Sha'th in Safad; Shafiq al-Hut in Jaffa; Habash in Lod; Abdallah Franji in Beersheva. Qaddumi, though born in Nablus, grew up in Jaffa.

The second major constituency was those living under Israeli occupation on the West Bank and Gaza. This group was generally accorded a second-class status in the movement behind the more militant, exiled refugees, a situation the intifada only gradually and partially redressed. Arafat, recalling past Jordanian, Israel, and U.S. proposals to deal with West Bank/Gaza Palestinians instead of the PLO itself, continued to view them as a potential substitute leadership of the Palestinians, and therefore a threat to his own power.

Consequently, Palestinians from the West Bank and Gaza were always underrepresented in the PLO's institutions. Of the Executive Committee's fifteen members between 1988 and 1991, for example, only Muhammad Milhim—a pro-Fatah West Bank mayor elected in 1976 and expelled by Israel in 1980—had lived for any time in the lands under occupation. Even his family had problems with Fatah, which killed eight of his relatives in 1968 as alleged collaborators with Israel. At the 1991 PNC, Milhim was dropped from the Executive Committee.

The distribution of seats in Fatah's Central Committee during the intifada followed a similar pattern. Even after the 1989 Fatah meeting reserved three of its twenty-one seats for strugglers from the territories, these posts went to men whose careers were entirely outside the West Bank and Gaza, like Abdallah Franji, the PLO envoy in West Germany, and Nabil Sha'th, an advisor to Arafat living in Egypt.[40]

The thinking and interests of indigenous Palestinians in the West Bank and Gaza as a group diverged somewhat from those of the exiled 1948 refugees. While PLO leaders only saw Israelis, figuratively, through rifle sights, West Bankers who dealt with them as a matter of daily life for over two decades had a more realistic perception of Israel and the most immediate incentive to end the occupation. The West Bank, already their home, was for them a suitable location for their projected homeland. Thus, local leaders generally urged more moderation in PLO policy.

A significant minority of 1948 refugees living in camps on the West Bank tended to be more radical and bent on conquering Israel than historic residents. Still, they would also benefit more directly from the occupation's end and creation of a West Bank/Gaza state than would Palestinians altogether outside the land. This situation also applied in Gaza, though most people there were 1948 refugees living under terrible conditions, and the movement tended to be more radical and Islamic fundamentalist than its West Bank counterpart.

The radicalism of even West Bank Palestinians was not to be underrated. In a 1986 poll conducted by PLO supporters, West Bankers almost unanimously endorsed the PLO and Arafat as their leaders. By a wide margin, they also rejected UN Resolution 242 and demanded establishment of a Palestinian state incorporating Israel. Only a small plurality was willing to accept a West Bank/Gaza state even as an interim solution. Most surprising, only 30 percent endorsed the PLO's position that the state should be based on Arab and Palestinian nationalism, compared with 53 percent who preferred Islam. Only 10 percent said they wanted a democratic secular state, 7 percent opted for a Communist one, and just 2 percent wanted a democratic state along Western lines.[41]

The West Bank's relatively moderate elite came from powerful families that had accumulated wealth and influence by accommodating themselves to Ottoman, British, and Jordanian rule. This pattern continued under Israeli occupation and was one of the main reasons why the territory was fairly quiet for two decades. The same class also produced nationalist leaders as its children received modern educations and became politicized. Gradually, the PLO ensconced itself as a new patron, granting legitimacy in exchange for allegiance. Most of these people kept on reasonably good terms with both the Israeli authorities and the PLO.[42]

Faysal al-Husayni, the leading figure among them, was heir to the most politically prominent Palestinian family—son of a senior Palestinian military commander in the 1948 war, cousin of that era's main political leader, and brother of a top Fatah military commander. Having been trained by the Syrian army and briefly involved in Fatah terrorist activities during the 1970s, he was imprisoned by Israel. But Israeli officials, aware of his influence, also visited his cell to talk politics. Husayni uniquely combined high social prestige, excellent PLO and intifada connections, and an understanding of the need to build trust with Israelis. Yet his very charisma made the PLO headquarters in Tunis nervous, lest he threaten its monopoly of leadership.

Husayni understood more clearly than the PLO in Tunis what needed to be done. "The intifada is not a military operation," he said, but a political campaign concurrently mobilizing Palestinians for struggle while teaching them the need to compromise since the "absolute justice" of their "legitimate dream" to regain all Palestine was unrealistic. More moderation and less violence would also be needed to win over Israeli public opinion.[43]

But Husayni's priorities and timetable were not necessarily those of Arafat. Even if indigenous West Bank/Gaza leaders were relatively moderate in the Palestinian political spectrum, PLO headquarters in Tunis usually subordinated their interests to those of its exiled refugee constituency. West Bank leaders, awed by the PLO's legitimacy and power—including that of potential physical compulsion—privately expressed bitterness about Arafat's incompetence but, as *New York Times* correspondent Tom Friedman put it, were "too intimidated, divided, and politically suppressed to ever develop a coherent alternative leadership."[44]

Suffering from continuing occupation and rebellion gave the local elite a strong incentive to resolve a conflict that jeopardized their lives and status. They were less enthusiastic about endless struggle and more skeptical about the likelihood that militancy would bring success. The Palestinian middle class generally feared and hated Islamic fundamentalists, extolled the PLO while fearing its intimidation, and promoted the intifada, yet were wary of the militant street agitators.[45]

The elite did not control the young revolutionaries from poorer families and refugee camps, who favored continuing and escalating the intifada which was the source for their own authority and prestige. With their limited experience, they overestimated the uprising's chances for victory. Differences in background and politics made these young militants unlikely to follow the elite in any independent diplomatic initiative, often viewing them as cowards or even collaborators. Early in the intifada, for example, radical Palestinians accused the pro-Fatah Sari Nusayba, a Bir Zayt teacher from an elite family, of embezzling intifada funds and beat him up after a small show of independence on his part. A colleague said this was progress: "Ten years ago, [he] would have gotten a bullet in his head for saying those things."[46] Thus, even after the intifada began, the West Bank/Gaza constituency's entreaties for urgent action to reach a compromise negotiated solution only slowly and incompletely became more influential.

While the 1948 refugees wanted a revolutionary transformation of the situation to redress their grievances and the West Bank/Gaza Palestinian residents and refugees needed a change in the occupied territories' situation, a third group of Palestinians' status as citizens in Israel or Jordan gave them incentives to respect these states' sovereignty but were also attracted by the alternate loyalty the PLO offered them. Its claim to lead all Palestinians implied that these people not only owed it allegiance but might choose to bring their places of residence under its rule. The PLO called on Israeli Arabs to shake "the Zionist occupation off the land of Palestine" and denied any distinction between "Palestinian" and "Jordanian" since, as Arafat claimed in 1973, "we are one people, not two."[47]

For Jordan, the Palestinian problem was a domestic as well as foreign policy issue since more than half its people were of Palestinian origin. Jordan was the West Bank's natural hinterland and the two peoples were close enough in every respect for King Husayn to call them "twins."[48] Some wealthy Palestinian families linked their fate to the monarchy, and even those loyal to the PLO—remembering the 1970 civil war—knew that open allegiance to Arafat could result in repression. For its part, Jordan long sought to regain the West Bank and feared that a PLO-ruled state would subvert its own citizens. Consequently, there remained profound mistrust between King Husayn and the PLO—and between East Bank Jordanians and Palestinian Jordanians—no matter how much they cooperated in the short-term.

By the same token, the Arab minority in Israel supported a Palestinian homeland on the West Bank and Gaza but, being partly integrated into the country whose citizenship it held, also hesitated to endanger its status there. Nonetheless, the PLO urged them to rebel and subvert the state from within, campaigning in the 1980s to woo them. Each Palestinian group, including the Communists and Islamic fundamentalists, supported its own clients or counterparts in Israel. Yet while Israeli Arabs increasingly identified as Palestinians and favored the creation of a West Bank/Gaza Palestinian state, they had little direct involvement in the PLO.[49]

The PLO's demand for self-determination was designed to preserve Palestinian independence from either Israel's or an Arab state's control but also implied that Israeli and Jordanian Palestinians could demand incorporation in a Palestinian state. "In no way," said Arafat, "do we accept as a price for the independent state the enslavement of our people who remain in the territories occupied in 1948." One of the PLO's main slogans was that it represented "all our people in all places inside and outside their homeland." If the PLO ever obtained a state, it would have to construct some new interpretation of its relations with the large number of Palestinians living in Israel and Jordan.[50]

Thus, in addition to bridging gaps within Fatah and those among different ideologies, member groups, and Arab states, Arafat had to hold together several geographic constituencies. By the mid-1980s, the PLO was at a dead end, losing its base in Lebanon, its leverage in the Arab world, and its Soviet ally. Driven out of Jordan and Lebanon and tightly restricted in Syria, the PLO finally turned to the West Bank and Gaza. PLO groups and Palestinian Islamic fundamentalists built a network of social clubs, youth groups, and labor unions. Many of those serving sentences for terrorism came out of prison to do political organizing there. After two decades of occupation with no end in sight, they were tired of waiting for Arafat to liberate them and ready to act on their own. The inhabitants of the West Bank and Gaza, loyal to the PLO but disappointed with it, took the issue into their own hands with the intifada.

Khalid al-Hasan warned that these Palestinians might next establish their own "international popular leadership." In 1991 the West Bank's most influential newspaper, the pro-PLO *al-Fajr,* commented, "The PLO needs some serious reassessment of itself and its *modus operandi.* Maybe it is time that some new blood be introduced into the Palestinian leadership."[51] Such ideas made Arafat even more nervous. Only the debacle of the Gulf War and the willingness of Arab states to meet Israel without the PLO's participation persuaded the PLO leader to select a West Bank/Gaza team to negotiate with Israel in 1991.

But while much of the West Bank elite favored a compromise agreement with Israel, it would do nothing without PLO permission. The Westernized temperament that let them communicate so effectively with Israelis or Americans made them incapable of taking over a revolution. These people were ready to serve as the PLO's intermediaries with Israel and the United States while also acting as a moderating pressure group to revise the PLO's policy.

While the West Bank elite would remain loyal, other challenges to the PLO came from rivals even less palatable to Arafat. Outside the organization were several Palestinian nationalist groups enjoying Syrian or other Arab sponsorship. These groups included Abu Musa's Syrian-backed Fatah rebels (estimated at 2,500 to 3,600 men), Abu Nidal's small but deadly Fatah Revolutionary Council (which Fatah managed to split in 1990), and Jibril's PFLP-GC (about 800 men).[52]

While these forces were largely discredited and dependent on Arab state support, the rise of Palestinian Islamic fundamentalist groups, offering a more familiar and congenial doctrine than Arafat's other rivals, was more worrisome. Inspired by Egyptian counterparts, they began organizing in Gaza where, at first, Israeli authorities left them alone since they competed with the PLO and engaged in such peaceful pursuits as building mosques and doing educational or welfare work. By 1983 the Palestinian Muslim Brotherhood was defeating Fatah for seats in the doctors', engineers', merchants', and lawyers' associations.[53]

The main fundamentalist group became the Muslim Brotherhood's Hamas front, which extolled terrorism, opposed Israel's existence, and demanded an Islamic Palestinian state from the Jordan River to the Mediterranean. It was helped by close links to Jordan's Muslim Brotherhood and by Saudi aid after the 1991 Gulf War. Ahmad Yasin, Hamas's spiritual leader, said, "I do not believe that a person who joins Fatah is a Muslim militant when at the same time he does not pray." Next, they began smuggling in arms from Egypt and setting up cells which would help launch the intifada in 1987.[54]

There were also a half-dozen small, independent factions, collectively referred to as Islamic Jihad, promoting dramatic terrorist acts—like a February 1990 attack on an Israeli tourist bus in Egypt, killing nine and wounding seventeen passengers—and sponsored by Arab states or Iran. The most important such group was the Bayt al-Maqdis of As'ad Bayyudi al-Tamimi, a Hebron cleric deported by Israel and based in Amman. After flirting with Iraq, Tamimi looked to Iran for support. Arafat and Abu Jihad unsuccessfully courted Tamimi by making one of his sons, Nadir, Fatah's deputy religious advisor. Smaller factions worked with Syria, Sudan, and Iran. Arafat's Fatah even created its own Islamic fundamentalist front group, the Jordan-based Saraya al-Islam.

Hamas and Bayt al-Maqdis negotiated with Arafat about joining the PLO or PNC but were never able to reach an agreement with him. They demanded that the PLO escalate the armed struggle, reject negotiations with Israel, and give them 40 percent of the PNC seats. Arafat refused, knowing that an alliance between the fundamentalists and the smaller member groups might seize control of the PLO or at least further restrict his own power.[55]

But PLO leaders had enough troubles even aside from these outside rivals. The intifada and diplomacy offered large risks as well as great opportunities. They feared being trapped into concessions, or accused of betraying their cause and splitting the movement and its constituencies. They worried that one misstep would forever forfeit any chance to create a Palestinian state or result in their being excluded from a U.S.-mediated peace agreement.

In general, Arafat simply put internal political considerations first, as most politicians usually do. The need to hold together such a diverse people in such a volatile situation made Arafat seek consensus, building the PLO as a loose coalition with little authority over its constituent factions, freezing its policy in order to preserve its unity, competing with rivals by showing his militancy.

From failure to failure in the external world, the PLO had gone from success to success in the Palestinian setting. In terms of maintaining its survival and unity, the PLO worked very well; from the standpoint of making material gains or reaching a peace agreement, however, it functioned very badly. The PLO's great challenge was whether it could break the pattern and achieve something for Palestinians through a true commitment to a compromise peace with Israel, offering a real—if partial—realization of Palestinian needs and demands. There could be no negotiated solution without the PLO, but, equally, none until the PLO altered its stand toward the United States and Israel, to seek the benefits of a compromise negotiated peace.

When that moment finally came in September 1993, these structural factors would shape Arafat's peacemaking with Israel and ensuing events. Knowing that the organization's survival required ignoring democratic or coalition restraints and facing the loss of the most radical wing, Arafat did possess the power to change the PLO's historic course. Most of the smaller groups and a part of Fatah would reject the plan but could neither stop nor defeat him.

Arafat's failure to prepare his followers for necessary concessions and changes reduced their support but did not abrogate his mandate. Each Palestinian constituency would respond somewhat differently based on its situation, with the indigenous West Bank/Gaza Palestinians being most favorable, refugees living in the territories suspicious, and refugees outside the land fearful of being abandoned.

The loyalty of the West Bank/Gaza leadership proved a major asset for Arafat, forcing Israel to give up any hope of dividing them from the PLO. At the same time, however, Arafat's own suspicions and jealousy of those "inside" Palestinian leaders pushed him toward the concessions needed for direct PLO involvement. He felt it essential to avoid a sustained transitional period when the local people controlled the territories and the PLO leadership would be excluded.

9 >> Turning Points and Sticking Points

The PLO's images of the United States and Israel were important elements in its formulation of methods and goals. If the United States was inevitably at odds with Palestinian aspirations and if Israel was a fascist state doomed to extinction, negotiation was futile and compromise was unthinkable. But Israel's survival for over four decades, and the PLO's inability to defeat it despite a quarter century of struggle, suggested that the time had come for a new analysis of the enemy and a different view of the future.

Until then, the PLO's historic interpretation underestimated Israel's endurance and overestimated the value of its own Arab and Soviet support, armed struggle, and steadfastness. Believing that its power could compel a change in U.S. policy or force Israel's surrender made other options less attractive to the PLO, while expecting that Washington could be persuaded to abandon Israel or order it to yield territory reinforced these miscalculations. As long as the PLO believed that Israel would be destroyed, it could not develop a serious policy to negotiate, compromise, and reach a diplomatic settlement with that state, or gain much credibility in Israel as a negotiating partner and future neighbor. The PLO's resulting continued use of radical means and rhetoric, in turn, hardened Israel's aversion to negotiating with it—much less yielding territory.

The PLO always had an option of announcing its readiness to accept Israel's existence in exchange for a West Bank/Gaza Palestinian state and of stopping terrorism as a sign of its willingness to reach a compromise solution. Yet the PLO never took such a course until 1993. By changing its policy and goals earlier, it could have entered negotiations in the eras of the 1979 Camp David peace talks, the 1982 Reagan Plan, or on other occasions.

Even when the PLO did make important alterations in 1988, it did not go far enough to be accepted as a diplomatic partner. PLO leaders acted in this manner for understandable reasons: their desire to hold together a diverse assemblage of competing member groups; pressure from radical Arab states; constituents' expectations of total victory; the leaders' own political need to prove their militancy; the adoption of terrorism as an integral part of the PLO's strategy; and a deep, ideologically based distrust of the United States and Israel.

The hope of eliminating Israel and ruling all Palestine was the ideological and political source of the PLO's internal unity as well as the basis of its legitimacy among Muslims, Arabs, and Palestinians. As refugees from 1948, the PLO's main supporters and leading cadre mourned lost homes in Israel that could be regained only by conquering that land. An uncompromising radicalism was a natural element in the psychological and political revival from defeat and displacement, responding to a sense of having suffered injustice and a passion for revenge.

A spate of events damaging the PLO's interests in the 1980s and early 1990s made this historical analysis harder to maintain, though it still served a useful function within Palestinian politics. If the PLO and its allies could not expel U.S. influence or defeat Israel on the battlefield, the diplomatic route became the only viable option, though few Palestinians were willing to admit this publicly. Whatever moral or historical arguments Palestinians might employ, the reality was that not one inch of land could be obtained without some agreement with the only two states that might materially affect the Palestinians' fate for the better.

The PLO was pushed toward tough decisions and irreversible choices as West Bank/Gaza Palestinians demanded action, Arab rulers reduced support for the PLO and involvement in the conflict, the USSR collapsed, U.S. power grew, and Israel became stronger and more deeply entrenched in the territories. The opening of direct Arab–Israeli and Israeli–Palestinian negotiations in 1991 further challenged PLO leaders to bridge the gap between opportunities and limits imposed by internal politics or ideology in order to advance from revolutionary movement to governing authority. This situation made the PLO's view of its foes even more central in determining its strategy and fortunes.

In the 1970s and into the 1980s, some U.S. policymakers and opinionmakers had at times believed—as Arafat did—that the Arab–Israeli conflict was the region's overriding central issue, uniting all Arabs and Muslims, guaranteeing their active, energetic support for the PLO, and determining their relations with the United States. This attitude gave the PLO some leverage in the minds of these Westerners, but the PLO's inability to advocate a credible compromise solution made it unable to take advantage of this limited approbation. Instead, the PLO offered no prospect of a viable solution to those overestimating its power and no actual concessions to those overestimating its moderation.

U.S. policymakers were thus frustrated in efforts to work with Arafat and did not pursue them. The appeal of changing the U.S. position in the Middle East was gradually undermined as the impossibility of finding an Israeli–Palestinian settlement, the PLO's hostility to U.S. interests, and the limitations of the PLO's power all became apparent. Failing in its attempt to endanger U.S. interests or to fulfill the U.S.'s desire of achieving a diplomatic breakthrough, the PLO found U.S. policymakers largely ignoring its concerns. By the time the organization began moving toward a more flexible position, both its psychological and material advantages had very much eroded.

Those American officials, experts, and journalists highlighting the PLO's importance had earlier predicted that unless the Palestinian problem was solved as soon as possible on terms acceptable to the PLO, the Middle East would explode, U.S. interests and influence would be destroyed, and pro-U.S. regimes would be overthrown or decide—from anger or self-preservation—to embrace Moscow or Islamic fundamentalism. Terrorism, anti-Americanism, radicalism, revolution, Islamic fundamentalism, and every other regional phenomenon was attributed to this single-cause explanation, appealing in its simplicity and focus on the regional issue with which Americans were most familiar.

All the area's problems were said to be rooted in this dispute. Zbigniew Brzezinski wrote in 1975: "It is impossible to seek a resolution to the energy problem without tackling head on—and doing so in an urgent fashion—the Arab–Israeli conflict." Otherwise, "any stable arrangement" was impossible. But in fact the oil crisis and related financial issues were handled successfully on their own. "Unless the United States makes a real concession to the Palestinians soon by recognizing the PLO," The London-based *Middle East* magazine wrote in 1979, "It may find it has burnt its bridges." In 1980, the influential scholar Malcolm Kerr claimed that because the issue "has continuously been the number-one preoccupation" of the area, "the decline in American prestige hangs like a cloud over . . . any other form of diplomatic initiative in the Middle East that Washington might wish to pursue."[1]

No matter how much ground the USSR lost or the United States gained, some were ready to argue this was only a mirage. The Arabs, wrote Professor Edward Said in 1979, were "losing hope" in U.S. credibility and turning "to Moscow . . . because they felt they had been left with no alternative. America has been paying heavily for the unresolved conflict in many large and small ways. These include the radicalization of half a dozen Arab regimes, the strengthening of their ties with Moscow . . . their hostility to the United States; [and] the destruction of Lebanon."[2] A leading regional expert, John Campbell, insisted in 1981, "The Palestine question remains a formidable obstacle and burden to U.S. relations with the Arab world. It undermines the moderates and strengthens the wild men. It plays into the hands of the Soviet Union. It threatens to isolate the United States with Israel as the only friend in the region."[3]

"The way to increase security of Western interests in the area and to promote common shares in cooperation is through progress on the Palestine problem, not around it," claimed Professor William Zartman in 1981.[4] Yet U.S. policymakers understandably concluded that since the issue was unresolvable at a time when U.S.–Arab cooperation was possible on other urgent concerns, the matter was better avoided than highlighted.

In 1983 the journalist David Lamb wrote that U.S. policy had convinced most Arab governments "that the Reagan Administration cannot be an honest broker in the stalemated Arab–Israeli conflict." *Time* magazine opined in 1986, "On the Arab side, the sense of betrayal is deep. The Arabs feel that Washington has moved closer to Israel than ever before, thus endangering U.S.

strategic interests and abandoning claims of being an honest broker."[5]

The Arabs of the Persian Gulf were supposedly obsessed about the Arab–Israeli conflict and allegedly mistrusted the United States as a result. "We should not assume," warned author Robert Lacey in 1982, that the Saudi royal family "will continue to be as pro-Western as it is at present . . . [It] could very easily shift itself in a more radical direction." Professor Udo Steinbach wrote in 1983 that until a settlement of the Palestine question was achieved "which will correspond approximately to [Arab] views of a 'just' solution—then close cooperation with the United States cannot fail to operate in a destabilizing manner for the states of the [Persian Gulf] region."[6]

But the role of mediator and protector was precisely the part Arab states were repeatedly asking the United States to play. At that very moment, Saudi Arabia was cooperating with the United States, buying vast amounts of arms from it and building larger military facilities than it needed so that the United States could use them if the Saudis ever needed U.S. protection. In 1987 Kuwait put American flags on its tankers and asked the U.S. navy to convoy them in order to deter Iranian attacks. An Arab summit meeting endorsed the arrangement although no progress had been made on resolving the Arab–Israeli conflict. Saudi Arabia did not hesitate—just a few months after the United States broke off its dialogue with the PLO—to invite U.S. troops to save it when Iraq invaded Kuwait in 1990. Egypt, Syria, and other Arab states aligned with Washington against Baghdad in the Gulf War.

By the same token, anti-Americanism was no mere reaction to U.S. help for Israel or opposition to the PLO. A U.S. policy defending the regimes in Saudi Arabia, Jordan, Lebanon, Libya, and Iraq in the 1950s against radical forces—at a time it had only minimal links with Israel—angered both radicals seeking to overthrow incumbent rulers and expansionist states eager to take over neighbors. American power frightened Pan-Arab nationalists and Muslims who thought a Western cultural and political invasion threatened to swamp their way of life, destroy their independence, and block their plans for unity. Radicals would have fomented revolution and regimes would have battled over regional hegemony even if Israel had never existed.

In fact, while the Palestine issue was undoubtedly an important one for Arab states, it neither pushed them into the Soviet camp nor prevented them from cooperation with the United States when it was otherwise to their advantage. They were more preoccupied with their own problems and strife, largely a natural aftermath of their independence, search for identity, and traumas of development comparable to those elsewhere in the Third World. These factors generated crises often having little or no relation to the Arab–Israeli one, constantly drawing attention and resources away from the PLO's cause and dragging it into costly diversions.

The inter-Arab competition for leadership and frequent coups of the 1950s and 1960s were followed by such strife as Qadhafi's takeover in Libya and subversion of neighbors, instability in Sudan, Lebanon's civil war, the displacement of Iran's shah by an Islamic republic, Kurdish revolts and the Iran–Iraq war, the Soviet invasion of Afghanistan, Islamic fundamentalism, the upward spiral of oil prices, and Iraq's invasion of Kuwait. In these circumstances, Arab support for the PLO was limited or distorted by state interests.

Unwilling to fight Israel—as respect for its strength grew—and increasingly concerned by threats from Iran or Iraq, internal problems, and internecine quarrels, Arab states devoted only diminishing resources to help the PLO. Pro-PLO statements did not stop Saudi Arabia and Egypt from strengthening ties with the United States, nor did Iraq let PLO interests stand in its way when it needed U.S. aid to defeat Iran during their war.[7]

Arab rulers attacked the PLO in the name of the Palestinian cause, assassinating or jailing its leaders, helping anti-Arafat factions, and withholding aid. The PLO had to compete with Jordan's claim to represent the Palestinians and rule the West Bank, as well as Syria's claim to Palestine as "southern Syria" and its demand for veto power over PLO policies. Arafat found no consistent champion in any Arab leader or government.

Instead, these regimes gradually accepted Israel's existence. Egypt and Israel made peace. In practice—though not formally—Jordan and Israel settled into peaceful coexistence; Syria and Israel avoided direct strife. Competing with Israel for U.S. favor, many Arab rulers improved relations with the world's strongest state. The very anxiety that U.S. power might be used against them made radicals more cautious. Assistant Secretary of State Richard Murphy explained that close U.S. ties "to both Israel and Arab states [made it] the only superpower trusted by both." In contrast, "the Soviet Union, without diplomatic relations with Israel and with limited diplomatic ties and bilateral relations in the Arab world, has only a peripheral role to play."[8] Even Kerr conceded that alliance with Israel aided U.S. interests, "as long as the Arabs let the United States get away with . . . managing to befriend Israel without sacrificing important interests in the Arab world."[9]

Despite Moscow's role as the PLO's superpower patron, its influence declined in the Arab world, which found the USSR to be an unreliable champion, a miser on aid, and ineffective in exerting diplomatic or military leverage. Egypt and Sudan expelled the Soviets; Iraq turned its back on them. Even South Yemen—whose close alignment with Moscow was hardly inspired by the Palestinian issue—gave up and merged with conservative North Yemen. Constantly proving superior in technology, reliability, and power to the USSR, the United States had clearly won the Cold War in the Middle East several years earlier than elsewhere.[10] Despite the many times when the U.S. position was said to be on the verge of ruin, it succeeded in limiting regional instability, defeating its Soviet rival, containing extremist regimes, protecting allies, maintaining influence, and ensuring access to oil.

Thus, through the 1970s and 1980s, the PLO had only limited and declining Arab and Soviet backing, no capacity to defeat or destroy Israel, and little leverage in changing U.S. policy. While Arafat was aware of these general trends, he also continued to overestimate his assets, banking on the PLO's centrality in the Arab–Israeli conflict and that issue's alleged primacy for the region, repeatedly threatening to unleash a volcano destroying U.S. interests unless Washington met his demands.

Yet as history moved in the opposite direction, the PLO, unable to force a U.S. retreat, needed a strategy capable of inducing U.S. policy to be more favorable. In short, the power balance meant that the more moderate the PLO's position, the greater its chance to enter negotiations and achieve some form of Palestinian self-determination; the more ambiguous or hardline was the PLO's stand, the less likely the United States would deal with it, endorse its direct inclusion in talks, or accede to a West Bank/Gaza Palestinian state. Since only the PLO and the Palestinians gained nothing from the status quo—and U.S. interests were protected whether or not it resolved Palestinian grievances—the burden of proof for achieving any change was placed on the PLO.[11]

As long as the PLO was disinclined to change policy in order to alleviate current Palestinian suffering, the United States could hardly be expected to do so. But as early as the mid-1970s, U.S. policy did provide a way to involve the PLO in a diplomatic process by giving Arafat a choice. He could show a readiness to change the conflict's terms, and hence move toward a resolution, by meeting three conditions—recognizing Israel, accepting UN resolutions 242 and 338, and rejecting terrorism—or, alternatively, he could choose pro- but non-PLO delegates to represent Palestinian interests.

Such a strategy's requirements, however, clashed with the PLO's historic goals, structure, tactics, and worldview. For the PLO, anti-Americanism had been both ideological tenet and a reaction to the U.S.–Israel alliance. On the one hand, it assumed that U.S. imperialism sought to conquer the Arabs. Arafat called the United States in 1986 "the controlling force of neo-colonialism, imperialism and racism [which] employs Israel to spearhead its strategy of domination in the Middle East."[12] There could be no rapprochement with—only a struggle against—an America trying to rule and exploit the Middle East, using Israel as a tool and inevitably opposing Palestinian rights.

According to an advocate of this determinist view, the Palestinian–American PNC member Edward Said, "The United States, as a government and as a society, is hostile to us." It was not an arbiter but "a party to the conflict." He urged the PLO to turn military defeat into political victory by dealing "with the United States the same way the Vietnamese dealt with Henry Kissinger in Paris."[13] This stance implied that the PLO could subvert domestic U.S. support for the client state, erode U.S. willpower by protracted struggle, and make agreements only to break them as soon as possible.

On the other hand, the PLO could hardly expect to achieve its somewhat contradictory goal of splitting the American patron from its Israeli client if the United States was so irredeemably hostile to the Arabs. Arafat claimed that the way for the PLO to succeed was by forcing America to submit through the PLO's own strength and persistence rather than by enticing it to accede through a change in the PLO's own policy.

Yet was U.S. opposition to Palestinian rights so inevitable, or did the PLO also fail to exploit opportunities to change U.S. policy? The PLO's own behavior and professed goals were among the main reasons the United States became the PLO's enemy. The PLO view of America as hostile was, in no small part, a self-fulfilling prophecy. During the long Cold War decades, a PLO policy aligned with Moscow, putting a priority on armed struggle, employing terrorism even against U.S. citizens, and seeking to destroy Israel gave the United States no compelling political or strategic incentive to change policy, take risks, or weaken its own ally.[14]

Even Said thought that "negligence, corruption, and incompetence" damaged the PLO's attempt to improve its image in the United States.[15] It failed to take advantage of such elements in American political culture as sympathy for "underdogs" and support for self-determination. Moreover, an American tendency to attribute conflicts to misunderstanding or poor communication—rather than to clashing interests—created an expectation that proof of good intentions and concessions might transform enemies into friends. Yet, even those journalists, experts, or officials eager to recognize or even exaggerate moderation from the PLO were usually denied evidence of its predicted "pragmatism" in recognizing Israel or stopping terrorism.

The extent of U.S. support for Israel, of course, was no mere illusion. Aside from a large, politically active Jewish community, American public opinion was positive toward Israel for such reasons as memory of the Holocaust, Israeli support of U.S. interests, mutual opposition to Soviet influence and to radical Arab states, and greater cultural proximity. Still, the PLO exaggerated this attachment, a factor which affected its own policy toward the United States. A PLO newspaper claimed in 1991 that pro-Israel forces "terrified all U.S. presidents of the past 40 years and became so strong that any state wanting to move closer to the White House and to enjoy its care and loans had to obtain Israeli approval first." Abu Iyad claimed in 1989 that Israel "to a large extent controls the United States." Hani al-Hasan said in 1990, "It is regrettable that a superpower . . . the greatest one at present, is governed by the Zionist lobby."[16]

By the mid-1980s, however, the PLO was already exploring an approach based on its long-standing idea that the United States was Israel's master rather than its servant. The PLO Charter had defined

Israel not as a homeland for a Jewish nation but as a "base for world imperialism placed strategically in the midst of the Arab homeland to combat . . . Arab liberation, unity, and progress . . . to secure continued imperialist robbery and exploitation of our country."[17]

Commented Khalid al-Hasan in 1989, "We don't consider ourselves as fighting Jews but the U.S. military. Israel itself cannot do anything. And if Israel is left alone without this kind of military support we could have solved the problem long ago."[18] Even as late as 1993 he quoted an old antisemitic forgery to make the point: "As George Washington said [Jews] cannot live except by sucking the blood of others. The Israeli political leadership is like a coward seeking protection from a strong man . . . Israel is the United States' slave."[19]

But now the view of Israel as a U.S. puppet was deemed a factor that might be turned to the PLO's advantage. Concluding that "nothing can get done in the region without the United States," Arafat sought serious talks with Washington by meeting its long-standing conditions for a dialogue in December 1988.[20] Instead of trying to defeat America, the PLO sought both to pressure and woo it as a substitute for making peace with Israel. If, as Arafat suggested, Israel merely did what America said, "Peace is not in Israel's hand, but in the hand of the United States, because Israeli decisionmaking is in Washington and not in Tel Aviv."[21]

PLO Executive Committee member Abdallah Hourani explained, "The party that decides . . . is neither us nor Israel. It is the two superpowers and the [UN] Security Council's permanent member states." Nabil Sha'th insisted, "The United States is a realistic country. The longer the uprising continues and the wider Palestinian peace movements spread or gain supporters in the world, the more the United States is forced to change its line."[22]

The PLO's own internal needs encouraged such official optimism in the late 1980s that continued struggle, and support for the organization's leaders, would produce success. Several factors were said to be forcing U.S. policy to accommodate itself to the PLO. Especially important was the intifada, whose extensive coverage in the U.S. media brought more sympathy for the Palestinians. "People are being killed," said a Palestinian newspaper, "Muslims and Christians, children and women, using American taxpayers' money."[23] In speech after speech, Arafat assured the Palestinians that a few more months of steadfastness and struggle would bring total victory. Muhammad Milhim, the PLO's coordinator with the intifada, asserted, "The maintenance of the current PLO policy and the continuation of the PLO's firm strategy will force Israel and the United States to accept the Palestinian peace initiative."[24]

The PLO also thought its hand was strengthened by the end of the Iran–Iraq war—letting Arabs, Arafat claimed, "devote more of their attention to supporting the Palestinian people's cause"—and of the Cold War. Khalid al-Hasan suggested the latter event would undermine U.S. support for Israel: "When the Zionist entity becomes an obstacle in the vital American interests, Washington will be the first to jettison Israel." Qaddumi asserted, "International detente has diminished Israel's strategic value."[25] But rather than subverting U.S.–Israel relations, the Cold War's end reduced any American need to woo the PLO or Arab states away from the Soviet camp, extinguishing the old argument that only concessions to the PLO could prevent a pro-Moscow Middle East.

Furthermore, while the United States knew that only an Israeli–Palestinian agreement could bring a breakthrough, the PLO argued that internal weaknesses and U.S. pressure would force Israel's withdrawal without requiring a clear and major revision of PLO policy, tactics, or goals. In short, PLO leaders thought that they could negotiate with the United States as a substitute for dealing with Israel, an idea which also undermined chances for rapprochement with the United States.

The PLO's inability to conceive of its main enemy as a legitimate, genuine, or viable state had long intensified such miscalculations. By divorcing Israel from any Jewish historical, national or philosophical context, the PLO found the country's survival inconceivable.[26] Rather than seeing Zionism as a Jewish nationalist movement, it was defined as imperialist, racist, fanatic, aggressive, expansionist, colonial, and fascist. The PLO argued that Jews could not be a legitimate nation and that neither their religion nor their heritage had a historical connection with Palestine.[27] Israel must disappear because it was, in Khalid al-Hasan's words, "an alien entity in the region . . . moving against the historical trend."[28]

Even when acknowledging some Jewish rationale for Israel's existence, the PLO sometimes did so by arguments paralleling traditional antisemitism. Abu Iyad commented in 1990, "The enemy exists in the world politics and economy; it controls money and media. We are not facing only 3 million Israelis on the Palestinian territories but 16 million Zionist Jews spread around the world and supported by others in the world. The battle . . . cannot be counted by years. The Crusades lasted more than 200 years, and this war is more serious."[29]

One of the PLO Executive Committee's most sophisticated members—Jamal al-Surani, the organization's expert on negotiations—could say in 1990, "Israel was built on a Torah Talmud racist foundation."[30] On the popular level, the Palestinian masses were told by a 1992 Fatah leaflet that the PLO "realizes it is negotiating with Jews, and knows the Jews to be what they are: 'Descendants of monkeys and pigs' . . . Fatah will continue to carry a gun in one hand and an olive branch in the other until Allah has had his say on the matter."[31]

Arafat himself called Israel's government a "military junta" and insisted that its relentless expansionism was signified by the two blue lines on Israel's flag—a traditional Jewish motif—said to show Israel's claim to all the land between the Nile and Euphrates rivers. If Israel's motive was expansionism, the PLO could logically conclude that Israel was not able to either make or maintain peace.

The Zionists, exclaimed Abu Iyad in 1988, complain about Nazi concentration camps, but "the atrocities that they are perpetrating are more terrible and uglier than the atrocities and crimes perpetrated by the Nazis." Arafat repeatedly equated Israel with the Nazis and spoke of "Israeli concentration camps" as equivalent with "the notorious Auschwitz death camp."[32] Seeing Israel as illegitimate, insatiable, and genocidal—as well as riven with internal contradictions and doomed to disappear—hardly inclined Arafat to compromise with it. "The arrogant forces in Israel," Arafat commented in 1988, could only be stopped "with another Masada," referring to the place where Jews committed mass suicide at the end of the Roman conquest. "We are going with the course of history, and they are going against it."[33]

There were some gestures of conciliation from the Tunis leadership or hints that the PLO might find mainstream partners in Israel with whom to make peace. Arafat in 1990 once cited polls showing that the majority of Israelis wanted "peace and reconciliation." One intifada communique greeted "progressive and democratic forces and the Jewish peace forces which support our people's national rights." A 1989 leaflet tried to appeal to Israeli soldiers. But such statements were still rare.[34]

In 1992 Arafat asserted: "I have never made the mistake of attacking the Jews [verbally] . . . In the Palestinian movement we have Jewish strugglers of whom we are proud. We have friendly forces in Israel, such as the Peace Now Movement . . . We were the first movement in the Arab world to call for a democratic state in which Jews, Muslims, and Christians could coexist."[35] But this statement again suggested that the PLO was not ready to recognize Israel and was made in response to an event undermining Arafat's claim. When the French government expelled PFLP leader Habash who had come there for medical treatment in February 1992, Arafat told the PLO's representative in Paris, "The Jews at work. Damn their fathers. The dogs. Filth and dirt . . . I took care of and treated their ill and sick. But trash is always trash."[36]

Abu Iyad expressed a similar ambiguity. In 1989 he said, "It is incontrovertible fact that Palestine is Arab–Islamic and that the Jews are the scum of humanity that gathered from the four corners of the earth and conquered our land, encouraged by the powers. Will the Jews keep a promise? Treachery flows in their blood, as the Qur'an testifies. The Jews are the same as they have always been."[37] About the same time, he also wrote a moderate article in the U.S. magazine *Foreign Policy* calling for a West Bank/Gaza Palestinian state that would live peacefully alongside Israel.[38] It was impossible to say how much of this type of contradiction expressed by PLO officials was an attempt to appeal to different audiences and how much was a result of contradictory ideas held by the individuals.

Thus, making peace with Israel was long repugnant to PLO leaders because of that country's alleged nature; unimaginable because such a deed would sell out Palestinian rights; unnecessary because the United States would concede to Palestinian demands or Israel would collapse any way; and dangerous since many Palestinian people and groups would reject it. The PLO's statements and views on Israel were conducive neither to making peace nor to convincing its adversaries that the PLO was a negotiating partner able to reach a stable settlement. Only strong leadership, moderated thinking, preparation of the masses for compromise, and more influence by the West Bank/Gaza constituency could overcome these powerful forces.

The point, Henry Kissinger once remarked, was "not so much how to start negotiations as to define their objective."[39] The PLO had to convince Israel that it would make a stable, final peace settlement on the basis of a West Bank/Gaza state. As Secretary of State Baker told the PLO in 1989, "Translate the dialogue of violence in the intifada into a dialogue of politics and diplomacy. Violence will not work. Reach out to Israelis and convince them of your peaceful intentions. You have the most to gain from doing so and no one else can or will do it for you. Finally, understand that no one is going to 'deliver' Israel for you."[40]

Only the PLO's leadership could persuade Israel to relinquish the West Bank and Gaza by showing its readiness for a compromise peace ensuring Israeli security and Palestinian rights. But whatever its intentions, as long as the PLO leadership felt no need of convincing Israelis to change policy by showing moderation, any effort to do so remained a low priority for the organization.

As long as Israelis deemed their survival to be at stake, they would prefer a continuation of a status quo which, while difficult, entailed far less suffering for them than for Palestinians in the occupied territories. Despite some Israelis' support for keeping the territories on religious grounds and despite a strong settlers' lobby, the occupation's chief motive was security. Most Israelis believed, as Prime Minister Yitzhak Shamir argued in 1988, that the PLO "does not want peace with Israel but to destroy it . . . We know this from the Palestinian Charter and their ideology."[41] Remembering the Holocaust, a half-dozen wars, PLO and Arab threats to annihilate them, and terrorist attacks, Israelis would not return to something close to the narrow pre-1967 borders in exchange for anything less than the conflict's end, not the onset of a new stage of struggle. No Israeli government would accept terms—regardless of pressure— openly announced as a way to promote its destruction nor negotiate with an organization proclaiming this as its goal.

From the PLO's standpoint, diplomatic progress was impeded by the fact that the United States and Israel rejected an independent Palestinian state and preferred dealing with West Bank/Gaza Palestinians rather than itself. It feared a permanent Israeli occupation might be hidden behind an offer of local autonomy. Yet these problems were not so insuperable as they might appear at first glance.

Whatever reluctance the PLO's two enemies had shown to a fully independent state, they were open to a Palestinian federation with Jordan, which the PLO had officially accepted. In addition, the peace process was designed with an interim stage of self-rule in the territories, which the PLO could use in order to consolidate power, creating, step-by-step, an infrastructure which would ensure its own future rule and make any loosening of Israeli control an irreversible process.

Seeing Israel's conservative Shamir government—opposed to yielding territory and rapidly building settlements—as uncompromising, the PLO could have worked to shore up the arguments of the opposition Labor party, committed to trading territory for peace. Indeed, the Shamir coalition's efforts to entrench further Israel's presence in the territories and Israeli repression there, which the PLO painted in nightmarish terms, made a Palestinian diplomatic effort all the more urgent.

Such an effort would have had a big impact on Israeli politics. Despite all the factors militating for intransigence in Israel, the Labor party, favoring territorial compromise and talks with pro-PLO Palestinians in the territories, still nearly won the 1984 and 1988 elections and in early 1990 came within one vote of forming a cabinet ready to negotiate with them.

Moreover, if the Palestinian people were as united behind the PLO as it claimed, the organization could certainly negotiate through a screen of West Bank/Gaza Palestinians. This arrangement even arguably had advantages for the PLO, since it would not have to make the concessions—ceasing armed struggle, for example—that would be necessary if it were to enter negotiations directly.

But for a long time the PLO did not act to defuse U.S. and Israeli suspicions deriving from its own acts and goals nor did it, even while moderating its stand, develop a comprehensive strategy for advancing the diplomatic process. Instead, it remained enamored of the idea that the United States and Israel could be defeated or outmaneuvered with the minimum modification of its own policies. The PLO was more concerned with proving itself to be an indispensable rather than an acceptable negotiating partner. Palestinians easily rationalized their stands on the basis of historical and current injustice, but the real issue was that the PLO's approach was ineffective.[42]

Thus, with massive support from Palestinian constituents, the PLO leapt on Saddam Husayn's bandwagon. At a January 1991 Baghdad rally, a few days before fighting began, Arafat said that if the United States wanted war, "then I say welcome, welcome, welcome to war." "Iraq and Palestine," he continued, would be together, "side by side" in battle. In February he proclaimed, "If they want to have o-i-l, then they have to also take P-L-O," and called for military attacks on Israel.[43]

The result of this strategy was another debacle for the PLO, again demonstrating that it could get nowhere except through negotiations, mutual compromise, and an agreement with Israel. "The Palestinians," an Arab writer said, "do not accept the proposition that, in the age of the people's right to self-determination, they should be singled out for denial of this right."[44] Yet they could not achieve this goal while denying it to Israel.

In explaining its objectives, the PLO tried to give the West the impression that it only sought a West Bank/Gaza state, while it claimed the whole land to Arab and Palestinian audiences. Resolving that distinction was vital if the PLO were to shift toward compromise, obtain U.S. or Israeli recognition, reach an agreement to end the occupation, and gain control over any territory. Without such a transformation, Arafat and his colleagues might easily remain the PLO's leaders but not become rulers over part of Palestine—the West Bank and Gaza. Whatever the extent of opposition from Israeli or U.S. policy, the PLO could only gain ground through flexibility and moderation, thereby establishing its credibility in Washington and Jerusalem and strengthening the hand of forces within those governments willing to negotiate and compromise with it.

By maintaining a hard line in doctrine and tactics, the PLO ensured that U.S. and Israeli policy would exclude it, and that very exclusion became the PLO's rationale for preserving its hard line. But by 1993, having gotten nowhere with strategies dependent on Arab unity, guerrilla warfare, terrorism, the USSR, Saddam Hussein, or the United States, the PLO finally chose to try the hitherto rejected option of making peace with Israel itself.

10 >> Breaking the Mold, 1991–1993

The speech of Haydar Abd al-Shafi, the Palestinian delegation's leader, to the Madrid peace conference on October 31, 1991, was a historic moment in a process which at last might help to resolve Palestinian problems and grievances. "We, the people of Palestine, stand before you in the fullness of our pain, our pride, and our anticipation, for we long harbored a yearning for peace and a dream of justice and freedom. For too long, the Palestinian people have gone unheeded, silenced and denied. Our identity negated by political expediency; our right for struggle against injustice maligned; and our present existence subdued by the past tragedy of another people . . . It is time for us to narrate our own story . . . We seek neither an admission of guilt after the fact, nor vengeance for past inequities, but rather an act of will that would make a just peace a reality."[1]

But even though every word was no doubt approved by the PLO, it was still Abd al-Shafi, not Arafat, standing on this podium, representing the people of Palestine. The veteran nationalist from Gaza, who had been a delegate at the PLO's 1964 founding conference, paid tribute to the organization without mentioning it directly: "We have been denied the right to publicly acknowledge our loyalty to our leadership and system of government."[2]

More than a half-century earlier, Palestinians had faced parallel challenges, opportunities, debates, dangers, and temptations. In 1939 a British White Paper had offered Palestinian Arabs more self-government immediately and full independence within a decade.

Egypt's government urged them to accept the compromise: "You shall be able to control your country's administration; to stop persecution, exiles and harsh measures." Building a state would require such an interim period to train officials, organize security, and win popular legitimacy. If this chance was missed, the Egyptians warned, the great powers would lose patience, Arab rulers would become preoccupied with other issues, the Jews would grow stronger, and the Palestinian Arabs would lose everything. The Palestinian leaders rejected the proposal, however, saying, "When the revolution started, we had aims in view to attain. We cannot now tell our people, 'Stop the revolution because we got some high posts.'"[3] But the Egyptian prophecy had proven correct in the 1940s: by rejecting compromise solutions, the Palestinians had lost the chance to rule any part of the country.

In 1973 Arafat had set his generation's task as one of "suffering, of sacrifice . . . it is the next generation that will win the victory [and] reach the sea." Like the Vietnamese, who fought for twenty years, "The Arab peasant will also impose his conditions one day."[4] Indeed, the Vietnamese Communists did implement a two-stage strategy, first acquiring the country's northern part, then using it as a base when conditions were ripe a quarter-century later for conquering the rest. This triumph's cost, however, was hundreds of thousands dead and Vietnam's devastation. The PLO, too, had the possibility of choosing to fight on into the indefinite future, an alternative it had preferred in the past.

But now once again, the situation was analogous to that of 1939. The Palestinians were being offered rule over part of the country for a transitional testing period, at a time when their friends were weakening or deserting them and their historic enemies were growing stronger. Yet a great deal had changed, with a constellation of new pressures: the PLO's own experience, defeats, and failures; its current financial crisis; the rising influence of West Bank Palestinians; declining Arab and Soviet support; and the growing power of the United States and Israel had all slowly moved the PLO along an equivocal but steady path toward moderation.[5]

The political situation after the Gulf War had further narrowed the PLO's choices. The Kuwait crisis and the war, said Arafat, "dealt our Arab nation a great blow, hit Arab solidarity, and paralyzed the Arab position toward the Palestinian question." The weakening of the USSR was destroying the PLO's strongest remaining ally, leaving "American power" to dominate "the fate of international politics."[6] This new atmosphere was reflected in the UN's December 1991 repeal—over PLO objections—of its 1975 resolution equating Zionism with racism.[7]

At the regional level, forty years of Arab rejection of Israel, a quarter-century of PLO armed struggle, and a mass uprising had brought no tangible material gain for the Palestinian people. Any hope of destroying Israel and regaining all the land seemed futile in the light of repeated military defeats. Arab states, tired of the conflict and of supporting the PLO, were meeting with Israel. Having itself made peace with Israel, Egypt urged the PLO to do the same. Lebanon's reviving government disarmed PLO forces outside the refugee camps and made them surrender their heavy weapons. "Palestinian guns have not liberated one inch of Palestine for the past 16 years," said Defense Minister Michel al-Murr. "Under no circumstances will we allow the Palestinians to use their weapons to establish a state within our state," as had existed before 1982.[8]

Arab rulers in the Persian Gulf worried more about Iran and Iraq than about Israel. They expelled about half as many Palestinians as had become refugees in 1948 and stopped aid to the PLO in revenge for its support of Iraq, forcing the PLO to cut its budget and further impoverishing West Bank/Gaza Palestinians. At the 1991 Islamic Conference Organization summit in Senegal, Saudi Crown Prince Abdallah had refused to embrace Arafat, and the meeting did not repeat past sessions' calls for the liberation of Palestine. In a message to two million Muslim pilgrims to Mecca in June 1993, King Fahd predicted that talks with Israel would inevitably bring "security and peace for all." History proved, he said, "that conflicts and wars achieve no victory and produce no gains." Israel could achieve security guarantees not through "ignoring the rights of the Palestinian people . . . but by peaceful coexistence between neighboring states and peoples."[9]

On the local front, more than five years of intifada had not forced Israel's withdrawal but had brought the Palestinian economic and social infrastructure to the verge of collapse. Fundamentalist or PLO squads had killed as many Palestinians as had Israel's army. Moreover, almost half a million Soviet and Ethiopian Jewish immigrants had arrived in Israel between December 1989 and September 1993, greatly increasing that country's Jewish population. The building of new Jewish settlements in the territories made the occupation look even more permanent unless a negotiated settlement was reached. A refusal to face the need to redefine its structure, strategy, and goals would make continued Palestinian suffering and Israeli occupation a certainty. No words or deeds could achieve anything material for Palestinians until Arafat persuaded both Washington and Jerusalem that the PLO was ready to change its objectives and methods. No matter how historically sustainable a Palestinian claim to all the land or how justifiable the PLO's policies, these positions could not be effective.

Having lost its veto power over talks between Israel and the Arab states—the PLO's greatest fear since its inception—the organization could not leave Palestinians unrepresented as these negotiations were about to begin. Arafat said, "It is entirely impossible for the PLO to remain an onlooker because the Palestinian people will have to live with its results." By being outside such a peace conference, the PLO would have "betrayed the trust put in us by the Palestinian people."[10]

The PLO's predicament made it easier for West Bank/Gaza Palestinians to push for flexibility and to overcome the leadership's reluctance to let them sit at the negotiating table with Israel. Haydar Abd al-Shafi said that the Palestinians had laid the foundation for this step by having "formally abandoned the strategy of liberation and clearly and unambiguously adopted the principle of a two-state solution." He called this change a major concession but one which took reality into account, accepting the need to seek "pragmatic justice" rather than "absolute justice."[11]

The West Bank and Gaza leadership urged the PLO to adopt a flexible policy and suggested such reforms as increasing West Bank/Gaza representation in the organization's top ranks, electing PNC delegates in the territories, and establishing a provisional government staffed by themselves. "We have our own will," Faysal al-Husayni said in April 1991, "and we are capable of choosing our own leadership."[12]

Thus, the September 1991 PNC in Algiers was under intense pressure to shift the PLO's strategy. Yasir Abd Rabbu summed up the PLO's dilemma as being "between the options of suicide and suicide."[13] Faysal al-Husayni and Hanan Ashrawi, a Bir Zayt Uni-

versity professor and U.S.-educated Christian Palestinian who
served as spokesperson, secretly attended the meeting and spoke to
press their case for participation. In his opening speech Arafat said
the PLO would "show the utmost seriousness in dealing with this
opportunity" and expressed readiness to participate in an international peace conference. He also once again called Israel a racist,
fascist state seeking to rule the Middle East from the Euphrates to
the Nile.[14]

Khalid al-Hasan pointedly warned that time was running against
the PLO and inaction might make it irrelevant. "Can the PLO revert
and once again become an underground movement? Do we have
to start from square one? Will the enemy wait for us until we rebuild our strength and change the balance of power . . . Does this
serve the interests of the future of our people? It is not enough for
us to say that our conscience rejects, and therefore we have to reject
everything. We are dealing with politics, with the future of a
people, and not with wedding arrangements."[15]

Echoing these sentiments, the PNC's political resolution asserted,
"The current situation requires us to deal with it in the spirit of
political responsibility and national realism." It called for a peace
conference based on UN Resolutions 242 and 338; full Israeli withdrawal from the occupied territories, including East Jerusalem; an
exchange of land for peace; a halt to Israeli settlements; acceptance
of Palestinian national and political rights; a strong connection between the interim and final stages of negotiations; a confederation
between Jordan and Palestine; and the PLO's role in making all Palestinian decisions.[16]

In terms of doctrine, the meeting went only slightly further toward recognizing Israel or pledging to stop terrorism—steps which
might have allowed a direct PLO role in talks—than did its 1988
predecessor. But, more significantly, it permitted a radical departure
from all previous policy by authorizing pro-PLO Palestinians in the
territories—whom the organization could control behind the
scenes—to negotiate on its behalf. In practice, this let Arafat form
a delegation of West Bank/Gaza Palestinians to attend the proposed
Middle East peace conference in Madrid, Spain, and the Israel–
Palestinian negotiations to follow.

"No one can hide the sun with their fingers," said Arafat in defending his decision. "Everyone knows that the Palestinians will be

represented by the PLO. Every Palestinian is a member of the PLO, inside and outside the territories."[17] But such sentiments did not change the fact that he had rejected this approach many times before as unacceptable; nor did the reality that the PLO was operating behind a thin screen negate the organization's continued exclusion from direct participation.

The West Bank leadership praised the PLO decision to attend the Madrid meeting, and the list of Palestinian delegates—worked out between local leaders and the PLO—was handed by Husayni to Secretary of State Baker in October. Arafat again expected, as he had in 1988, that the U.S. connection would bear fruit. "America says Jerusalem is an occupied territory. We say Jerusalem is an occupied territory," he explained. "With whom do they intend to make peace? If it was not with the Palestinians then with whom?"[18]

Thus, when the conference, co-chaired by the United States and USSR, opened in Madrid on October 30, 1991, PLO officials advised the delegation—which had quietly met with Arafat to receive his authorization—but stayed in the background. The spotlight was held by Abd al-Shafi, Husayni, and Ashrawi.

Abd al-Shafi had to deal carefully with the fact that only the West Bank/Gaza Palestinians were present at the meeting, standing in for the PLO and Palestinian constituencies outside the occupied territories. Thus, he emphasized that "the Palestinian people are one," even though the invitation to discuss "the peace we all desire and need comes to only a portion of our people." He maintained that "each of us represents the rights and interests of the whole" and, referring obliquely to the PLO, added: "Our acknowledged leadership [was the] justly democratically chosen leadership of all the Palestinian identity, the guardian of our past, the protector of our present, and the hope of our future. Our people have chosen to entrust it with their history and the preservation of our precious legacy." The delegation's duty was "not to surrender or forget."[19]

Defining the demands which the delegates were supposed to champion was an equally important task. Abd al-Shafi stated these goals as a Palestinian state "on all the territories occupied by Israel in the war of 1967," including East Jerusalem. A transitional stage was acceptable, "provided interim arrangements are not transformed into permanent status. The time frame must be condensed."[20]

The diplomatic framework set at Madrid was not incompatible with this approach. The United States would host a series of bilateral meetings bringing together Israel with Syria, Lebanon, and a joint delegation representing Jordan and the West Bank/Gaza Palestinians. The purpose of talks between Israel and the neighboring Arab states would be to work out peace treaties. Israeli–Palestinian negotiations—excluding direct PLO involvement—would first set the parameters for a phase of self-rule in the occupied territories supposed to last five years. Within three years of the onset of this period, the sides would begin negotiations for a permanent settlement to determine the territories' future.

The West Bank/Gaza Palestinian delegation began periodic sessions of bilateral talks in Washington, which would total eleven sessions during 1992 and 1993. Israel began meeting separately with these Palestinians, rather than only as part of a joint delegation with Jordan, the formula sanctioned in Madrid. Simultaneously, there were a series of multilateral talks involving Arab states, Israel, and the Palestinians on such issues as arms control, economic development, and refugees.

A critical turning point was the June 1992 election of a new government in Israel—led by Prime Minister Yitzhak Rabin and Foreign Minister Shimon Peres—not only committed but eager to trade territory for peace. It was the first time the Labor party held power without a conservative partner since 1977, and its main coalition colleague, the Meretz party, favored talks with the PLO. As the general who captured the West Bank and Gaza in the 1967 war and a tough defense minister in fighting the intifada, Rabin had proven credentials on defending Israel's security. This reputation allowed him to act flexibly as a negotiator and to muster broad Israeli support for a compromise peace with the Palestinians.

Declaring many of the Jewish settlements in the territories "political" and unnecessary for Israel's security, Rabin's new government quickly cut funding and stopped new construction. He and Peres predicted that they would soon reach agreement with the Palestinians. In 1993 Israel's parliament repealed a law barring citizens from talking to the PLO, and legislators from Meretz and Labor began meeting with PLO officials. Israel also permitted the return of twenty-five prominent pro-PLO deportees to the West Bank and Gaza in April 1993 and accepted Husayni as the Palestinian delegation's leader in June, a step it had previously rejected lest his East Jerusalem residency compromise its claim to that part of the city. Rabin's goal was to reach an agreement with local Palestinians as a branch of the PLO, since he doubted that Arafat would make the concessions necessary for an accord with the organization's Tunis headquarters.

Furthermore, the negotiating framework agreed to in Madrid restricted the PLO to an indirect, behind-the-scenes role, despite the accurate claim that, in the words of PLO official Nabil Sha'th, "the United States . . . cannot deny that in talking with any member of the Palestinian delegation to the peace conference, it is talking with delegates chosen directly by the PLO [who] do not utter one word or statement and do not make any decision except by specific instructions from the PLO leadership, led by president Yasir Arafat."[21]

The Palestinian delegates had to refer all questions to PLO headquarters and felt extreme pressure from their own constituents—as well as from Islamic fundamentalist groups outside the PLO and radical factions within it—to give no ground in either the literal or figurative senses. The PLO wanted ironclad advance assurances that any process would inevitably produce a Palestinian state, with East Jerusalem as its capital. Aside from concerns that limited self-rule might become a permanent situation, the PLO also sought to deemphasize the interim period, since local Palestinians would hold all the power during that time. The obdurate Abd al-Shafi often disagreed with the more flexible Husayni, but both sought reforms in the PLO and criticized Arafat; Arafat tried to ensure his own control over Husayni—and the West Bank Palestinians generally—by showing that he was giving the orders.[22]

Thus, progress was still difficult, even though the chances for agreement were better than ever before. Both sides still had to contend with mutual mistrust, domestic politics, the knotty Jerusalem question, and a belief that patience—or U.S. intervention favoring one's own interests—would win concessions from the other side. Israel remained suspicious of the PLO, claimed East Jerusalem, wanted to have some limits on self-rule, refused to make a prior commitment to the establishment of a state, and demanded that the PLO abandon claims to pre-1967 Israel and a right of return.

Many Palestinians—even in the PLO itself—not only were reluctant to make a definitive diplomatic settlement but also were opposed to negotiations altogether. Both PLO leaders and their rivals saw the interim stage as a potential trap, enabling a permanent Israeli occupation. The decision to go to Madrid and participate in bilateral talks with Israel had been intensely criticized not only by Habash, Hawatmah, and the Islamic fundamentalist Hamas but also by high-ranking Fatah officers in Lebanon. Within the territories, frustrated militants pushed for more attacks on Israeli soldiers and civilians.

The PLO itself, at least for a transitional period, remained partly the prisoner of its history and structure, frozen between a two-state solution or an attempted two-stage destruction of Israel; between mobilizing constituents through militancy and persuading Israelis that a deal could bring them peace and security; between a lack of control over member groups and the need to curb violence or extremism to make the compromises needed for any treaty.

Under these conditions, outside observers could not so easily distinguish between face-saving myth and operational program. As a February 1990 article in the PLO's theoretical organ put it, a Palestinian state "will be able, if only gradually, to cause the disintegration of the Zionist–Jewish framework of the State of Israel." Khalid al-Hasan's effort to straddle this gap was typical among PLO leaders: "An Israeli withdrawal will totally undermine the basic foundations of Zionism. An Israel that has been reduced in size will be a non-Zionist Israel, beside which the Palestinian state can live in peaceful coexistence, although ultimately the non-Zionist state of Israel will, of its own volition and in a perfectly peaceful manner, be swallowed up by the surrounding Arab cultural milieu. Thus will the democratic Palestinian state [encompassing all of Palestine] be born."[23]

Qaddumi, the PLO's second-highest-ranking leader, as late as January 1993 called the negotiations "no more than a futile debate by which each party wishes to pass the time until the current stage ends . . . We are not about to sign any document that will prevent us from laying claim to the 1948 territories and the right of return," lest the leadership be accused of selling out. "We are certain that the appropriate time will come to rebuild the 'jihad' front and restore collective action" against Israel by Arab and Muslim states. At present, the Palestinians would merely "take advantage" of Israel's weakness to advance. "Every Israeli withdrawal from the land means that Israel has been forced to recognize that this land does not belong to it, that it is Arab land . . . The Fatah movement started before 1965 [i.e., before Israel captured the West Bank and Gaza]. It's objectives are known. We said that we adopted the step-by-step course. We must pursue this course to liberate our holy land. We are still on the same course."[24]

Abd al-Shafi himself, once off the stage at Madrid, also took a tough stand. The negotiations' value, he commented, was in improving the Palestinians' image, focusing attention on the issue, and depicting Israel as the obstacle to peace. But he, too, assumed the talks would fail and that a deadlock would benefit the PLO by reaping it more concessions, including a renewed U.S.–PLO dialogue. He preferred dealing with a hardline Israeli government, Abd al-Shafi declared, since Israeli intransigence would bring the Palestinians more international sympathy. Like Qaddumi, Abd al-Shafi felt that the PLO's weak position did not compel it to give up anything more since this was no ordinary dispute, where bargaining was appropriate, but a case of Israeli "aggression" and violation of "international law."[25]

Thus, on the one hand, the PLO might at last be ready and able to achieve a compromise peace, having begun to speak in terms of recognizing Israel as part of a two-state solution. The end of the occupation and conflict, along with the realization of Palestinian sovereignty, would be great achievements. On the other hand, politics made PLO officials and Palestinians in general reluctant to abandon the idea animating their struggle and mobilizing their most loyal constituency. "What more can we offer?" Abu Iyad had asked in 1989. "Are we required to give up the PLO, the right to self-determination, a state, and all our national rights while Israel gives up nothing?"[26]

PLO leaders worried that giving up their historic demands would undermine Palestinian unity and threaten their own survival or legitimacy. Yet these factors were less important than on previous occasions. The financial pressures on the PLO had reached unprecedented levels, with Saudi Arabia withholding aid unless progress was made toward an agreement. The PLO was forced to lay off employees, sell off properties, and drastically cut its subsidies in the territories. According to a Palestinian economist and delegate to the multilateral economic talks, Samir Hulayla, PLO funding to the territories had fallen from $350 million in 1988, to $120 million in 1990, to only $40 million in 1993.[27] Abd al-Shafi, Husayni, and other Palestinians from the territories were now far more vocal in criticizing Arafat. In addition, contrary to the PLO's rhetoric, for the first time it had a common interest with Israel in opposing the rising power of Palestinian Islamic fundamentalists.

When Israel responded to Hamas's escalated terrorism in December 1992 by deporting over four hundred Islamic fundamentalist activists from the territories, Hamas demanded that the PLO stop the talks. Friction between fundamentalists and nationalists ran so high that Abd al-Aziz al-Rantisi, head of the Hamas deportees in Lebanon, denied that the PLO was the Palestinians' leader. Hamas's spokesman in Jordan, Ibrahim Ghawshah, explained that his group favored Israel's withdrawal from the territories as long as the Palestinians did "not recognize [Israel] or give up our rights to all of Palestine from the Jordan River to the Mediterranean sea." Hamas also demanded forty percent of the PNC seats, to match the proportion it claimed to have won in student and professional groups' elections in the territories.[28] While paying lip service to solidarity with Hamas, however, the PLO refused to meet its demands and continued negotiations with Israel into 1993.

To make progress, the PLO not only had to confront its historic enemies in the talks but also its own self and the people it represented. The fate of negotiations was bound up with the PLO's need to decide between the mutually exclusive alternatives of remaining a revolutionary group or transforming itself into the government of part of historic Palestine. "We must live with the idea of peace ourselves first if we are to transmit it to others," the late Abu Iyad once said. "The test of courage is when such extremism is countered head on, rather than surrendered to."[29]

A breakthrough to peace would require Arafat to use his status as Palestinian nationalism's symbol and the masses' idol to galvanize popular support and educate his people to the need for a historic compromise. He would have to pull Fatah into line and force, persuade, coopt, divide, isolate, or repress radicals and fundamentalists who opposed the moves necessary to reach a compromise peace with Israel. All successful Third World nationalist movements had undergone such a process.

Khalid al-Hasan's brother, Hani, had already suggested an ideological escape route for the PLO. While affirming that Palestinians would "never abandon our hope and our dream that there will one day be a secular, democratic state of Palestine of the kind we proposed in 1968," he acknowledged in 1989 that "the world will not give us more than" a West Bank/Gaza state. "We are realistic, not dreamers." It was hard to accept this outcome, but "for us Palestinians the brutal, heartbreaking truth is that if we want peace and an absolute minimum of justice, we have to pay for it with three-quarters of our homeland." To win part of Palestine would require giving up the claim on Israel, a psychological revolution requiring broad Palestinian support. The PLO had to "tell our people what they did not want to hear."[30]

The only man who could dispense this medicine and break the impasse was Arafat himself. Arafat, as the journalist Youssef Ibrahim noted, unlike his colleagues or rivals, "always managed to convey to [Palestinians] the notion that while he is far from perfect, he is unequivocally devoted to fight for the cause."[31] During its thirty years of struggle, the PLO had tried a wide variety of strategies: hoping Arab states would destroy Israel in battle, initiating its own guerrilla warfare and terrorist attacks, seeking Soviet patronage, promoting a mass uprising in the occupied territories, and trying to persuade the United States to pressure Israel into surrender. At last, having exhausted every other alternative, Arafat chose the only route that could bring success and Palestinian liberation: making peace with Israel directly.

The very deadlock in the Washington talks gave both sides an incentive to conduct secret, direct exchanges. Arafat needed progress to deal with the PLO's financial problems, growing criticism of his leadership, and the surge of Islamic fundamentalist rivals. The PLO was unable to provide salaries to employees or payments to the families of Palestinian "martyrs" and activists at a time when Arafat himself said that Gaza "has reached the point of starvation" and the West Bank was enduring "the utmost economic hardships."[32] The organization reportedly suffered a deficit of $140 million in its $300 million annual budget. The Saudis and Europeans promised help, but only if the PLO reached an agreement with Israel.

In addition, Arafat wanted a solution that would avoid putting the West Bank/Gaza leaders—whom he did not entirely trust—in control of that territory during a prolonged autonomy period while he remained in Tunis. The extent of the PLO's crisis and rising friction between the local leaders and Arafat was suggested by Faysal al-Husayni's warning to a West Bank meeting: "We are facing a total national collapse of all our institutions. The only solution in these circumstances is to form a national salvation government."[33] A degree of conflict was also reflected by the short-lived resignation in August 1993 of Husayni and his colleagues Ashrawi and Sa'ib Arikat, angry that Arafat was bypassing them in his secret dealings with Israel.

Rabin, too, had linked his political future with success in the peace process, repeatedly predicting an imminent agreement with the Palestinians from the time he took office. Ironically, he was pushed toward direct talks with the PLO by the conviction that the local Palestinian leadership was totally loyal to the organization, a view opposite that pushing Arafat toward direct negotiations with Israel. "For a long time," Rabin acknowledged in August 1993, "I believed that a Palestinian force would possibly be able to arise among the residents of the territories and develop its own capabilities."[34] But more than a year of talks had led him to conclude that the West Bank/Gaza Palestinians were unable to act on their own. Only Arafat could make a deal.

Secret Israeli–PLO contacts in Norway started after the Norwegian Institute for Applied Science offered to facilitate them. A meeting between two Israeli scholars and Abu Ala, a Fatah Central Committee member in charge of the multilateral talks, was held on January 20, 1993. Peres favored Norway partly because it agreed to keep the exchanges secret from the United States. Norway's Foreign Minister, Johan Jorgen Holst, aided by four other mediators—including his wife, Marianne, a Middle East specialist—hosted fourteen rounds in their Oslo home and other places, mostly over weekends, bringing together a small group of Israelis and Palestinians in an informal atmosphere. The PLO's side was supervised by Abu Mazin, a PLO Executive Committee member; Abu Ala, Director-General of the PLO Economic Department and a member of Fatah's Central Committee; and Nabil Sha'th, chairman of the PNC Political Committee and a Fatah Central Committee member. By March, exchanges seemed to be progressing. Peres brought the

Israeli government into the picture directly by sending an Israeli official—Uri Savir, Director-General of Israel's Foreign Ministry—in May and raised the idea of offering full autonomy to Gaza first. The PLO rejected this plan because it did not include any place on the West Bank. Israel then suggested adding Jericho but stressed that it would continue to control the frontier crossing to Jordan.[35]

Nevertheless, realizing that the Washington talks were going nowhere—even with Husayni leading the Palestinian delegation there—Rabin and Peres decided to seek an agreement through the Norwegian channel. A June 23rd personal letter from Bassam Abu Sharif in Tunis to Peres, delivered by an Israeli journalist, helped convince Israel's leadership that the PLO was serious. Other Israel–PLO contacts in Jerusalem and Cairo confirmed this perception. In July, negotiators realized that a breakthrough was possible and worked out a draft agreement. The peace agreement was finalized on August 19 in Oslo, with Peres and Abu Ala coming to Norway the next day to meet and to watch lower-level envoys initial it. Peres stressed to Abu Ala that any agreement required that Arafat clearly recognize Israel.[36]

During this process, Arafat consulted neither such high-level colleagues as Qaddumi—who he knew would oppose this initiative—nor leaders in Syria, Jordan, or the West Bank/Gaza Palestinian negotiating team. Similarly, Peres only briefed U.S. Secretary of State Warren Christopher about the details on August 27, as news of the accord was already leaking into the media. This endeavor also required a new PLO cognizance of Israel's nature and independent policymaking. As Sa'id Kamal, PLO ambassador to Cairo and one of those preparing the agreement, later commented, "The PLO felt that in its alliance with the United States, Israel makes its own decisions, and the American role is to provide support and guarantees, no more."[37]

In addition, while Arafat was acting out of necessity to save the PLO and Palestinian cause, he had also grasped fully—and even become an enthusiastic advocate for—the idea of a transitional solution taking several years and stages to build confidence. Kamal defended the accord as "the beginning [of] a long and hard road towards the building of an 'independent national entity' for the Palestinians by the Palestinians. Unless that entity is built, the Palestinian cause will be 'gone with the wind.' The Palestinians realized that after the end of the Cold War, it was a matter of 'to be or not to be.'"[38] Fifteen years after rejecting self-rule under the Camp David agreements, the PLO had turned a dead end into a new beginning.

This advance also required, however, that the PLO take a clear, irrevocable position on the central issues, compared with the ambiguity of its 1988 position. An Israeli official noted that the PLO's stand "must be very precise, without any loopholes, without any chances for misinterpretation."[39] Arafat had to accept Israel's demand—originally formulated by a Rabin–Peres government in 1975—that the PLO recognize Israel's right to exist as well as UN Resolutions 242 and 338 and cease using terrorism.

In exchange, Israel recognized the PLO as the Palestinians' representative and accepted an arrangement providing for a rapid withdrawal of Israeli forces and transfer of power to a PLO-appointed authority in the Gaza Strip and in Jericho—symbolizing the West Bank's future inclusion in the process—under conditions Israeli politician Yossi Sarid characterized as "autonomy plus and sovereignty minus."[40]

The accord, called the "Declaration of Principles on Interim Self-Government Arrangements," stated that it was "time to put an end to decades of confrontation and conflict, recognize . . . mutual legitimate and political rights, and strive to live in peaceful coexistence and mutual dignity and security and achieve a just, lasting and comprehensive peace settlement and historic reconciliation" through peaceful negotiations. Elections would be held to choose a Palestinian council, with the participation of East Jerusalem Palestinian residents, which would soon gain limited control over the rest of the West Bank as well as Gaza and deploy a strong police force to preserve security. Israel would remain in control of foreign relations, over-all security, and Jewish settlements.[41]

Within two years, negotiations would begin over the remaining issues—including the future of East Jerusalem, Palestinian refugees, the territories, and the Jewish settlements—and the agreed solution would be implemented within five years. In short, the PLO would obtain some control over the territories immediately and the chance to gain more—including the prospect of a Palestinian state—if it fulfilled its pledges during the interim period.

On August 30 Israel's cabinet approved the agreement. "Every change has its risks," Rabin commented, "but the time has come to take a chance for peace."[42] Arafat won endorsement from the Fatah Central Committee on September 4 and then cleared away the last barrier by obtaining the PLO Executive Committee's backing, albeit only after a long, bitter debate and by a 9-to-3 vote, with five opponents boycotting or abstaining and one supporter absent.[43]

Immediately thereafter, on September 9, Arafat and Rabin released letters in which Israel recognized the PLO "as the representative of the Palestinian people" and agreed to negotiate with it. "The PLO has changed completely," Peres stated. "Many Israelis had hoped for years for these changes. Israel has achieved in this document all the points it had demanded."[44]

"The signing of the Declaration of Principles marks a new era in the history of the Middle East," wrote Arafat. His statement was absolutely clear on the critical issues, stating that the PLO "recognizes the right of the State of Israel to exist in peace and security," "accepts United Nations Security Council Resolutions 242 and 338," "commits itself to the Middle East peace process, and to a peaceful resolution of the conflict between the two sides" through negotiations. He committed himself not only to renounce the use of terrorism and other acts of violence but also to "assume responsibility over all PLO elements and personnel in order to ensure their compliance, prevent violations and discipline violators." He also abandoned the ideological basis of the PLO's consensus by declaring "inoperable and no longer valid" those parts of the Palestinian Charter which "deny Israel's right to exist," promising to submit the necessary changes to the PNC.

On September 10 President Bill Clinton announced the renewal of the U.S.–PLO dialogue. Events swept forward quickly. On September 13, with Clinton and the Russian foreign minister—as co-sponsors of the Madrid conference—acting as hosts, a remarkable ceremony was held on the White House lawn. Peres and Abu Mazin signed the agreement in the presence of Rabin and Arafat. Rabin shook hands with Arafat in a moment symbolizing the advent of peace.[45]

"My people are hoping that this agreement which we are signing today marks the beginning of the end of a chapter of pain and suffering that has lasted throughout the century," said Arafat. Addressing Israelis, he continued, "The difficult decision we reached together was one that required great and exceptional courage . . .

Our people do not consider that exercising the right to self-determination could violate the rights of their neighbors or infringe on their security." On the contrary, he added, doing so was the "strongest guarantee" for coexistence. "Such a shift will give us an opportunity to embark upon the process of economic, social and cultural growth and development, and we hope that international participation in that process will be as extensive as it can be."

Rabin, in his speech, said that it was not easy to achieve peace after there had been so many casualties and victims; but, he went on, those who had fought were now saying, "Enough of blood and tears. Enough," the last phrase echoed Arafat's 1988 Geneva statement. "We have no desire for revenge . . . We, like you, are people who want to build a home, to plant a tree, to love, live side by side with you—in dignity, in empathy, as human beings, as free men . . . We wish to turn over a new chapter in the sad book of our lives together—a chapter of mutual recognition, of good neighborliness, of mutual respect, of understanding. We hope to embark on a new era in the history of the Middle East."[46]

That morning, Hamas had closed down Gaza by ordering a strike. The streets were largely empty and black flags of mourning were put up by the agreement's enemies. But at 3 p.m., as agreed in advance with Arafat's supporters, the Hamas cadre melted away and tens of thousands of people poured into the streets to celebrate, waving Palestinian flags which, up until that day, had been banned by Israeli authorities. The scene was repeated in Jericho and east Jerusalem, where Palestinian flags were raised over the Old City's walls and Orient House, Husayni's headquarters.

Despite these street celebrations and the international praise, however, there was also much criticism in the Arab world and from many Palestinians, accusing Arafat of selling out to Israel, giving up the Palestinian aspiration for a state, and accepting permanent occupation in exchange for dominion over only Gaza and Jericho. Arafat had decided to recognize Israel literally overnight, without preparing supporters or constituents. While Egypt and Saudi Arabia praised the move, the Jordanian and Syrian press—motivated partly by those two governments' anger at being left out—were quite critical.

Now Arafat had to consolidate support in the PLO and among Palestinians themselves. Within the PLO, Arafat's coalition endors-

ing the agreement included Fatah, its three tiny satellite groups—
Abd Rabbu's wing of the DFLP, the Palestine Peoples (Communist)
Party, and the Palestine Popular Struggle Front (PPSF) plus most of
the independents. Against them were arrayed four PLO member
groups: the Damascus-based PFLP and the DFLP of Naif Hawatmah,
as well as the pro-Iraq ALF and PLF. "The PLO is not Yasir Arafat,"
the PFLP's Riyad Malki told a West Bank protest meeting. "We are
the real PLO," said another PFLP activist.[47]

Arafat's own Fatah group was also not immune from dissent.
Three of eight pro-Fatah independent members on the PLO Executive Committee—Mahmud Darwish, Shafiq al-Hut (the PLO's representative in Lebanon), and Abdallah Hourani—had rejected his
policy and quit the Executive Committee. "We have taken two generations to their death in the project of liberation and independence," Darwish wrote, "and it now appears as if we are abandoning them completely." Hourani said that he feared the agreement
would be a "prelude to the abandonment of Palestinian rights."
Faruq Qaddumi, the most popular Fatah leader after Arafat himself,
also opposed the agreement, proclaiming, "No leadership body has
the right to commit our people to renounce their just struggle to
achieve their legitimate national goals—liberation of their homeland from Israeli occupation, repatriation, and the establishment of
their independent state on their national soil."[48]

More surprising was the disapproval of Khalid and Hani al-
Hasan, Fatah founders and generally Arafat's allies, who were often
deemed to be moderate. Khalid al-Hasan complained that the
agreement gave nothing to the refugees from 1948, a group comprising about half of Palestinians, who could no longer dream of
going back to homes in what was now Israel. He predicted that
Arafat's move could split the Palestinian people and destroy the
PLO. Hani al-Hasan claimed, "The PLO which Israel has recognized
is one that has submitted to Israeli demands [and] all but buried
the refugees' right to return."[49]

Nonetheless, Arafat did control Fatah and the PLO as a whole.
His standing as symbol of Palestinian nationalism, along with the
patronage and repression available to him, made him able to deliver
the great majority of the PLO for a peaceful settlement with Israel.
Being in the gunsights of radical groups which called him a traitor
gave Arafat ample incentive to defeat them. Further, unless he

helped to curb their terrorism, Israel would not proceed with transferring power in the West Bank and Gaza.

Bringing along the Palestinians themselves was another challenge he could meet, though not with ease or unanimity. Outside the PLO, the Islamic fundamentalist Hamas and Islamic Jihad—along with the militant anti-Arafat, Syrian-backed groups—rejected the accords. They passionately opposed the deal not only from hatred of Israel but also from fear of PLO rule. Even the PLO's handpicked head of the Palestinian negotiating team, Abd al-Shafi, was critical and refused to attend the ceremony in Washington. Given his prestige and organized following, though, Arafat's problem was not so much winning a big majority as imposing order on a large minority. At the same time, the personal nature of Arafat's leadership required his physical survival to succeed.

Palestinians opposing the new PLO stand cited three arguments. First, many of them still supported the organization's historic policy of seeking to destroy Israel and create an Arab state from the Jordan river to the sea. Zuhayr al-Rayiss, a founder of the PLO and an author of its Charter living in Gaza, declared, "I am not ready to give up any part of the Palestine."[50] Arafat's radical foes echoed this sentiment.

The second, related complaint, voiced by the Hasan brothers among others, was that the refugees from 1948 would remain displaced. Palestinians living in Jordan, Lebanon, Syria, and other Arab countries received nothing immediately from the deal and worried that they might remain permanently in exile. Habash, for example, said the agreement offered no solution to the problem of "the three million Palestinians living outside Palestine."[51] Even the September 20, 1993, Arab League resolution endorsing the Israel–PLO accord made support conditional on the redress of this group's grievances, implying a right of return. Palestinians in Syria, Iraq, and Lebanon were exposed to influence from the Damascus or Baghdad regimes and the anti-Arafat Palestinian nationalist groups they supported. In the long run, the PLO could try to solve this problem by planning to resettle those who so wished in the West Bank or to find compensation for their lost property from donor nations.

Finally, many Palestinians believed that Arafat had given up the possibility of creating a Palestinian state, fearing the pact would either remain restricted to Gaza and Jericho or merely produce limited self-rule in the territories under permanent Israeli dominion. As Shafiq al-Hut put it, they worried that "Gaza and Jericho first" might be "Gaza and Jericho last."[52] Those refugees in the West Bank and Gaza still hoping to regain pre-1948 homes and anxious about being permanently trapped in the camps were more likely to support Hamas. The PLO could respond by trying to show that the agreement would increase Palestinian rights, improve living standards, and end the occupation.

Arafat and his colleagues also knew that their power and popularity would grow as they returned to the territories, distributed money and patronage, brought back other deportees, built a police force to protect themselves and punish adversaries, secured the Israeli army's withdrawal from populated areas, and showed progress toward achieving a state and better Palestinians' lives. Radwan Abu Ayyash, one of the few West Bank mainstream leaders from a refugee background, claimed, "People have to taste the fruits of peace to be convinced that it is positive and genuine." Once the PLO "gets busy building the homeland and changing the old stereotypes and psychology, they will feel the difference and see that is not just talks and slogans [but] the first step toward a comprehensive peace settlement."[53]

Israel, the United States, the Europeans, and the Saudis also had a stake in Arafat's being able to defeat adversaries and create a stable regime in the territories. The breakthrough gave all these parties some parallel interests in regard to the regional situation while, in turn, the PLO's new function made it dependent on Saudi money, Egyptian diplomatic support, and Jordanian cooperation.

Jordan was especially concerned since the PLO's empowerment could subvert the Palestinian citizens of Jordan, where they were now a majority. Thus, King Husayn needed to curb popular support within his own country and to block any radical or Islamic control over a Palestinian state. Although disturbed by the PLO's separate deal, King Husayn signed his own preliminary agreement with Israel on September 14 and soon reconciled himself with Arafat, given their mutual interest in cooperating to keep any Palestinian entity stable and peaceful. The fact that the anti-Arafat Hamas worked closely with the militant Jordanian Muslim Brotherhood was an additional incentive to help Arafat against his competitors.

Arafat's regional enemies—Iraq, Iran, Libya, and Lebanese Islamic fundamentalists—were now the same as those of the United States and Israel. They backed his rivals and would like to see him eliminated but could do relatively little given their own weakness and remoteness from the scene. Syria's stance was less certain and more dangerous, given its domination of Lebanon, sponsorship of anti-PLO Palestinian groups—ranging from the PFLP to the PFLP-GC, which threatened to kill Arafat—and willingness to use terrorism and assassination. Syrian President Asad was neither ready to give up his veto on Palestinian decisionmaking nor to have his effort to regain the Golan Heights pushed aside by the Israel–PLO agreement. He wanted to gain leverage or exact revenge by showing himself able to sabotage a separate deal. While Arafat could voice support for a solution also resolving Syrian demands, he was unlikely to sacrifice Palestinian interests by conditioning them on Damascus's requirements.

To solve these problems and survive these obstacles, the PLO leadership would need every bit of popularity and power to galvanize support among Palestinians. While bargaining on behalf of its own demand for a Palestinian state in all the West Bank and Gaza with its capital in East Jerusalem, the reality—probably for at least five years—would be an Israeli security presence in the territories, control over foreign borders and east Jerusalem, constraints on Palestinian authority, the continued existence of Jewish settlements, and other features not so congenial to Arafat's constituents. Arafat might have to make more concessions to reach agreement with Israel. The PLO faced another set of difficult talks with Jordan over their future relationship in a confederation. Even coping with the economic disarray of overcrowded Gaza alone would be a Herculean task.

In ruling the territories, the PLO bureaucracy also intended to govern the local residents. Arafat had long applauded the "Algerian model," in which a government and army in exile returned after independence to command the country's compliance, excluding from power the internal leaders who had actually fought the French. The pattern was similar in Vietnam, where the Hanoi government ignored the National Liberation Front when it conquered the south. Relations between the PLO's "inside" and "outside" forces could parallel Namibia where, on independence, few of the former leaders held important posts and the new president, having been abroad thirty years, hardly knew the country. "When I left Windhoek it was a little village; now it is a little New York," remarked one of the returning exiles.[54]

The most promising factor for a successful outcome providing security for Israel and a better life for Palestinians was the completely new shape of the PLO's interests. Hani al-Hasan once argued that the Palestinians would be far to weak to pose any "military threat to Israel's security and existence." A Palestinian state would have difficulty obtaining arms and would retain a strong interest in stopping terrorists since "violence of any kind would provoke an Israeli response which would threaten the very existence" of any Palestinian state and the fruit of forty years of struggle. Its leaders "would have every conceivable incentive to keep the peace." If Israel had to take reprisals, the international community would support it. The day could come, he suggested, when Israeli and Palestinian leaders would join forces to fight terrorism targeting them both.[55]

As long as the PLO itself employed terrorism and did not clearly accept Israel's existence, such claims remained mere abstractions. Now everything has changed. The PLO has no Soviet Union or radical Arab states to back it: the former does not exist; the latter have become its sworn enemies. The policy of the United States, the world's sole superpower and victor over Iraq, strongly backs Israel. Arafat still needs to act moderately in order to obtain Israel's help and cooperation since even if Rabin cannot reverse the process, he can certainly halt it. The same radical Palestinian nationalists and Islamic fundamentalists who want to continue the war to destroy Israel are also contesting Arafat's authority. To uphold its commitments, the regime will forcefully have to defeat indigenous radicals and Islamic fundamentalists—with Arab or Iranian backers—trying to seize power, break commitments made in the peace agreement, or start cross-border terrorist attacks against Israel.

The agreement could redefine Palestinian and PLO interests, dramatically shift the political situation, and change the lines of conflict and cooperation in the region. A President Arafat threatened by radicals, fundamentalists, and radical Arab states would need cooperation with the United States, Israel, and Jordan. Perhaps remittances from Palestinians abroad and aid from Arab states as well

as the West would help create a stable—whether or not democratic—order, while the relatively large and educated Palestinian
middle class might find an economic niche in the area.

Having better living conditions and a homeland to protect could
make Palestinians increasingly committed to peace. Extremists
might become insignificant given the popularity of those who led
the struggle to victory and the repression these leaders could unleash. The USSR's collapse removed radicalism's main sponsor,
while Arab states that had made peace with Israel would be reluctant to reopen the struggle. The overall level of conflict could be
very much reduced, even if it were not completely eliminated.

Nonetheless, PLO leaders might still find it hard to administer a
state after so many years of fomenting a revolution, a factor further
curbing its taste—and certainly its resources—for engaging in new
adventures. They face a tremendous reconstruction and development task, especially in the overpopulated Gaza strip. The massive
resettlement of Palestinian refugees, both those moving out of
camps in the West Bank or Gaza and those returning from abroad,
might stir a patriotic enthusiasm encouraging cooperation.[56] But
this ordeal could also be divisive. Many new states soon became
politically erratic and economically unstable in modern times.[57]
Arab oil-producing countries—especially Kuwait, still resenting
PLO help to Saddam Husayn—might not give so generously to
build Palestine, using the conflict's end as a rationale for stinginess.
At an international conference held in Washington on October 1,
1993, where over $2 billion was pledged for Palestinian develop-
ment efforts (including more than $1 billion from European states,
$200 million from Japan, and $500 million from the United States),
only $125 million was pledged by Arab states—Saudi Arabia and
the United Arab Emirates.

Palestine might also be rendered less stable by the machinations
and appeal of some new claimant to Arab or Islamic leadership, like
a Saddam Husayn or Ayatollah Ruhollah Khomeini. Although it
might be hard to envision the people turning against leaders who,
at first, would enjoy near-unanimous support, the cases of Bangla-
desh, Algeria, and Afghanistan among others show how quickly
nationalist heroes can come to be considered incompetent tyrants.[58]
Irish history graphically demonstrates how the creation of a state
in one part of a claimed homeland does not automatically bring
permanent peace.

Sandwiched between Israel and Jordan, a Palestinian state would be less threatening, but this strategic situation could also create explosive resentments. Indeed, since about forty percent of Palestinians live in Jordan and approximately fifteen percent are Israeli citizens, even if several hundred thousand refugees were repatriated, Arafat would still be leading only a minority of Palestinians. Such factors could turn Palestinian energies inward or cause trouble for his neighbors. In short, the difficulty of building a solution in which Israel and Palestine coexist side by side in untroubled harmony should not be underestimated. A bright future for a PLO-ruled Palestine is even more open to question.

More certain, though, is the fact that international and regional events forced the PLO to shift its policy as a final, necessary catalyst in its own unfinished evolution. "Our days of military actions were a means to this end," Abu Mazin said in defending the Israel–PLO agreement. "Now we must concentrate on meeting new challenges."[59] On one hand, the PLO—always meant to be an interim structure designed to obtain a state for the Palestinians—was only fulfilling its basic function. On the other hand, the U.S. and Israeli strategy—at times purposeful, at other times implicit in their actions—of trying to force the PLO to change to a point where it could participate in peacemaking had succeeded. In the end, it would be Arafat's task to transform the PLO's historic positions and structure, fulfilling Palestinian self-determination by redefining it to abide with the existing states and to avoid new rounds of conflict, bloodshed, and instability.

The PLO failed in achieving total victory but it succeeded in becoming a key force in deciding the conflict's conclusion. This latter success came about not because the PLO's position was so strong, but because the Palestinians were in the dual situation of having a veto power over change while being those who most needed it. "We are fed up with this bloodshed," Arafat said in 1989. "We are looking to have peace for our children and also for their children." The PLO's fate will be to incarnate, for better or worse, the epitaph Arafat made for it then: "This is the historical chance. If we lose it, we are criminals."[60] If they succeed, Arafat and the PLO will seem to be the saviors of the Palestinian nation. Certainly, the politics and history of the PLO already hold a unique place in the annals of revolutionary and nationalist movements.

> Notes

1. Chameleon in the Labyrinth, 1964–1968

1. On the early history of Palestinian nationalism, see Y. Porath, *The Emergence of the Palestinian Arab National Movement, 1918–1929* and *The Palestinian Arab National Movement, 1929–1939* (London, 1977).
2. The Palestinian Arab rejection of the Peel, Woodhead, and White Paper proposals in the 1930s and other diplomatic proposals in the 1940s concluding with the 1947 partition resolution set a pattern essentially followed by the PLO in later years.
3. Albert Hourani, "The Decline of the West in the Middle East," *International Affairs*, April 1953, p. 166.
4. These issues are discussed in detail in Barry Rubin, *The Arab States and the Palestine Conflict* (Syracuse, N.Y., 1981).
5. Constantine Zurayk, *The Meaning of the Disaster* (Beirut, 1956), p. 2.
6. Mirza Khan, "The Arab Refugees: A Study in Frustration," in Walter Laqueur, *The Middle East in Transition* (New York, 1958), pp. 233–248. Khan puts the original number of refugees at 610,000.
7. On Arafat, see for example Alan Hart, *Arafat, a Political Biography* (Bloomington, Ind., 1989); Andrew Gowers and Tony Walker, *Behind the Myth: Yasir Arafat and the Palestinian Revolution* (London, 1992); and John Wallach and Janet Wallach, *In the Eyes of the Beholder* (New York, 1991).
8. Arafat's nom de guerre was Abu Ammar. Abu Iyad's real name was Salah Khalaf; Abu Jihad's actual name was Khalil al-Wazir. To avoid confusion, they will be referred to by their best-known appellation. Abu means "father of" and is a common alternative name in Arab society, incorporating the name of one's first son. Arafat has no son but was given the title as an honorific. Other founders of Fatah include Mahmud Abbas (known as Abu Mazin), Yusuf al-Najjar, and Kamal Adwan. The last two were killed in an Israeli raid on Beirut in 1973.
9. Many writers claim that the facts of Arafat's life are obvious, then present contradictory accounts. Al-Mustaqbal, December 4, 1982 (*Foreign Broadcast Information Service*, hereafter *FBIS*), December 6, 1982;

Journal of Palestine Studies (hereafter *JPS*), Vol. 12, No. 2 (Winter 1983), p. 211; "Yassir [sic] Arafat," *Third World Quarterly,* Vol. 8, No. 2 (April 1986); John Cooley, Green March, *Black September* (London, 1973), p. 88; *New York Times,* August 4, 1988.

10. Department of State, 784.00/2–2259, Jernegan to Herter, December 22, 1959.

11. Muhammad al-Hallaj, director of the Institute of Arab Studies, cited in Cheryl Rubenberg, *The Palestine Liberation Organization: Its Institutional Infrastructure* (Belmont, Mass., 1983), pp. 1–2. Fourth Fatah conference political platform, May 1980. Text in Raphael Israeli, *PLO in Lebanon: Selected Documents* (London, 1983), pp. 12–13.

12. Among several possible Islamic views of Jews, the PLO and Palestinian Islamic fundamentalists have chosen negative ones. As an Arab scholar summarizes this school, it views Jews as "invaders who, contrary to the account in the Torah, had no original contact with the area" and never formed a majority or stable community in the land of Canaan. It interprets the Qur'an as saying that Jews worship money, are arrogant and ungrateful, murdered prophets sent by God, and are punished by God for spreading evil. Therefore, the prophet Muhammad killed or expelled them from Arabia. According to this view, the Torah used by Jews today is a document rewritten to serve their self-interest: "The Israelites equipped the deity with their own morals and disposition . . . fond of war, attack, revenge, and destruction." The Talmud was held to be antagonistic to other peoples, portraying Jews as superior and permitting them to steal from non-Jews. M. Y. S. Haddad, *Arab Perspectives of Judaism* (The Hague, 1984), pp. 7 –8, 65, 89–160, 184, 228–230, and 304. PLO organs periodically echoed such views. For example: "The War of Liberation being fought by our people today against oppressive Zionism" is a continuation of the fight under Muhammad which would also purify Palestine, "defiled by aggressors, oppressive and mean Jews." *Filastin al-Thawra,* August 15, 1969, p. 57.

13. Fatah platform, cited in Israeli, *PLO in Lebanon.*

14. Arafat, May 1969, *International Documents on Palestine* (hereafter *IDOP*) 1969, pp. 691–692.

15. Ibid.

16. In 1965 and 1966 only seven and twelve Israeli civilians, respectively, were wounded by Palestinian terrorism. Guy Bechor, *Lexicon Ashaf* (Tel Aviv, 1991), p. 149.

17. May 21 and June 1, 1967, *IDOP* 1967, p. 537 and pp. 550-590.

18. Nasir, May 14, 1967, *IDOP* 1967, pp. 531–532.

19. Robert Stephens, *Nasser: A Political Biography* (London, 1973), p. 480.

20. Shuqayri, June 14, 1967, *IDOP* 1967, p. 605.

21. *Al-Hurriya*, October 2, 1967, in *IDOP* 1967, p. ۱81.

22. *Al-Ahram*, February 25, 1971.

23. Shuqayri's speeches of October 13 and 30, 1967, in *IDOP* 1967, pp. 686–687, 690. Ahmad Shuqayri, *Liberation, Not Negotiation* (Beirut, 1966).

24. Text in Walter Laqueur and Barry Rubin, *The Israel–Arab Reader* (New York, 1984), pp. 365–366.

25. Fatah rejection, December 12, 1967, *IDOP* 1967, p. 723.

26. PLO statement, November 23, 1967, *IDOP* 1967, pp. 715–716; Fatah rejection, December 12, 1967, *IDOP* 1967, pp. 721–723.

27. See, for example, Uriel Dann, *King Hussein and the Challenge of Arab Radicalism: Jordan, 1955–1967* (New York, 1969).

28. Fatah Press Release No. 1, January 1, 1968, *IDOP* 1968, p. 305.

29. CIA Directorate of Intelligence, *Anti-Israel Arab Terrorist Organizations*, Special Report, October 4, 1968, p. 8; Bechor, *Lexicon Ashaf*, p. 149.

30. Arafat interviews, *IDOP* 1969, p. 695, and August 1968, *IDOP* 1968, p. 413.

31. Interview, *al-Usbu al-Arabi*, January 22, 1968, in *IDOP* 1968, p. 298; August 1968 statement, *IDOP* 1968, p. 413. Habash, July 25, 1970, *IDOP* 1970, pp. 878–882. Arafat, May 1969, *IDOP* 1969, pp. 691–692.

32. For translations of the Charter, see Y. Harkabi, *The Palestinian Covenant and Its Meaning* (London, 1979); Leila Kadi, *Basic Political Documents of the Armed Palestine Resistance Movement* (Beirut, December 1969), pp. 130 ff.; and *IDOP* 1968, pp. 390 ff.

33. Al Ahram, February 2, 1969, in *IDOP* 1969, p. 582.

34. *IDOP* 1968, pp. 399–403; Harkabi, *Palestinian Covenant*, p. 73.

35. *IDOP* 1968, pp. 402–403.

36. Israeli, *PLO in Lebanon*.

37. *IDOP* 1968, p. 298; *al-Usbu' al-'Arabi*, January 22, 1968, p. 300.

2. The Poisoned Fruits of Terrorism, 1969–1973

1. Oriana Fallaci, *Interview with History* (Boston, Mass., 1977), p. 131.

2. Wadi Haddad, head of the PFLP's terror apparatus, was a doctor from a wealthy Palestinian Christian family. He split with that group in the mid-1970s and died in 1978 of cancer in East Berlin.

3. Ariel Merari and Shlomo Elad, *The International Dimension of Palestinian Terrorism* (Boulder, Co., 1986), p. 5.

4. Fouad Moughrabi, "The Palestinians after Lebanon," *Arab Studies Quarterly*, Vol. 5, No. 3 (Summer 1983), p. 214.

5. *The Economist*, October 3, 1970.

6. Habash, July 25, 1970, *IDOP* 1970, pp. 878–882.
7. "Any armed resistance can be condemned as a terrorist activity," Arafat commented. "Yassir [sic] Arafat," *Third World Quarterly*, Vol. 8, No. 2 (April 1986); Khalid al-Hasan, *Al-Riyad*, December 5, 1978 (Joint Publications Research Service, hereafter *JPRS*, No. 72836, February 16, 1979).
8. Habash, March 4, 1969, *IDOP* 1969, pp. 630–631.
9. PFLP, February 1, 1969, *IDOP* 1969, pp. 597–98.
10. For one of many examples of this thinking, see Gerard Chaliand, *The Palestinian Resistance* (Hammondsworth, Eng., 1972).
11. Abu Iyad, June 1969, *IDOP* 1969, p. 705.
12. Fallaci, *Interview with History*, p. 135.
13. Arafat interviews, *IDOP* 1969, p. 695, and August 1968, *IDOP* 1968, p. 413.
14. *Filastin al-Thawra*, June 1968. Harkabi, *Palestinian Covenant*, p. 9.
15. Ibrahim Sous, *Nouvelle Observateur*, August 14, 1981.
16. Interview, *IDOP* 1969, pp. 691–692.
17. Arafat, July 25, 1970, *IDOP* 1970, pp. 887–888.
18. "Yassir Arafat," *Third World Quarterly*, Vol. 8, No. 2 (April 1986), and also South, January 1986, p. 18; al-Anwar symposium of March 8, 1970, cited in Harkabi, *Palestinian Covenant*, p. 12; Arafat, May 1969, *IDOP* 1969, pp. 691–692.
19. *IDOP* 1968, p. 400.
20. Abu Iyad, *IDOP* 1969, pp. 719, 728; Speech by PLO Official Spokesman at the International World Conference of Christians for Palestine Beirut, May 7, 1970, *IDOP* 1970, p. 797. The author witnessed Hasan Abd al-Rahman, later PLO representative in the United States, telling a Christian group in 1972 that the Zionists controlled both America and Palestine. On this issue, see M. Y. S. Haddad, *Arab Perspectives of Judaism* (The Hague, 1984).
21. *IDOP* 1968, pp. 301, 379. When Senator Robert Kennedy was assassinated by a Palestinian in 1968, Fatah claimed the killer "must undoubtedly have been a tool employed by world Zionism, by persons having political, personal or capitalistic interests, and by the American CIA."
22. Interview, January 22, 1968, in *IDOP* 1968, p. 300.
23. *Filastin al-Thawra*, January 1970, p. 8. Compare this statement with a remarkably similar PLO document a dozen years later, cited in Raphael Israeli, *PLO in Lebanon: Selected Documents* (London, 1983) p. 31: The enemy's "greatest weakness is his small population. Therefore, operations must be launched which will liquidate immigration into Israel" by attacking immigrant absorption centers, sabotaging water

and electricity, "using weapons in terrifying ways against them where they live . . . attacking a tourist installation during the height of the tourist season." Holidays were said to be the best time for assaults since there were more human targets on the street.

24. Habash, June 12, 1970, *IDOP* 1970, pp. 836–839. Some of the world was easily convinced. The Greek government released a Palestinian terrorist from Abu Nidal's group, stating that "the actions for which he was being accused fall within the domain of the struggle to regain the independence of his homeland and consequently suggest action for freedom." The act in question was a 1982 attack on a Rome synagogue in which 34 worshippers were wounded and a two-year-old boy was killed, a startlingly uninhibited definition of national liberation as a rationale for any kind of violence. *Washington Times,* December 9, 1988.

25. This is not to say the PFLP was a mere Syrian instrument. The Syrian government imprisoned Habash in 1968. That same year, it unified its client Palestinian Ba'thist groups into al-Sa'iqa, led by Zuhayr Muhsin, the second-largest group in the PLO until the mid-1970s. It proposed that the Palestine built on Israel's destruction become part of Syria's empire. Iraq created the puppet Arab Liberation Front (ALF) in 1969.

26. In 1972 Habash suffered a heart attack and was out of action for some time, receiving medical treatment in the USSR and rest in Bulgaria.

27. First PFLP political statement, *al-Hurriya,* December 11, 1967, *IDOP* 1967, p. 724; PFLP to Fourth PNC, *IDOP* 1968, p. 389.

28. Habash, *IDOP* 1970, p. 804.

29. Habash, May 1970, *IDOP* 1970, p. 805; Hawatmeh, *JPS,* Vol. 12, No. 4 (Summer 1978), p. 192.

30. PFLP Basic Policy Document, August 1968, *IDOP* 1968, p. 423; PFLP, "Political Strategy," *IDOP* 1969, pp. 613–614.

31. Habash, July 25, 1970, *IDOP* 1970, pp. 878–882. As Habash expressed his dream, "If the Arab regimes become revolutionary everything will be different. Damascus will not be the Damascus of today, but a Damascus on a war footing and Cairo, too, will be . . . on a war footing. Everything will be for the battle, men, women and children, the six or seven millions in Syria will work non-stop on the production of food and arms, by organizing themselves."

32. Ibid. See, for example, al-Yom (Beirut), December 2, 1968, where Fatah complains that the PFLP falsely claimed responsibility for a bomb in Jerusalem's Mahane Yehuda market.

33. Abu Iyad, *IDOP* 1969, pp. 712–718, 728.

34. Harkabi, *Palestinian Covenant,* p. 94.

35. Nasir told the February 1969 PNC, "Our preparations to recover our

lost territories by force must not be allowed to impede our political action to recover what we have lost, if there is any hope of its succeeding." February 1, 1969, *IDOP* 1969, p. 583. Arafat, July 25, 1970, *IDOP* 1970, pp. 887–888.

36. Habash, July 25, 1970, *IDOP* 1970, pp. 878–882. He warned that the way to liberation was not to accept U.S. initiatives but "to attack its interests and to go on fighting it until it is forced to evacuate every inch of Arab territory."

37. Statements of Palestinian Commando Organizations in Amman, August 9, 1970 and May 6, 1970, *IDOP* 1970, pp. 887–888, 795. This is a persistent problem. Some PLO groups—like the DFLP and PFLP—still talk in these terms, not because they think "Jordan is Palestine" but because they claim that Jordan and Palestine are one. Such a stand legitimized a Jordanian claim to rule the Palestinians as well as a Palestinian claim to rule Jordan. Similarly, when the PLO called itself the representative of all Palestinians everywhere, this meant an assertion that it was legitimate leader of over half Jordan's population.

38. Abu Iyad, speech of January 9 and interview of October 1971, in *IDOP* 1971, pp. 350 and 540. Sadiq al-Azm, "The Palestine Resistance Movement Reconsidered," in Edward Said, ed., *The Arabs Today: Alternatives for Tomorrow* (Columbus, Ohio, 1973), pp. 121–29.

39. King Husayn speech, April 3, 1971, *IDOP* 1971, p. 423. The PNC's eighth session, March 4, 1971, pledged, "Resolute opposition to those who advocate the establishment of a Palestinian statelet in part of the territory of Palestine," *IDOP* 1971, p. 398.

40. Eric Rouleau, "The Palestinian Quest," *Foreign Affairs*, Vol. 53, No. 2 (January 1975), p. 276.

41. Christopher Dobson, *Black September: Its Short, Violent History* (London: 1975), pp. 11–21; *JPS*, Vol. 2, No. 2 (Winter 1973), p. 174; U.S. Defense Intelligence Agency, *International Terrorism: A Compendium*, Vol. 2, *The Middle East* (1979), in *Documents from the U.S. Espionage Den*, Vol. 43.

42. U.S. Department of State, dispatch of December 16, 1971, *Documents from the U.S. Espionage Den*, Vol. 42, p. 1; John Cooley, *Green March, Black September* (London, 1973), p. 26. An official U.S. government report stated that Fatah "used the name Black September Organization from 1971 to 1974," U.S. Department of Defense, *Terrorist Group Profiles* (Washington, 1988), p. 12.

43. *London Times*, March 8, 1973; State Department telegram, Beirut March 5, 1973, and Khartoum cable, March 7, 1973. The pattern was similar to the *Achille Lauro* hijacking of 1985.

44. Moshe Ma'oz, "The Palestinian Guerrilla Organizations and the Soviet Union," in Moshe Ma'oz, *Palestinian Arab Politics* (Jerusalem, 1975),

pp. 91–94, 101–102; Israeli, PLO in Lebanon, pp. 170–83; Ma'oz, "The Palestinian Guerrilla Organizations and the Soviet Union," p. 98.

45. Ion Mihai Pacepa, *Red Horizons* (Regnery Gateway, N.Y., 1987), pp. 12–36. Pacepa was former director of Romanian intelligence. See also *Washington Post*, December 24, 1989; *Washington Times*, December 27, 1989.

46. Arafat, May 1969, *IDOP* 1969, pp. 695–696; Bechor, *Lexicon Ashaf*, p. 149.

47. David Ignatius, *Wall Street Journal*, February 10, 1983; Lally Weymouth, "Andy Young Wasn't Alone," *Washington Post*, June 4, 1989. There were reportedly 35 meetings between U.S. diplomats and the PLO between 1978 and 1981 to discuss embassy security and the release of U.S. hostages in Iran but not political issues. U.S. Ambassador John Gunther Dean coordinated his travels with the PLO, and Abu Jihad may have helped release thirteen hostages from Tehran. The PFLP had assassinated U.S. Ambassador Francis Meloy in 1976. Salama reportedly visited the United States to meet with CIA officials in 1976, early in the relationship.

48. One of Abu Nidal's victims was Abu Iyad's bodyguard during an April 1979 ambush in Belgrade.

49. Fifth PNC, February 4, 1969, *IDOP* 1969, pp. 589–590; DFLP, draft resolution for PNC, September 1, 1969, *IDOP* 1969, p. 777; Arafat, October 1968, *IDOP* 1968, pp. 453–454.

50. Habash and others suggested that Palestine become part of a Pan-Arab state to ensure that any remaining Jews would be a tiny minority. Hawatmeh, March 11 and December 12, 1969, in *IDOP* 1969, pp. 801–806, 830; Habash, May 1970, in *IDOP* 1970, pp. 801–802.

51. Abu Iyad, January 9, 1971, *IDOP* 1971, p. 346; Nabil Sha'th, May 1971, *IDOP* 1971, p. 472; PLO statement, January 1971, *IDOP* 1971, p. 362.

52. Arafat, August 1968, *IDOP* 1968, p. 413; Abu Iyad, January 9, 1971, *IDOP* 1971, p. 352. Arafat used almost precisely the same words in December 1977—*IDOP* 1977, p. 458—and again in 1988, "Knowing the Enemy," *Time*, November 11, 1988, pp. 47–48.

53. Interview, March 4, 1969. *IDOP* 1969, p. 630–631.

54. Fallaci, *Interview with History*, p. 134.

55. Al-Azm, "The Palestine Resistance Movement Reconsidered," p. 130; Paul Jureidini and William Hazen, *The Palestinian Movement in Politics* (Lexington, Mass., 1976), p. 16.

56. Abu Iyad, June 1969, in *IDOP* 1969, pp. 711, 733.

57. Abu Iyad, June 1969, *IDOP* 1969, p. 732.

58. Arafat, August 1968, *IDOP* 1968, p. 413.

3. A Bastion in Beirut, 1973–1983

1. Albert Hourani, *Political Society in Lebanon: A Historical Introduction* (Cambridge, 1985), p. 14. "The purpose of the political system of Lebanon was to balance interests: those of the politicians themselves, their clients, and their communities and districts." The 1958 civil war was the first sign of the coming contest, but the system survived with minor changes.

2. Rashid Khalidi, "The Palestinians in Lebanon: Social Repercussions of Israel's Invasion," *Middle East Journal*, Vol. 38, No. 2 (Spring 1984), p. 258.

3. The Maronites, linked culturally and politically to the West, favored their own continued rule, Lebanese nationalism, and a Western-oriented foreign policy. Sunni Muslims favored Pan-Arabism and were often friendly to Nasir and Syria, but were slow to learn the new tools of mass mobilization. The Druze followed their traditional aristocratic heads, the Joumblatts, who held leftist ideas. The Shi'a, historically the poorest, least organized group, began demanding more rights under a charismatic mullah, Musa al-Sadr, and his Amal movement.

4. Arafat's speech in Kuwait, February, 20, 1974, *JPS*, Vol. 3, No. 3 (Spring 1974), p. 197.

5. The 1977 Palestine National Council reiterated this plan, seeking "the realization of the Palestinian people's rights to return and self-determination within the context of an independent Palestinian national state on any part of Palestinian land, without reconciliation, recognition or negotiations, as an interim aim of the Palestinian Revolution." Laqueur and Rubin, *Israel–Arab Reader*, p. 602.

6. Ibid., pp. 198–199. Khalid al-Hasan, "The Future of the Palestinian Struggle after the Ramadan War," *al-Jumhuriyya*, June 17, 1974.

7. Jureidini and Hazen, *Palestinian Movement in Politics*, pp. 22–23.

8. The plan, said the official PLO magazine, was an achievement, "On the road of continuous and unremitting struggle for the liberation of all the soil of the Palestinian homeland." *Filastin al-Thawra*, February 20, 1974. When Tunisian President Habib Bourguiba suggested in 1974 that the Arabs recognize Israel within the smaller boundaries proposed in the UN's 1947 partition lines—in order to weaken it and make possible a gradual, total Arab victory—Arafat criticized and attacked him.

9. The extremist PFLP-GC accepted both the 1974 and 1977 programs. At the Palestine National Council's 1977 session it adopted a resolution defining the PLO's "strategic goal" as "the liberation of Palestine from racist Zionist occupation, to make it the homeland of the people

of Palestine where they may establish a democratic Palestinian state." The PLO and Arab states would decide how to help Jews who wanted to return to Arab states. *IDOP* 1977, p. 347; *Los Angeles Times,* October 26, 1980. The PFLP, DFLP, PFLP-GC, and PLF of the Steadfastness and Confrontation front agreed in December 1977 to endorse the 1977 Palestine National Council plan. *IDOP* 1977, p. 461.

10. Text in Laqueur and Rubin, *Israel–Arab Reader,* p. 518.

11. Ibid., pp. 504–518.

12. Bechor, *Lexicon Ashaf,* p. 149.

13. Samir Franjieh, "How Revolutionary Is the Palestinian Resistance? A Marxist Interpretation," *JPS,* Vol. 2, No. 2 (Winter 1973), pp. 54–57.

14. Rex Brynen, "PLO Policy in Lebanon: Legacies and Lessons," *JPS,* Vol. 18, No. 2 (Winter 1989), pp. 55–56; Kamal Joumblatt and Philippe Lapousterie, *I Speak for Lebanon* (London, 1982), p. 55. See also Rashid Khalidi, "Lebanon in the Context of Regional Politics: Palestinian and Syrian Involvement in the Lebanese Crisis," *Third World Quarterly,* Vol. 7, No. 3 (July 1985), p. 500: "Eventually, a clear majority of Lebanese came to feel that the PLO was using Lebanon for its own ends, without concern for the harm visited on the country in the process."

15. Syria obtained Arab League support to allow its troops to enter Lebanon as a "peacekeeping force." Adeed Dawisha, "Comprehensive Peace in the Middle East and the Comprehension of Arab Politics," *Middle East Journal,* Vol. 37 (1983), pp. 147–148. Ahmad Jibril, leader of the pro-Syrian PFLP-GC, was seriously wounded in the leg fighting Arafat's forces.

16. Asad proposed as candidates two pro-Syrian Palestinians—Zuhayr Muhsin, leader of al-Sa'iqa, and Palestine National Council speaker Khalid al-Fahum—along with the more pro-Arafat Fatah founder Khalid al-Hasan.

17. Syria's troops stayed out of the far south, having been warned by Israel that an advance to the border could bring war. Knowing that Israel would blame it for PLO terrorist attacks launched from its own territory, Syria kept the PLO away from the Israel–Syria front in the Golan Heights. But since Syria did not try to stop the PLO from attacking Israel altogether, Arafat and Asad managed to patch up their relations.

18. W. F. Abboushi, "Changing Political Attitudes in the West Bank after Camp David," in Emile Nakhleh, *A Palestinian Agenda for the West Bank and Gaza* (Washington, D.C., 1980). Arafat, December 1977, *IDOP* 1977, p. 459.

19. Arafat speech of September 19, in U.S. Embassy dispatch of September 27, 1978, in *Den of Spies,* Vol. 42, p. 5.

20. Ibid., p. 6. Vance dispatch, January 26, 1979; May 3, 1979, Newton

dispatch, p. 7. This very argument about Camp David was made secretly by PLO Executive Committee Secretary Muhammad Zuhdi Nashashibi, who feared the organization would lose support if it stood in the way of progress.

21. Arafat, February 20, 1977, *IDOP* 1977, p. 331.

22. Defense Intelligence Agency, *International Terrorism: A Compendium: Vol. 2, The Middle East* (Washington, D.C., 1979), pp. 16–18, 22, in *Documents from the U.S. Espionage Den,* Vol. 43.

23. Ibid.

24. David Hirst, "The Other Hostage in Beirut," *Guardian,* June 30, 1985, p. 7; Nashashibi, U.S. State Department dispatch, May 3, 1979, *Den of Spies,* Vol. 42, pp. 7–9; Khalid al-Hasan, *al-Anba,* August 31, 1981; Ibrahim al-Sus, "My Statements Have Been Distorted and I Did Not Discuss the Recognition of Israel," in *al-Nahar,* December 21, 1978 (*JPRS* 72836). The PFLP demanded Sus's recall.

25. *Time,* May 4, 1981.

26. *Middle East,* July 1979, p. 26, and October 1980, p. 15.

27. On the common features of different Third World dictators and their realms, see Barry Rubin, *Modern Dictators: Third World Coupmakers, Strongmen, and Populist Tyrants* (New York, 1987). On the Iranian revolution and its relations with the United States, see Barry Rubin, *Paved with Good Intentions: The American Experience and Iran* (New York, 1980), and *Cauldron of Turmoil: America in the Middle East* (New York, 1992).

28. Christos Ioannides, "The PLO and the Iranian Revolution," *American–Arab Affairs* (Fall 1984), pp. 89, 95.

29. Ibid.

30. Ibid.

31. "Under PLO Rule," *The Economist,* August 7, 1982, pp. 28–29; Israeli, *PLO in Lebanon,* pp. 234–299; David Shipler, "Lebanese Tell of Anguish under the PLO," *New York Times,* July 25, 1982; William Haddad, "Divided Lebanon," *Current History,* January 1982.

32. *New York Times,* June 11, 1980, and January 29, 1981; *Monday Morning,* July 13, 1980; David Hirst, *The Observer,* June 22, 1980; Musa al-Sadr quoted in Fouad Ajami, *The Vanished Imam: Musa al Sadr and the Shia of Lebanon* (Ithaca, N.Y., 1986), p. 178. On the view of Lebanese Prime Minister Elias Sarkis, see Karim Pakradouni's account cited by Ajami.

33. Rex Brynen, "PLO Policy in Lebanon: Legacies and Lessons," *JPS,* Vol. 18, No. 2 (Winter 1989), pp. 59–60.

34. "The PLO Papers," *The Economist,* July 10, 1982, p. 48.

35. The pro-Saudi PLO theoretician Khalid al-Hasan pointed out that the plan "does not call for an official recognition of Israel." *Ukaz,* August

24, 1981; *al-Hawadith,* December 4, 1981; Khalid al-Hasan, *al-Anba,* August 31, 1981; *al-Sharq al-Awsat,* October 14, 1981. *Al-Majalla,* August 1, 1981.

36. *New York Times,* June 21 and 30 and July 25, 1982; *London Times,* June 19, 1982.

37. On Israeli policy and the invasion see, for example, Avner Yaniv, *Dilemmas of Security: Politics, Strategy and the Israeli Experience in Lebanon* (New York, 1987); Zeev Shiff and Ehud Yaari, *Israel's Lebanon War* (New York, 1984); Itamar Rabinovich and Hanna Zamir, *War and Crisis in Lebanon, 1975–1981* (New York, 1982).

38. Voice of Palestine, July 5, 1982 (*FBIS,* July 6, 1982).

39. Rashid Khalidi, *Under Siege: PLO Decisionmaking during the 1982 War* (New York, 1986), p. 2; Michael Hudson, "The Palestinians after Lebanon," *Current History,* January 1983, p. 5.

40. Arafat, *Middle East,* May 1983; Khalid al-Hasan, *al-Madina,* August 31, 1982 (*FBIS,* September 9, 1982); Arafat speech, Voice of Palestine (Aden), September 8, 1982 (BBC, *Survey of World Broadcasts,* September 11, 1982.)

41. Salah Khalaf, *JPS,* Vol. 11, No. 4; Vol. 12, No. 1, pp. 309–311. South Yemen and Algeria also accepted some PLO forces.

42. *Al-Ra'y al-Amm,* April 27, 1985; Arafat, *al-Shira'a,* July 18, 1983. Moughrabi, "The Palestinians after Lebanon," p. 215; *South,* September 1982, p. 24. See also Souhayr Belhassen, "La traverss du desert arabe," *Jeune Afrique,* September 8, 1982, pp. 22–25; Radio Amman, June 14, 1982; BBC, *Survey of World Broadcasts,* June 16, 1982; Arafat, Voice of Palestine, June 17, 1982; Ali Hashim, "The Media Repeats Its 1967 Performance and the Lebanese Are Strangled," *al-Nahar al-Arabi w-al Duwali,* August 23, 1982, pp. 24–25; Ahmad Shahin, "The Extent of Arab Participation in the War and Factors Behind It," *Shu'un Filastiniyya,* August 1982, pp. 33–37; *al-Dustur,* "Khalid al-Hasan: Why Did Syria Not Take Advantage of the Opportunity to Liberate the Golan?" December 13, 1982, pp. 20–21; Tamam al-Barazi, "Hisham Sharabi: 'These Are Arafat's Mistakes,'" *al-Watan al-Arabi,* August 12, 1983, pp. 24–26; 'Isam Ni'man, "Peace between the Arabs," *al-Watan al-Arabi,* July 1, 1983, pp. 36–37.

43. Text in *New York Times,* September 2, 1982. The plan favored "territory for peace," with Resolution 242 "as the foundation stone of America's Middle East peace effort . . . Jerusalem must remain undivided, but its final status should be decided through negotiations."

44. Text, Laqueur and Rubin, *Israel–Arab Reader,* pp. 679–686; Qaddumi, "The Union with Jordan after the Establishment of the Palestinian state," *al-Dustur,* December 13, 1982.

45. Muhammad Anis, "An interview with Isam Sartawi," *al-Musawwar,* March 25, 1983; Avner Yaniv, "Phoenix of Phantom? The PLO after Beirut," *Terrorism,* Vol. 7, No. 3 (1984).

46. Anis, "An interview with Isam Sartawi"; "Sartawi: They prevented me from speaking in the Palestine National Council because I would demand a Palestinian commission of inquiry," *al-Hawadith,* March 4, 1983. Syria rewarded Abu Nidal for murdering Sartawi by bringing his headquarters to Damascus.

47. Karen House, *Wall Street Journal,* April 14 and 15, 1983.

48. Ibid.

49. Eric Rouleau, "The Future of the PLO," *Foreign Affairs,* Vol. 62, No. 1 (Fall 1983); *Filastin al-Thawra,* November 20, 1982. The first PLO official to hint at suggesting recognition of Israel was Sabri Jiryis, *Shu'un Filastiniyya,* May 1977. See *JPS* Vol. 6, No. 4 (Summer 1977), p. 150 ff. But such expressions were rare over the next decade. As early as 1977, PLO leaders had met with a delegation from the Israeli Communist Party.

50. Rashid Khalidi describes these basic tenets as: "The independence of Palestinian decisionmaking from external interference; a balance between those Arab states with the potential for interference in Palestinian affairs; the freedom to organize Palestinians throughout the Arab world; increased military and political strength; and the freedom to pursue a settlement when and if one becomes possible." Rashid Khalidi, "The Asad Regime and the Palestinian Resistance," *Arab Studies Quarterly,* Vol. 6, No. 4 (Fall 1984), p. 265.

51. Rouleau, "The Future of the PLO," p. 145.

52. Luyis Faris, "Asad avoids welcoming Arafat," *al-Majalla,* December 4, 1982; Damascus television, December 15, 1982 (BBC, *Survey of World Broadcasts,* December 17, 1982); Abu Musa, NIN (Belgrade), October 30, 1983 (*JPRS,* November 22, 1983); Memorandum of January 27, 1983, text in *JPS,* Vol. 13, No. 1 (Fall 1983), pp. 170–173.

53. Abu Salah's real name was Nimr Salih; Abu Musa's was Sa'id Musa Muragha.

54. *Al-Watan,* May 26, 1983; *al-Anba,* October 3, 1987; *JPS,* Vol. 27, No. 2 (Winter 1988).

55. Moughrabi, "The Palestinians after Lebanon," p. 211.

56. Yezid Sayigh, "Fatah: The First Twenty Years," *JPS,* Vol. 13, No. 4 (Summer 1984), p. 115; *al-Anba,* October 3, 1987, *JPS,* Vol. 27, No. 2 (Winter 1988).

57. Arafat, *al-Watan al-Arabi,* December 16, 1983; Agence France Presse, April 11, 1983.

58. Abu Iyad, *Qatar News Agency,* February 6, 1984 (*FBIS,* February 6,

1984); Khalid al-Hasan, *al-Nahar al-Arabi wal-Duwali*, May 24, 1982; *al-Hadaf*, "Arafat's Downfall Is Our Main Objective," February 20, 1984.

59. *Al-Khalij*, October 6, 1982, and December 19, 1983; Kuwait News Agency, December 15, 1983; *Jordan Times*, April 17, 1984.

60. *Al-Jazira*, November 4, 1983; *al-Khalij*, June 2, 1983.

61. *Al-Hawadith*, March 1, 1985.

4. In Search of a Program, 1984–1987

1. Text, *JPS*, Vol. 14, No. 3 (Spring 1985), p. 201.

2. November 22, 1984 speech, text in *FBIS*, November 26, 1984, pp. A-13–18.

3. *Al-Sharq al-Awsat*, March 1, 1984; on Husayn's meeting with Palestinians, see *FBIS*, November 30, 1984, p. F-1.

4. Ironically, even Qawasma, shortly before his murder, advocated this position. Interview, *al-Sharq al-Awsat*, December 8, 1984; text, *FBIS*, November 28, 1984, pp. A-4–A-14.

5. Ibid.

6. Speech, November 22, 1984, *FBIS*, November 26, 1984, pp. A-8–A-12.

7. Abu Iyad, *al-Qabas*, November 11, 1984. See also *al-Watan*, December 19, 1984; Shafiq al-Hut, *al-Anba*, March 20, 1983.

8. Text, *FBIS*, February 25, 1985, p. F-1, and *American–Arab Affairs*, No. 12 (Spring 1985), p. 140.

9. *Al-Hawadith*, March 1, 1985 (*JPS*, Vol. 14, No. 3, Spring 1985, p. 155); *al-Sharq al-Awsat*, March 1, 1985 (*JPS*, Vol. 14, No. 3, Spring 1985, p. 159).

10. *FBIS*, February 26, 1985, p. A-2; February 4, 1985, p. A-1; and February 15, 1985, p. A-2.

11. Ibid.

12. Voice of the PLO (Baghdad), April 9, 1983; Kuwait News Agency, April 11, 1983.

13. *Washington Post*, February 27, 1985; *Jordan Times*, February 7, 1985.

14. *Al-Sharq al-Awsat*, March 1, 1985 (*FBIS*, March 5, 1985, p. A-2); *al-Ahram*, February 21, 1985 (*FBIS*, February 26, 1985). Khalid al-Hasan said that land for peace was the starting point for a series of stages that must end with the elimination of either Arab nationalism or Zionism. Hani al-Hasan said there could be no solution without a Palestinian state from the Jordan river to the Mediterranean. *al-Anba*, June 1 and 12, 1985; *al-Sayyad*, June 15, 1985.

15. *Al-Dustur*, "The Syrian 'Peace' Following the Israeli 'Peace,'" June 3, 1985; *al-Nahar*, May 29, 1985.

16. *Arab Times,* July 9, 1985.

17. Khalid al-Hasan, *FBIS,* July 1, 1985, p. A-4; Abu Iyad, *FBIS,* July 25, 1985, p. A-2; *al-Dustur,* December 2, 1985, pp. 8–13.

18. *Le Monde,* July 26, 1985.

19. *La Republica,* October 22, 1985; *La Stampa,* November 13, 1985.

20. Musa Sabri, "Open Letter to Arafat," *al-Akhbar,* October 20, 1985 (*FBIS,* October 24, 1985, pp. D-3, 4).

21. L. Paul Bremer III, "Countering Terrorism: U.S. Policy in the 1980s and 1990s," speech at George Washington University, November 22, 1988, pp. 10–11; Shultz, in John Goshko, "Arafat Threat Against Truce Advocates Hit," *Washington Post,* January 5, 1989.

22. *Washington Times,* October 16, 1987.

23. King Husayn speech, August 7, 1985 (*FBIS,* August 8, 1985, p. A-5). Both Husayn and Peres made last-minute efforts to save the initiative in UN speeches. Husayn said, "We are prepared to negotiate, under appropriate auspices, with the government of Israel, promptly and directly, under the basic tenets of Security Council Resolutions 242 and 338" through an international conference as an umbrella for direct talks rather than as a substitute for them. Peres accepted an international forum and Jordan-Palestinian delegation "comprising delegates that represent peace, not terror."

24. *Al-Siyasa,* March 1, 1986; King Husayn's speech, Amman television, February 19, 1986 (*FBIS,* February 20, 1986, pp. F 1–16). See also *New York Times* and *Washington Post,* February 20, 1986.

25. *Sawt al-Sha'b,* March 12, 1986 (*FBIS,* March 12, 1986, p. F-1). Lamis Andoni, "Hussein Stakes His Claim," *Middle East International,* February 21, 1986, pp. 7–8.

26. David Hirst, "The Pressure on Arafat to Cross the Jordan," *Guardian,* December 19, 1985, p. 17; Matti Steinberg, "The Pragmatic Stream of Thought within the PLO According to Khalid al-Hasan," *The Jerusalem Journal of International Relations,* Vol. 11, No. 1 (1989), pp. 54–55. Jonathan Randal, "Husayn's Move Isolates Arafat," *Washington Post,* February 22, 1986; Alain Gresh, *The PLO: The Struggle Within* (London, 1985), p. 247.

27. Sabri Jiryis, "A Different Kind of 'Discussion' about 'the Discussion' and National Unity," *Shu'un Filastiniyya,* May-June 1987, pp. 3–32.

28. *Washington Post,* April 21–23, 1987. The other returning groups were the Arab Liberation Front and the Palestine Liberation Front led by Abu al-Abbas. The radicals demanded a collective leadership and a break with Egypt but settled for cosmetic changes. For the March 16, 1987, agreement, see *JPS,* Vol. 25, No. 4 (Summer 1987).

29. Qaddumi, Kuwait News Agency, October 19, 1987 (*FBIS,* October 20,

1987, p. 3), called the PLO–Syria dispute a family row between brothers who should face the common enemy together. On PLO–Jordan relations, see *New York Times,* February 17 and 18, 1987.

30. Helena Cobban, "The PLO in the Mid-1980s: Between the Gun and the Olive Branch," *International Journal,* Vol. 38 (Autumn 1983), p. 649.

31. American Enterprise Institute, *A Conversation with the exiled West Bank Mayors: A Palestinian Point of View* (Washington, 1981), pp. 3 and 5. See also p. 15.

32. Ibid., pp. 9–10;

33. Ibid.

34. Daoud Kuttab, "The PLO Must Not Forget the Palestinians," *Middle East International,* October 10, 1986.

35. See Robert Satloff, "Islam in the Palestinian Uprising," *Policy Focus,* Number 7 (Washington, D.C., 1988); Zuhair Kashmeri, "Islamic Fervour Growing among PLO," *Manchester Guardian Weekly,* May 18, 1986; Barry Rubin, *Islamic Fundamentalists in Egyptian Politics* (New York, 1991).

36. Patrick Seale, "Paymasters Desert Beleaguered Arafat," *Observer,* June 22, 1986.

5. The Intifada and the Diplomatic Option, 1987–1988

1. Daoud Kuttab, "Will Arafat Back Elections?" *Washington Post,* April 16, 1989.

2. Speech in *al-Ra'y al-Amm,* September 11, 1989, p. 16 (*FBIS,* September 14, 1989, pp. 6–7).

3. Khalid al-Hasan said in a speech that Palestinians had a right to kill collaborators as the Jews had killed the Nazi war criminal Adolf Eichmann. "Two Years of Intifada: Its Impact on the American, Israeli, and Palestinian Political Climates," December 7, 1989.

4. Jamal al-Surani, *al-Sharq al-Awsat,* December 15, 1989 (*FBIS,* December 20, 1989). p. 4.

5. PLO spokesman Kamal Nasir, February 1972, *JPS,* Vol. 1 No. 3 (Spring 1972), p. 174.

6. Voice of Palestine (Algiers), November 28, 1987 (*FBIS,* December 1, 1987, p. 5); Voice of Lebanon, December 3, 1987 (*FBIS,* December 4, 1987, p. 3).

7. Palestine National Council Political Report, November 15, 1988; *Washington Post,* April 11, 1988.

8. *New York Times,* February 22, 1988; *Washington Post,* May 11, 1988.

9. Paul Taylor, "West Bank, Gaza Palestinians Urge a PLO Political Initia-

tive," Reuters, October 5, 1988; Youssef Ibrahim, "A Palestinian Revolution without the PLO," *New York Times*, February 14, 1988.

10. *Al-Tadamun*, September 11, 1989, p. 14 (*FBIS*, September 15, 1989, p. 5); Jim Hoagland, "Will the PLO Break with its Past?" *Washington Post*, November 16, 1989; Palestine National Council Political Resolution, U.S. State Department translation; Nabil Sha'th, speech to National Press Club, March 16, 1989.

11. He was at that time the second-ranking official in Jordan's Foreign Ministry. U.S. State Department dispatch, 784.00/5–2857, Cole to Dulles.

12. Daoud Kuttab, *al-Fajr,* May 31, 1987.

13. Daoud Kuttab, "A Profile of the Stonethrowers," *JPS*, Vol. 17, No. 3. (Spring 1988), p. 14.

14. Satloff, "Islam in the Palestinian Uprising"; Charter of the Islamic Resistance Movement of Palestine, August 18, 1988; *al-Anba*, October 8, 1988, pp. 24–25 (*FBIS*, October 13, 1988, pp. 3–10).

15. *Ha'aretz*, April 25, 1989.

16. Text in *FBIS* August 8, 1988, pp. 26–28. See also *Jerusalem Post*, August 12, 1988; Sari Nusayba lecture, Oxford Arab Committee, *Middle East Mirror,* February 12, 1990.

17. Khalid al-Hasan, interview in *Yediot Aharnot*, September 5, 1988, p. 17 (*FBIS* September 7, 1988, p. 5). For the Husayni document, see *Jerusalem Post*, August 12, 1988, p. 10, and *FBIS*, August 12, 1988, pp. 30–32. "A Critical Palestine National Council Session," *al-Fajr,* August 14, 1988, p. 5. Text of Call No. 27, *al-Ra'y al-Amm*, October 10, 1988, p. 37 (*FBIS*, October 12, 1988, pp. 6–7).

18. See, for example, Vladimir Nosenko, "The Transformation of the Soviet Stand on the Palestinian Problem," Dayan Center Occasional Paper No. 109, January 1991.

19. *Al-Thawra*, April 22, 1989 (*FBIS*, April 25, 1989, p. 3); *al-Quds al-Arabiyya*, February 7, 1990; *al-Majalla*, April 5–11, 1989 (*FBIS*, April 7, 1989, pp. 1–8); *Agence-France Presse*, April 18, 1989 (*FBIS*, April 18, 1989 p. 1); Mubarak in Middle East News Agency, August 12, 1988 (*FBIS*, August 15, 1988, p. 4), and *al-Ahram* (*FBIS* October 20, 1988, p. 14). Abu Iyad, *al-Muharrir,* November 25, 1989 (*FBIS*, November 29, 1989, p. 4); Khalid al-Hasan, *al-Watan*, October 13, 1989 (*FBIS*, October 17, 1989).

20. Text, *American–Arab Affairs*, Number 25 (Summer 1988), pp. 194–98 and *FBIS*, September 14, 1988, pp. 27–32. Interviews in Tunis, July-August 1989; Jonathan Wright, "PLO Rethinking How to Use Uprising in West Bank and Gaza," Reuters, September 30, 1988; Bassam Abu Sharif, *Jerusalem Post*, September 16, 1988.

21. Speech to Council on Foreign Relations, June 14, 1988, in U.S. Department of State, "Middle East Peace: Facing Realities and Challenges," *Current Policy*, No. 1082.

22. Interviews, Algiers, November 1988; Tunis, July–August 1989.

23. "Palestinian Document Circulated at Arab Summit in Algeria, PLO View: Prospects of a Palestinian–Israeli Settlement."

24. Abu Iyad, *Der Spiegel*, August 29, 1988, pp. 131–136 (*FBIS*, August 31, 1988, p. 6); *al-Ra'y al-Amm*, June 19, 1988 (*FBIS*, June 22, 1988, p. 5); Ihsan Hijazi, "An Aide to Arafat Comes under Fire," *New York Times*, June 22, 1988; Alex Efty, "Arafat Aide's Peace Proposal Stirs Palestinian Feud," *Washington Post*, June 23, 1988; Abu Iyad, Radio Monte Carlo (*FBIS*, July 3, 1988, p. 5); Radio Damascus, July 6, 1988 (*FBIS*, July 7, 1988); Nihad al-Jahiz, "Independent Palestine Need Not Be Castrated," *al-Fajr*, September 18, 1988. Mubarak text, *FBIS*, July 21, 1988, p. 11.

25. PFLP leader George Habash said he could accept a state or government only if it "does not offer concessions in its programs or hide the PLO role[,] . . . does not contradict the PLO Charter and rules, [and] includes all the Palestinian revolutionary factions." Salam Musafir, "PFLP Official Views U.N. Role, Soviet Talks," *al-Anba*, September 19, 1988, pp. 1 and 30 (*FBIS*, September 22, 1988, p. 25). Hawatmah rejected "establishing a government of the so-called moderates which will be accepted by the West and America's allies in the region." Gail Fitzer, "Israel Expects More than 50 States to Recognize Any PLO State," Reuters, October 11, 1988.

26. Text in Laqueur and Rubin, *Israel–Arab Reader*, pp. 113–122.

27. Voice of Lebanon, December 3, 1987 (*FBIS*, December 4, 1987, pp. 3–6); Voice of Palestine (Algiers), November 28, 1987 (*FBIS*, December 1, 1987, pp. 5–6); *al-Watan*, October 2, 1988. Harkabi, *Palestinian Covenant*, p. 76; interview, *al-Anba*, September 7, 1988, p. 23 (*FBIS*, September 9, 1988, p. 3–5).

28. Ibid.

29. Kuwait News Agency, September 23, 1988 (*FBIS*, September 26, 1988, p. 6); *Der Spiegel*, p. 5; Kuwait News Agency, September 1, 1988 (*FBIS*, September 2, 1988, p. 3); *al-Siyasa*, October 17, 1988, pp. 1 and 20 (*FBIS*, October 20, 1988, p. 5). *Al-Majalla*, August 31-September 6, 1988, p. 11 (*FBIS* September 2, 1988, p 4).

30. *London Times*, November 14, 1988.

31. *Le Monde*, July 1, 1988.

32. Jonathan Wright, "PLO Rethinking How to Use Uprising in West Bank and Gaza."

33. Kuwait News Agency, September 1, 1988 (*FBIS*, September 2, 1988,

p. 3); interview, *al-Siyasa,* October 17, 1988, pp. 1 and 20 (*FBIS,* October 20, 1988, p. 5).

34. Middle East News Agency, April 19, 1989 (*FBIS* April 21, 1989, p. 7).

6. Rehearsals for a Moment of Truth, 1988–1990

1. Key sources for the Palestinian National Council Resolution were the September 1982 Fez Arab summit resolution, Text in Laqueur and Rubin, *Israel–Arab Reader,* pp. 663–665, and Arafat's speech to the June 1988 Arab summit, text, *FBIS,* June 10, 1988, p. 6.

2. *New York Times,* November 16, 1988.

3. Quotations of Palestine National Council resolution are from the official translation.

4. Quotations are from official Palestine National Council translation; Kuwait News Agency, September 1, 1988 (*FBIS,* September 2, 1988, p. 3).

5. "Arafat flew to Amman," Reuters, January 6, 1989; text of September 14, 1988 speech in *FBIS,* September 15, 1988. p. 6.

6. Cited in James Dorsey, "PLO State to Seek United Nations Birth," *Washington Times,* December 5, 1988, p. A-6. This echoes the June 1988 Arab summit resolution, text in *FBIS,* June 10, 1988, p. 12.

7. *Washington Post,* October 25, 1988; Interview, Voice of Lebanon, December 3, 1987 (*FBIS,* December 4, 1987, pp. 3–6); *Washington Post,* January 4 and 5, 1989, and March 1, 1989; L. Paul Bremer III, "Countering Terrorism: U.S. Policy in the 1980s and 1990s," speech at George Washington University, November 22, 1988, pp. 10–11. On PLO attacks just prior to the Council meeting, see also *Los Angeles Times,* October 25 and November 14, 1988.

8. "Knowing the Enemy," *Time,* November 7, 1988, pp. 47–48.

9. *Al-Siyasa,* December 5, 1988 (*FBIS,* December 7, 1988, p. 2); *al-Sharq al-Awsat,* January 13, 1989 (*FBIS,* January 18, 1989, p. 5). Abd al-Hamid al-Sa'ih was born in 1904, trained at Egypt's al-Azhar mosque-university, and was a supporter of the dominant Husayni faction in the pre-1948 Palestinian movement, for whom he handled finances at times. Expelled by Israel in September 1967, he went to Jordan and at times served as minister of religious affairs there. In 1984, after the Palestine National Council's chairman defected to the Syrians, he was elected as Fatah's candidate. On PLO ambiguity, see Robert Pear, "The PLO's Many Voices Differ about its Commitments to the U.S.," *New York Times,* May 2, 1989; *Washington Times,* December 5, 1988, p. A-6.

10. "Yes, We Will Recognize Israel in Return for an Independent Palestinian State," *al-Dustur,* September 26, 1988 (*FBIS,* October 5, 1988,

p. 33); *al-Siyasa,* December 21, 1988, p. 18 (*FBIS,* December 23, 1988, p. 4).

11. Ibid.

12. Text, *Washington Post* and *New York Times,* November 27, 1988, December 6 and 7, 1988; Menachem Rosensaft, "Meeting the PLO," *Reform Judaism,* Spring 1989, p. 13.

13. Text, Voice of the PLO (Baghdad), December 15, 1988 (*FBIS,* December 15, 1988, p. 3); *New York Times,* December 14, 1988.

14. Text, Voice of the PLO (Baghdad), December 15, 1988 (*FBIS,* December 15, 1988, p. 3); *Washington Post,* December 15, 1988.

15. Voice of the PLO (Baghdad), October 16, 1989 (*FBIS,* October 17, 1989, p. 6).

16. *Al-Watan,* October 13, 1989 (*FBIS,* October 17, 1989). For the effect of the Cold War's end on the region, see Barry Rubin, "Reshaping the Middle East," *Foreign Affairs,* Summer 1990.

17. Al-Ra'y al-Amm (*FBIS,* October 19, 1988, p. 12).

18. *FBIS,* January 25, 1989, p. 4; al-Musawwar, January 19, 1990. Sadat's comment, February 17, 1977, *IDOP* 1977, p. 329.

19. Voice of Palestine (Algiers), March 9, 1989 (*FBIS,* March 21, 1989, p. 11);

20. *New York Times,* December 5, 1989.

21. *New York Times,* December 5, 1989; Youssef Ibrahim, "A Palestinian Revolution without the PLO," *New York Times,* February 14, 1988.

22. *Al-Ra'y Al-Amm,* September 11, 1989, p. 16 (*FBIS,* September 14, 1989, pp. 6–7); *FBIS,* October 4, 1989, p. 4; *al-Sharq al-Awsat,* September 17, 1989 (*FBIS,* September 22, 1989, pp. 4–5).

23. *Al-Musawwar,* January 19, 1990.

24. *Ma'ariv,* December 3, 1989.

25. *New York Times,* February 12 and 22, March 11, 14, and 16, 1989; *Washington Times,* February 16, 1989; *Washington Post,* February 24 and May 2, 1989.

26. *New York Times,* March 22, 23, and 31, April 4, and May 24, 1989; *Washington Post,* January 21 and May 24, 1989.

27. Carol Giacomo, Reuters, "Secretary of State Baker Toughening U.S. Attitude toward Israel," July 11, 1989; *Washington Times,* July 17, 1989; *Washington Post,* July 18, 1989. Aharon Papo, *Yediot Aharnot,* cited in *Middle East Mirror,* February 7, 1990, p. 6.

28. *Al-Anba,* September 19, 1989 (*FBIS,* September 22, 1989, pp. 5–7); Voice of the PLO (Baghdad), March 26 1989 (*FBIS,* March 27, 1989, p. 7); *al-Sharq al-Awsat,* April 8 (*FBIS* April 18, 1989, pp. 6–7); *al-Musawwar* and *Sawt al-Sha'b* interviews (*FBIS,* April 13, 1989, pp. 3–4).

29. *Al-Ahram,* February 14, 1989 (*FBIS,* February 22, 1989, p. 10). See

also Kuttab, "A Profile of the Stonethrowers"; Sari Nusayba, *Christian Science Monitor,* April 14, 1989, p. 6; Faysal al-Husayni, *al-Fajr (FBIS,* April 25, 1989, p. 34); *al-Anba,* March 24, 1989 *(FBIS* March 28, 1989, p. 4); Voice of Palestine (Algiers), April 3, 1989 *(FBIS* April 4, 1989, p. 3.).

30. Ahmad Abd al-Rahman, editorial, *Filastin al-Thawra,* May 14, 1989.

31. *Al-Ittihad,* March 17, 1989 *(FBIS* March 20, 1989, p. 18); *International Herald Tribune,* November 16, 1988; Abu Ahmad Fuad, PFLP Political Bureau and commander of its forces in Lebanon, *al-Qabas,* March 13, 1989 *(FBIS,* March 22, 1989, pp. 7–9); Hawatmah, *al-Fajr,* December 18, 1989 *(FBIS,* December 19, 1989, p. 5).

32. Text, *FBIS,* August 10, 1989, pp. 11–14. *New York Times,* August 11 and 15, 1989; *Washington Times,* July 13 and August 11, 1989. Occasional PLO articles did advocate a two-state solution. For example, Hasan al-Batal, "Different Nationality, Different Zionism," *Filastin al-Thawra,* July 2, 1989.

33. *Al-Bayan,* August 6 *(FBIS,* August 8, 1989); *al-Anba,* August 21, 1989 *(FBIS,* August 25, 1989, p. 3).

34. *New York Times,* March 31 and April 7, May 24 and 28, and June 25 and 30, 1989; *Washington Post,* May 24 and June 29, 1989; *Washington Times,* June 8 and July 19, 1989.

35. For the first version of Mubarak's plan, see *Jerusalem Post,* July 5, 1989. A copy of the later formulation, presented with some differences in August, is in the author's possession. *Al-Fajr,* September 18, 1989; Palestinian memo to John Kelly, *The Return,* September 1989, pp. 38–39.

36. Abu Iyad, *al-Bayan,* October 2, 1989 *(FBIS,* October 4, 1989, p. 5).

37. Text, *New York Times,* December 7, 1989. See also *Washington Post,* October 7 and 11, 1989; *New York Times,* October 8 and 11, 1989.

38. See, for example, testimony, House Appropriations Committee, March 1 and 7, 1990; text, Bush's press conference in Palm Springs, California, March 3, 1990. See also Thomas Friedman, *New York Times,* March 9, 1990.

39. *Washington Times,* November 2, 1989; *Washington Post,* November 9, 1989.

40. Robert Greenberger, ""Bush Administration at Last Is Optimistic on Progress for a Middle East Peace Plan, *Wall Street Journal,* November 13, 1989; *al-Anba,* December 3, 1989 *(FBIS,* December 5, 1989, pp. 6–7). *Jordan Times,* December 23, 1989, carried the purported text of the official PLO response to Baker.

41. Text of confidential talking points in author's possession.

42. Glenn Frankel, "West Bank Mayor Drops Truce Call," *Washington Post,* January 4, 1989; John Goshko, "Arafat Threat against Truce Advocates Hit," *Washington Post,* January 5, 1989.

43. *Al-Tadamun*, February 5, 1990 (*FBIS*, 5, 1990, pp. 5–6). For a similar statement by Abu Iyad, see *al-Thawra*, April 22, 1989, p. 2 (*FBIS*, April 25, 1989, p. 4).

44. Reuters, "Guerrillas Killed as Radicals Keep Up Attacks on Israel," March 2, 1989.

45. *Al-Qabas*, December 23 1988, p. 19 (*FBIS*, December 27, 1988, p. 4). *al-Ahram*, February 14, 1989 (*FBIS*, February 22, 1989, p. 4).

46. Lee Stokes, UPI, "Egypt's Ruling Party Newspaper Slams PLO in Unprecedented Attack," February 11, 1990. The Voice of the PLO (Baghdad) praised the attack in Egypt, arguing that the Zionist entity "enjoys no intrinsic requirements of survival because it is a body that stands outside history, logic, reason, and the constant essential facts in this part of the world." July 12, 1989 (*FBIS*, July 13, 1989).

47. Menachem Rosensaft, "A Letter to Yasir Arafat," *Newsweek*, December 11, 1989; Joel Brinkley, "Majority in Israel Oppose PLO Talks Now, a Poll Shows," *New York Times*, April 2, 1989.

48. See, for example, Algiers Television, March 22, 1990 (*FBIS*, March 23, 1990, pp. 4, 6).

49. *Washington Post*, August 28, 1990.

50. Arafat, October 1968, *IDOP* 1968, pp. 453–454; Vienna television (*FBIS*, December 19, 1988, p. 7); interview with author.

7. The PLO and the Arab States

1. *JPS*, Vol. 2, No. 2 (Winter 1973), p. 176.

2. Yezid Sayigh, "Fatah: The First Twenty Years," *JPS*, Vol. 13, No. 4, (Summer 1984), p. 115.

3. Walid Kazziha, *Palestine in the Arab Dilemma* (London, 1979), pp. 15–19; Abu Za'im, *al-Watan*, April 18, 1986.

4. Ibrahim Ibrash, "The Palestinians and Arab Unity: From the Disaster of 1948 through Today," *al-Mustaqbal al-Arabi*, July 1984, pp. 39–57.

5. Janice Stein, "The Alchemy of Peacemaking," *International Journal*, Vol. 38 (Autumn 1983), p. 1.

6. Speech, December 1980, cited in Daniel Pipes, "The Politics of Muslim Anti-Semitism," *Commentary*, Vol. 72, No. 3 (August 1981), p. 39. See also Rushdi Abbas al-Amara, "The Historical and Religious Influences on Israel's Behavior," *al-Siyasa al-Duwaliyya*, October 1982; Hassan Nafaa, "Arab Nationalism: A Response to Ajami's Thesis on the 'End of Pan-Arabism,'" *Journal of Arab Affairs*, Vol. 2, No. 2 (Spring 1983), p. 193.

7. Nafaa, "Arab Nationalism," p. 192.

8. Nizar Hamdoun, "The U.S.–Iran Arms Deal: An Iraqi Critique," *Middle East Review* (Summer 1982), pp. 35–36.

9. PLO Executive Committee member Milhim commented, "It makes no sense for a Palestinian in Lebanon to use his arms against Israel when he is being stabbed in the back." *Al-Anba*, September 19, 1989 (*FBIS*, September 22, 1989, p. 7).

10. Alain Gresh, *The PLO: The Struggle Within* (London, 1985), p. 246. See also Walid Khalidi, "The Asad Regime and the Palestinian Resistance," *Arab Studies Quarterly*, Vol. 6, No. 4 (Fall 1984), p. 265.

11. Abu Nidal's real name was Sabri al-Banna. U.S. Department of Defense, *Terrorist Group Profiles* (Washington, D.C., 1988). U.S. Department of State, *Abu Nidal Organization* (Washington, D.C., 1988), pp. 5–8. During the first half of 1978, his group assassinated three PLO officials—Sa'id Hamami, Ali Nasir Yasin, and Izz al-Din Qalaq, respectively the PLO representatives in London, Kuwait, and Paris—and four people in the PLO's office in Pakistan. Abu Nidal killed a PLO official in Rome in 1982, Sartawi in 1983, and an Arafat supporter in Rome in December 1984 (pp. 5–8). Among dissident terrorists Arafat took over were Colonel Hawari and others from the May 15 group who he put into his own security apparatus. *Al-Nahar Arab Report & Memo*, August 14, 1978 (*JPRS*, No. 71833, September 8, 1978).

12. James Adams, *The Financing of Terror* (New York, 1986), p. 109.

13. *Al-Quds al-Arabi*, cited in *Middle East Mirror*, February 15, 1990. Muhammad Milhim called the Arab states' support "peanuts" in comparison with their resources. *Filastin al-Thawra*, February 1, 1986, pp. 14–15. On Saudi complaints about Arafat, see *New York Times*, August 25, 1990.

14. *Al-Ra'y al-Amm*, April 27, 1985; Khalidi, "The Asad Regime," p. 260.

15. Sabri Jiryis, "The Important Five Years in Jewish National History in Palestine, 1931–1936," *Shu'un Filastiniyya*, February 1985.

16. Kazziha, *Palestine in the Arab Dilemma*, pp. 15–19.

17. Killgore dispatch, August 29, 1986, pp. 33–36, in *Den of Spies*, Vol. 42. When the PLO supported Iraq's invasion of Kuwait in 1990, Qatar expelled many of its leading Palestinian families. See *Middle East Monitor*, August 31, 1990, pp. 14–15.

18. Abu Za'im, *al-Watan*, April 18, 1986; Moughrabi, "The Palestinians after Lebanon," p. 211. Kazziha, *Palestine in the Arab Dilemma*, pp. 15–19.

19. Robert Neumann, "The Search for Peace in the Middle East: A Role for U.S. Policy," *American–Arab Affairs*, Summer 1982, pp. 9–10.

20. Hisham Sharabi, "Arab Policy and the Prospects for Peace," *American–Arab Affairs*, Summer 1982, p. 108.

21. Said, *The Arabs Today*, pp. 5–6.

22. U.S. Department of State, Memorandum of Conversation, 785.00/7–

2451, July 24, 1951; letter from Francis Russell, who met with Nasir, June 9, 1979.

23. The author was present.

24. Voice of the PLO (Baghdad), January 26, 1989 (*FBIS*, January 30, 1989, p. 6).

25. Hazem Saghiyeh, *al-Hayat*, August 21, 1990. Cited in *Middle East Mirror*, August 21, 1990, p. 20.

26. Arafat interview, *Vjesnik*, December 8, 1990 (*FBIS*, December 13, 1990, p. 1); *Washington Post*, January 18, 1991. See also Karen Laub, "Palestinians Fearful of Attack, But Proud of Iraq for Targeting Israel," Reuters, January 18, 1991.

27. *Le Quotidien de Paris*, November 9, 1990 (*FBIS*, November 14, 1990, p. 3); *Sawt al-Sha'b*, November 15, 1990 (*FBIS*, November 16, 1990, pp. 2–6). See also Monte Carlo Radio, November 20, 1990 (*FBIS*, November 21, 1990).

28. The Saudi Ambassador to Bahrain in *al-Sharq al-Awsat*, November 9, 1990; *al-Ahram* cited in *Middle East Mirror*, November 9, 1990, p. 25; Yusuf Hasin, *al-Nadwa*, October 1, 1990.

29. Mahmud Abd al-Monim Murad, *October* (*Middle East Mirror*, August 21, 1990, p. 20); Dunia al-Issa, *al-Qabas International* August 21, 1990.

30. See, for example, Saghiyeh, *al-Hayat*, August 21, 1990.

31. *The Economist*, September 22, 1990, p. 48. Arafat estimated that the PLO lost $6 million a month from Saudi Arabia, $2 million a month from Kuwait, and $4 million a month from Iraq, plus billions of dollars in income lost by Palestinians formerly employed in these countries. *New York Times*, March 15, 1991.

32. *Ha'aretz*, August 17, 1990, text in *Middle East Mirror*, August 17, 1990, p. 7.

33. Resolution cited in *The Economist*, "Egypt, and the Knocking at the Gates of Basra," November 21, 1987, p. 39.

34. Interview, Middle East News Agency, January 24, 1989 (*FBIS*, January 25, 1989, p. 15).

35. Fouad Ajami, "Arab Road," *Foreign Policy*, No. 47 (Summer 1982), p. 16; David Ottoway, "Syrian Connection to Terrorism Probed," *Washington Post*, June 1, 1986; Jim Hoagland, "A Clean State for Syria?" *Washington Post*, September 19, 1987.

36. Seale, *Asad*, p. 348; *Tishrin*, July 9, 1983.

37. King Husayn's throne speech, November 1, 1967, *al-Dustur*, November 2, 1967, *IDOP* 1967, p. 691; text, *American–Arab Affairs*, Number 25 (Summer 1988), pp. 194–198, and *FBIS*, September 14, 1988, pp. 27–32.

38. Moshe Zak, "Talking to Husayn," *Jerusalem Post*, April 19, 1985; *al-*

Ra'y, "West Bank Appeal for Cooperation," March 1, 1984, pp. 12–13. *Al-Fajr* reported that the Jordanian–Palestinian joint committee distributed $430 million in the West Bank between 1980 and 1985. *Al-Fajr,* December 3, 1985.

39. Satloff, *They Cannot Stop Our Tongues: Islamic Activism in Jordan* (Washington, D.C, 1986), p. 83: "Military dangers and economic blackmail have never permitted the Kingdom to act independently of the four powers of the Arab world—Egypt, Syria, Iraq, and Saudi Arabia. Instead, Husayn has accepted humiliation as the price for survival in a hostile environment."

40. Witnessed by the author.

41. Interview, *al-Anba,* September 7, 1988 (*FBIS,* September 9, 1988). See also Adam Garfinkle, "Jordanian Foreign Policy," *Current History,* January 1984.

42. Hasan Bin Talal, "Jordan's Quest for Peace," *Foreign Affairs,* Spring 1982, p. 807; Satloff, *They Cannot Stop Our Tongues,* p. 87.

43. Adeed Dawisha, "Saudi Arabia and the Arab–Israeli Conflict: The up and downs of pragmatic moderation," *International Journal,* Vol. 38, No. 4 (Autumn 1983), p. 680.44. *Al-Sharq al-Awsat,* July 15, 1985.

45. Author's observation.

46. Voice of Palestine (Algiers), December 10, 1983; Kuwait News Agency, May 24, 1984; Khalid al-Hasan, *al-Qabas,* January 21, 1981; on Abu Iyad's views, *al-Majalla,* March 10–16, 1984; *al-Watan al-Arabi,* January 13–19, 1984; *al-Jazira,* November 4, 1983. In April 1987, Soviet leader Mikhail Gorbachev tried all his famous charm to persuade Asad to support an international peace conference; Asad rejected the idea as a U.S.–Israel plot. Equally, the Soviets failed to avert Syria's invasion of Lebanon in 1975 or make it cooperate with the PLO after 1983. See *Pravda,* April 27, 1987 (*FBIS: USSR,* April 28, 1987, pp. H-7 to 14).

47. Ahmad Shahin, "The PLO from One Siege to Another," *Shu'un Filastiniyya,* July 1985.

8. Contentious Unity

1. Interview, *JPS,* Vol. 11, No. 2 (Winter 1982), p. 10.

2. Arafat, *al-Qabas,* May 10, 1990 (*Middle East Mirror,* May 10, 1990, pp. 10–13).

3. Interview, *JPS,* Vol. 11, No. 2 (Winter 1982), p. 6. Hani al-Hasan, Speech to Royal Commonwealth Society, December 11, 1989. Text, *Middle East Mirror,* December 12, 1989.

4. *Al-Majalla,* November 21, 1989.

5. *Al-Majalla,* August 30–September 5, 1989 (*FBIS,* September 7, 1989, p. 2).

6. Edward Said, *The Question of Palestine* (New York, 1980), p. 165.
7. Moughrabi, "The Palestinians after Lebanon," p. 214; Thomas L. Friedman, "West Bank Grows Critical of Arafat, But It's More from Love than Anger," *New York Times*, November 20, 1984, p. A-8.
8. Arafat, *al-Qabas*, May 10, 1990 (*Middle East Mirror*, May 10, 1990, pp. 10–13).
9. Ibid.
10. "Yassir [sic] Arafat," *Third World Quarterly*, Vol 8, No. 2 (April 1986); Hisham Sharabi, *Nationalism and Revolution in the Arab World* (New York, 1966), p. 93.
11. Arafat, *al-Qabas*, May 10, 1990 (*Middle East Mirror*, May 10, 1990, pp. 10–13).
12. Helena Cobban, "The PLO in the mid-1980's: Between the gun and the olive branch," *International Journal*, Vol. 38 (Autumn 1983), p. 642.
13. *Al-Majalla*, March 10, 1984; *al-Watan al-Arabi*, January 13–19, 1984.
14. *Al-Fajr*, September 12, 1986.
15. Jim Hoagland, "Arafat and the Fog Machine," *Washington Post*, June 30, 1988.
16. *Al-Ahram*, February 21, 1985, *JPS*, Vol. 14, No. 3 (Spring 1985), pp. 151–153. Military action, wrote a pro-PLO Palestinian intellectual, "is supposed to influence the other parties to the conflict and convince them of the inevitability of including the Palestinians in any political process." Yet military action had the exact opposite effect, Yezid Sayigh, "Palestinian Armed Struggle: Means and Ends," *JPS*, Vol. 16, No. 1 (Autumn 1986), p. 109. On Qaddumi's view, see David Ottoway, "U.S. Again Says PLO Violating Vow," *Washington Post*, March 1, 1989; "PLO Says Not Responsible for Raids, Criticizes Europeans," Reuters, February 28, 1989.
17. Arafat, *al-Qabas*, May 10, 1990 (*Middle East Mirror*, May 10, 1990, pp. 10–13). See also al-Azm, "The Palestine Resistance Movement Reconsidered," pp. 131–133.
18. Friedman, "West Bank Grows Critical of Arafat," *New York Times*, November 20, 1984, p. A-8.
19. Interviews in Algiers and Tunis, 1988 and 1989, and in Egypt and Jordan, 1990.
20. Moughrabi, "The Palestinians after Lebanon," p. 212.
21. *Al-Muharrir*, November 25, 1989 (*FBIS*, November 29, 1989, p. 4); *Ukaz*, November 16, 1989 (*FBIS*, November 27, 1989, pp. 5–6).
22. On the Black September connection, see Defense Intelligence Agency, *International Terrorism: A Compendium, Vol. 2: The Middle East*, p. 6.
23. "Farouk Kaddoumi [sic]," *Third World Quarterly*, Vol. 8 (April 1986). His nom de guerre was Abu al-Lutf. During the 1988–1990 U.S.–PLO

dialogue, the Political Department was represented on the PLO delegation by its director-general, Abu Jabir.

24. For a study of such institutions, see Laurie A. Brand, *Palestinians in the Arab World: Institution Building and the Search for a State* (New York, 1988).

25. Rubenberg, *The Palestinian Liberation Organization*, pp. 12–14. Barbara Rosewicz and Gerald Seib, "Aside from Being a Movement, the PLO Is a Financial Giant," *Wall Street Journal*, July 21, 1986; Hesh Kestin, "Terror's Bottom Line," *Forbes*, June 2, 1986. The leading PLO financial official was Jawad al-Ghusayn, son of a wealthy orange grower, who met Arafat at university in Cairo and became a wealthy building contractor in Abu Dhabi. *Euromoney*, September 1989, pp. 36–37; Shawn Tully, "The Big Moneymen of Palestine Inc.," *Fortune*, July 31, 1989, pp. 182–183; "Who Pays Arafat?" *U.S. News & World Report*, April 26, 1993, pp. 47–52.

26. His real name was Colonel Mahmud Ahmad Mahmud al-Natur.

27. See, for example, *New York Times*, November 6, 1986.

28. Hawari (whose real name was Abdallah Abd al-Hamid Labib) had belonged to the Baghdad-based May 15 organization headed by Husayn al-Umari (Abu Ibrahim), who left the PFLP in 1979. In 1982 Hawari was involved in bombing a U.S. airliner en route to Hawaii, killing one and injuring fourteen passengers. In December 1983 his group tried to blow up three airliners, and in January 1984 it attempted to bomb an El Al plane. The PLO worked in the late 1980s to block U.S. efforts to extradite a Hawari operative, Muhammad Rashid, from Greece for the 1982 bombing.

29. Abu Mazin's real name was Mahmud Abbas. He was a charter member of Fatah's Central Committee.

30. At the 1991 PNC, Ali Ishaq became the PLF's representative; Taysir Khalid was the delegate for Hawatmah's DFLP faction; and Abd Rabbu represented his own group. Arafat also controlled the 90-member Central Council which served under the Executive Committee. For a formalist but useful discussion of PLO structure, see Sami Mussalam, *The PLO* (Brattleboro, Vt., 1988).

31. Arafat's independent supporters on the eighteen-member Executive Committee as of 1993 included Elias Khuri, a Christian minister and the only non-Muslim; Jawad al-Ghusayn, head of finance and the Palestine National Fund; Abdallah Hourani, in charge of information; Mahmud Darwish, a poet and cultural chief who lived in France; and Jamil al-Surani, a veteran PLO negotiator and legal expert. Three new members chosen that year were Shafiq al-Hut, a PLO official in Beirut for many years; Muhammad Zuhdi al-Nashashibi, the Committee's

former secretary; and Yasir Amr, a veteran Fatah activist. Two members of the Committee elected in 1988 were not reelected in 1991: Muhammad Milhim, the Amman-based head of the PLO's Occupied Homeland Affairs Department, responsible for guiding and financing the struggle there; and Abd al-Razzaq Yahya, former PLO commander and representative in Jordan. Darwish and al-Hut left the Executive Committee in August 1993 to protest Arafat's management of the PLO and his peacemaking policy.

32. The August 1989 Fatah meeting in Tunisia elected eighteen Central Committee members. Some were relative hardliners: Qaddumi; Muhammad Ghana'im (Abu Mahir), Fatah's representative in Kuwait; Salim Za'nun, its delegate to the Gulf; and Brigadier Muhammad Jihad, a former Palestine Liberation Army officer who had briefly joined the 1983 revolt against Arafat. Intisar al-Wazir (Umm Jihad), Abu Jihad's ambitious widow, sometimes opposed Arafat (notably over control of intifada finances). High PLO officials said that Arafat opposed the election of al-Wazir and Umm Jihad. Abu Iyad and Abbas Zaki, PLO director of Arab and foreign relations responsible for armed operations through Amman, supported Arafat but had their own factional loyalty. The same could be said of Khalid and Hani al-Hasan. The other nine members were reliable Arafat supporters: Arafat himself; Abu Mazin; Hakim Bal'awi (Abu Marwan), the PLO's veteran representative in Tunisia and one of Arafat's closest lieutenants; PLO security man and head of the Western Sector, Abd al-Hamid Ha'il (Abu al-Hawl); Palestine Liberation Army officer Colonel Nasir Yusuf; Subhi Abu Qirsh (Abu al-Mundhir), former aide to Abu Jihad and deputy PLO representative in Saudi Arabia; Sakhr Abu Nazir, secretary of Fatah's Revolutionary Committee; Ahmad Khuri (Abu Ala), director-general of the PLO economic department; and Abu al-Tayyib Abd al-Rahim, PLO ambassador to Yugoslavia and later Jordan. The only active member not reelected was PLO envoy in Saudi Arabia, Rafiq al-Natsha (Abu Shakir), who voted against the 1988 PNC political resolution and attacked Arafat's policy at the Fatah congress. For Arafat's complaint, see *al-Majalla*, April 5–11, 1989 (*FBIS*, April 7, 1989, pp. 1–8).

33. The PFLP voted against the key provision in the 1988 PNC resolution; the PFLP, DFLP, and PLF openly continued terrorist attacks against Israel and rejected Arafat's Geneva statements, which made possible the dialogue with the United States, as unauthorized and non-binding on the PLO.

34. See, for example, *al-Anba*, February 1, 1989 (*FBIS*, February 15, 1989, pp. 13–15). For a Fatah critique of the DFLP, see Abu Mazin's open

letter to Hawatmah, *al-Anba*, March 2, 1989 (*FBIS*, March 10, 1989, pp. 14–15). See also Middle East News Agency, April 2, 1989 (*FBIS*, April 3, 1989, p. 3); Voice of the PLO (Baghdad), April 5, 1989 (*FBIS*, April 6, 1989, p. 11); and Khaled Abu Toameh, "Now We Don't Rely on Outsiders," *Jerusalem Report*, December 13, 1990, pp. 11–12.

35. He headed one of the three PLF factions. The others were those of Tal'at Ya'qub in Syria and of Abd al-Fattah Ghanim in Libya. The PLF emerged from the PFLP-GC after Jibril supported Syria's 1976 attacks on the PLO in Lebanon. It entered the PNC in 1981 but split over whether to support the 1983 anti-Arafat rebellion, with Abu al-Abbas backing Arafat.

36. Abd al-Rahim Ahmad, *al-Sharq al-Awsat*, October 3, 1989 (*FBIS*, October 11, 1989, p. 11). See also Abdallah Hourani's comments, *al-Majalla*, October 3, 1989 (*FBIS*, October 3, 1989, p. 3). For another PLO denial of an Abu Sharif statement, see *FBIS*, September 13, 1989, p. 7. Ahmad Abd al-Rahman was born in 1939 near Jerusalem. A University of Damascus graduate, he worked in the PLO's early radio station and became editor of *Filastin al-Thawra* in 1973.

37. This general breakdown of population figures is not exact, of course, and many Palestinians also live in the Western Hemisphere. Palestinians in Kuwait included both refugees and West Bank residents, most of whom went to Jordan after the 1991 Gulf War when Kuwait expelled them. Palestinians in large numbers were never welcome in Saudi Arabia or Egypt.

38. In 1971 Israel Defense Minister Moshe Dayan wanted to let West Bank and Gaza delegates attend the PNC. Prime Minister Golda Meir refused. The deportee closest to Arafat was Akram Haniyya, a Fatah activist who had been publisher of the PLO-subsidized East Jerusalem newspaper *al-Sha'b* and headed the Arab Journalists Association between 1983 and 1985. Israel expelled him from the West Bank in January 1987.

39. *JPS*, Spring 1977. "The Zionist enemy, which brings in Jews from all over the world to occupied Palestine, realizes that permitting the return of the Arabs to Palestine will destroy the ideological foundation of Zionism." *Ukaz*, August 24, 1981. When all Palestinians, Qadhafi explained, "are returned to their properties and homeland in occupied Palestine . . . there will be no more Israel." Interview, Barbara Walters, January 23, 1989, p. 7; Abu Iyad in interview with author, August 1989.

40. *Mideast Mirror*, March 19, 1990. The Central Committee failed to agree on a third candidate but was said to favor Colonel Abu al-Mu'tasim

(Ahmad Affana), a military aide to Arafat and leader of the Western Sector. Franji went to West Germany in 1963 to study medicine and, with Hani al-Hasan, set up student and labor groups there. During the 1967 war he was imprisoned a year in Israel, returned to Germany, and was one of 270 Palestinians deported after the 1968 killing of Israeli athletes in Munich but was allowed back again in 1974. Sha'th, chairman of the PNC's Political Committee since 1971, went to Egypt in 1948, earned a doctorate in economics at the University of Pennsylvania Wharton School, and taught there. He was dean of business administration at the American University of Beirut and headed the National Institute of Management Development in Cairo from 1963 to 1969. He was president of the Arab world's largest consulting and training company. The larger, lower-level Fatah Revolutionary Council reportedly added twenty deportees to its membership. On the membership of the Fatah Central Committee, see note 31, above.

41. *Al-Fajr,* September 12, 1986.
42. *Al-Ahram,* September 10, 1989, p. 5 (*FBIS,* September 13, 1989, p. 8). Leading notables in Gaza included: Fayiz Abu Rahma, head of the bar association and Abu Jihad's brother-in-law; Dr. Zakariyya al-Agha, head of the Gaza Medical Association; Dr. Hatim Abu Ghazala; lawyer Zuhayr al-Rayiss, a veteran nationalist; Khalid al-Qudra of the bar association; As'ad al-Siftawi, an independent-minded Fatah supporter; Mansur al-Shawwa, son of the late political boss; and Haydar Abd al-Shafi, a respected hardline elder statesman. In the West Bank, they included: Faysal al-Husayni, see below; Radwan Abu Ayyash, one of the few refugees in the West Bank leadership, head of the Arab Journalists Association; Hanna Siniora, the (Christian) editor of the pro-PLO newspaper *al-Fajr;* Ziyad Abu Ziyad, editor of a Palestinian Hebrew-language newspaper; the Communist Ghassan al-Khatib, a lecturer at Bir Zayt college; Jamil al-Tarifi, a former deputy mayor; Ghassan al-Shak'a, from a leading Nablus family; and pro-Jordan notables Elias Freij (Christian) mayor of Bethlehem, and Sa'id Kan'an, a Nablus businessman, as well as Muhammad Nasir, an independent political strongman in Hebron. Two West Bankers who became very important members of the negotiating team were Hanan Ashrawi and Sa'ib Arakat, both professors at Bir Zayt.
43. Radio Monte Carlo, December 7, 1989 (*FBIS,* December 8, 1989, p. 5).
44. *New York Times,* March 9, 1986.
45. Emile Sahliyeh, *In Search of Leadership: West Bank Politics since 1967* (Washington, D.C., 1988), and Moshe Maoz, *Palestinian Leadership on the West Bank* (London, 1984).

46. *Washington Post,* September 21, 1987. His ally Hanna Siniora's two cars were burned when he announced plans—quickly withdrawn—to run for Jerusalem's city council on a nationalist platform.

47. Voice of Palestine (Sanaa), March 30, 1989 (*FBIS,* March 31, 1989, pp. 6–8); Arafat, January 1973, *JPS,* Vol. 2, No. 3 (Spring 1973), p. 168.

48. *Mideast Mirror,* November 27, 1989, p. 25.

49. Ex-Israeli Arabs in the PLO hierarchy included Imad Shakur, Muhammad Darwish, and Palestine Research Center director Sabri Jiryis. While writing from a PLO perspective very critical of Israel, Jiryis was the first PLO figure to propose a compromise peace. Elie Rekhess, "Arabs in a Jewish State: Images vs. Realities," *Middle East Insight,* January-February 1990.

50. Arafat in *Middle East,* May 1983; "From our perspective," Jordan's Crown Prince Hasan insisted, these "Palestinians are Jordanian citizens." Hasan was referring to a U.S. report estimating that there were 1.2 million Palestinians in Jordan. Speech to Washington Institute for Near East Policy, September 12, 1989.

51. Steinberg, "The Pragmatic Stream of Thought," p. 45; *al-Fajr,* June 24, 1991.

52. Aharon Levran et al., *The Middle East Military Balance, 1987–88* (Boulder, Co., 1988), p. 362. Abu Iyad claimed that 1800 cadres had left Syria, refusing to support the anti-Arafat revolt, and that seven of ten rebel leaders were no longer active. *Al-Tadamun,* September 11, 1989 (*FBIS,* September 15, 1989, p. 5).

53. On the rise of this phenomenon, see Barry Rubin, *Islamic Fundamentalism in Egyptian Politics* (New York, 1991), and *Paved with Good Intentions: The American Experience and Iran* (New York, 1980).

54. Robert Satloff, "Islam in the Palestinian Uprising," Washington Institute for Near East Policy, *Policy Focus* series No. 7 (October 1988); Daoud Kuttab, *al-Fajr,* September 27, 1987. An interesting case was As'ad al-Siftawi, an UNRWA teacher and pro-Fatah activist in Gaza jailed between 1969 and 1974, who had been close to the Muslim Brotherhood in the 1950s. His sons, Imad and Ala, were active Islamic fundamentalist radicals. The PLO tried to portray Hamas as Israeli agents, fostered by the authorities in order to stymie it. See, for example, *Filastin al-Thawra,* July 8, 1990 (*FBIS,* August 9, 1990, pp. 7–15). As'ad al-Siftawi, a strong advocate of the Israel–PLO agreement, was murdered, probably in a Fatah power struggle, on October 21, 1993.

55. According to one report, Arafat only offered eighteen seats, about 4 percent of total. *Jordan Times,* October 3–4, 1991.

9. Turning Points and Sticking Points

1. *The Middle East,* June 1979, p. 14; Malcolm Kerr, "American Middle East Policy: Kissinger, Carter and the Future," *Institute for Palestine Studies Paper* #14, 1980, pp. 7–8, 27.
2. Edward Said, *The Palestine Question and the American Context* (Institute for Palestine Studies, Beirut, 1979), p. 17.
3. John Campbell, "The Middle East: A House of Containment Built on Shifting Sands," *Foreign Affairs,* Vol. 60, No. 3 (1981), p. 626.
4. I. William Zartman, "Power of American Purposes," *The Middle East Journal,* Spring 1981, pp. 165–166.
5. David Lamb, *Los Angeles Times,* July 14, 1985; William E. Smith, "Plight of the Moderates," *Time,* June 16, 1986, p. 19.
6. Robert Lacey, "Saudi Arabia: A More Visible Role," *The World Today,* January 1982, p. 11; Udo Steinbach, "The Iranian–Iraqi Conflict and Its Impact Upon the 'Arc of Crisis,'" *Journal of South Asian and Middle East Studies,* Summer 1983, p. 15.
7. For a broader discussion of these issues, see Barry Rubin, *Cauldron of Turmoil: America in the Middle East* (New York, 1992).
8. Testimony, House of Representatives Foreign Affairs Committee, March 6, 1986.
9. Kerr, "American Middle East Policy," p. 11. Its worst setback came from the revolution in non-Arab Iran, where the Arab–Israeli conflict was—at most—a marginal concern.
10. The PLO and radical regimes saw the USSR as a model for development, an enemy of the rulers against whom they rebelled, and an ally helpful in achieving their ambitions. Nasir's alliance with Moscow took place shortly after the United States saved his regime in 1956, preventing its own allies—Britain, France, and Israel—from overthrowing him. The Soviet regional position was strongest in the early 1960s, when the Arab–Israeli conflict was quiescent. Syria and Iraq sided with the USSR in exchange for its support against neighbors and such huge material benefits as virtually free loans, military advisers, and large amounts of arms.
11. Presidents only risk prestige and spend political capital when sensing a reasonable chance for success on a problem, given the number of other pressing or promising issues. As long as the PLO sought to destroy Israel through a terrorist, anti-American strategy, there could be no settlement with the PLO just as there could be none without it. Before engaging in any effort, commented Secretary of State George Shultz, "I should have at least a 0.1 probability of accomplishing something." *Washington Post,* January 6, 1989. Shultz spoke from experi-

ence. In his 1982 Senate confirmation hearings, he made resolving the conflict his top priority. But the PLO, Israel, Jordan, and others were less cooperative than he had been led to expect. U.S. mediation efforts in 1982–1983, 1985–1986, and 1988–1990 ended in failure as both sides pulled back from private promises or public hints of flexibility. Progress was possible only when the parties in the dispute were ready to take the necessary steps. Otherwise, the United States had neither the stake nor ability to break the deadlock. For a history of U.S. policymaking, see Barry Rubin, *Secrets of State: The State Department and the Struggle over U.S. Foreign Policy* (New York, 1985), and William Quandt, *Peace Process* (Washington, D.C., 1993).

12. "Yassir [sic] Arafat," *Third World Quarterly*, Vol. 8, No. 2 (April 1986).

13. Interview with *al-Anba* (*FBIS*, October 19, 1989). For the PLO's response, see Abd Rabbu in *al-Quds al-Arabi*, October 13, 1989 (*FBIS*, October 19, 1989, p. 6).

14. Terrorism was a particular cause of friction. Even on the eve of the U.S.–PLO dialogue in 1988, the PLO was blocking the extradition from Greece of Muhammad Rashid for bombing a U.S. airliner and killing a passenger. Rashid's boss, Colonel Hawari, a close associate of Arafat, had been convicted in court for attacking U.S. targets, including another bombing which killed four Americans, one an infant. The State Department denied Arafat himself a visa based on his direct involvement in attacks on Americans. Two years later, a terrorist act by a PLO member group, which the organization refused to denounce, destroyed the dialogue. See, for example, *Washington Post*, March 3, 1988.

15. *Al-Anba* interview.

16. Abd al-Bari Atwan, "Counter Storm?" *al-Quds al-Arabi*, September 16, 1991 (*FBIS*, September 19, 1991, p. 4.). On Abu Iyad, see *al-Madina*, July 7, 1989 (*FBIS*, July 19, 1989, p. 1); *al-Anba*, April 12, 1990 (*FBIS*, April 19, 1990, p. 5).

17. Harkabi, *The Palestinian Covenant*, p. 73.

18. Interview with author in Tunis, August 13, 1989.

19. *Al-Quds al-Arabi*, January 7, 1993 (*FBIS*, January 12, p. 10).

20. *FBIS*, December 28, 1988, p. 1.

21. Edward Said, *The Palestine Question and the American Context* (Institute for Palestine Studies, Beirut, 1979), p. 12; "Year-Old Palestinian Uprising Will Continue—Arafat," Reuters, December 9, 1988.

22. Voice of the PLO (Baghdad), January 26, 1989 (*FBIS*, January 30, 1989, p. 6); *al-Siyasa*, January 30, 1989 (*FBIS*, February 1, 1989, p. 4); *al-Dustur*, November 17, 1988 (*FBIS*, November 17, 1988, p. 4).

23. *Al-Quds al-Arabi*, February 12, 1990 (*Middle East Mirror*, February 12, 1990).

24. *Al-Anba,* September 19, 1989 (*FBIS,* September 22, 1989, p. 7).
25. Steinberg, "The Pragmatic Stream of Thought"; *al-Qabas,* October 3, 1989 (*FBIS,* October 5, 1989, p. 2).
26. *Rude Pravo* (Prague), October 21, 1989 (*FBIS,* October 26, 1989). See also Qaddumi, WAFA news agency, *Mideast Mirror,* December 17, 1991; M. Y. S. Haddad, *Arab Perspectives of Judaism,* pp. 341, 355. A PLO educational and cultural official, Ahmad Sidqi al-Dajani, said that the Palestinian people had absorbed whatever Jews were there in ancient times. The remaining ones were descendants of European Turkish Khazar tribes who never had anything to do with Palestine. *Al-Khalij,* August 31, 1988. Others may believe the "nonsense story in the Torah" about Jews being from Palestine, "but we know this is false." Dr. Ahmad Susa and Muhammad Khalifa, *al-Watan,* September 2, 1988.
27. The PLO opposed Soviet Jewish migration to Israel as strengthening the state and blocking the return of Palestinian refugees. "If it is every Jew's right to immigrate" from the USSR, said Arafat in 1990. "Why don't they go to France? Why have the United States stopped Jewish immigration? Why must they only come to Palestine?" Reuters, February 26, 1990. Abu Mazin said, "This goes to show what a bankrupt movement Zionism is; it is seeking to gather Jews in Palestine using coercion and terror." *Al-Siyasa,* November 18, 1989 (*FBIS,* November 22, 1989, p. 2). Rafiq al-Natsha, PLO representative in Saudi Arabia, said, "Every Jew should stay in the nation he belongs to. Likewise, the Soviet Jews should stay in their nation." *Saudi Gazette,* November 1, 1990. Arafat called the movement "not emigration, but forced expulsion." Amman Television, April 25, 1990 (*FBIS,* April 27, 1990, pp. 3, 7). "Palestine is now occupied by 3.4 million Israelis," Arafat said in 1990. "How can the United Nations and the superpowers permit Israel to bring in Jews who have no link whatsoever with Palestine? I am not the only one to say this, but also the original Jews. They say that these people do not belong to the twelve tribes . . . So I say: Why not go to Canada, Latin America which has room, Australia." Algiers Television, March 22, 1990 (*FBIS,* March 23, 1990, pp. 4, 6). See also Voice of Palestine (Sanaa), February 27, 1990 (*FBIS,* March 2, 1990). The PLO portrayed Soviet Jewish emigration as a plan to populate the West Bank, expel the Palestinians, and begin Israel's next step in seizing more land from neighboring Arab states. As Haddad summarized Arab thinking, "The more people immigrate to Israel the more there is need for territory and the greater the wish to expand." M. Y. S. Haddad, *Arab Perspectives of Judaism,* p. 434.
28. Matti Steinberg, "The Demographic Dimension of the Struggle with Israel—as Seen by the PLO," *Jerusalem Journal of International Relations,* Vol. 11, No. 4 (1989); *al-Watan,* October 13, 1989 (*FBIS,* October 17,

1989). The PLO's intellectual journal called Zionism the main cause of modern antisemitism which Nabil Amr, PLO representative in Moscow, designated "a Zionist invention designed to justify Israeli policies and blackmail the societies where there are Jewish minorities." *Al-Majalla*, March 13, 1990. Abd al-Wahab Muhammad al-Masiri, "The Phenomenon of Antisemitism between Evidence and Truth," *Shu'un Filastiniyya*, December 1991, pp. 72–92.

29. *Al-Qabas al-Duwali*, May 19, 1990 (*FBIS*, May 30, 1990, pp. 12–13).

30. *JPS*, Vol. 11, No. 2 (Winter 1982), pp. 4–5, 12–13. Jamal al-Surani, *al-Sharq al-Awsat*, February 8, 1990 (*FBIS*, February 9, 1990, p. 4). Such statements continue to be made frequently. See, for example, Arafat to *al-Anba*, March 12, 1990 (*FBIS*, March 14, 1990). In an interview with the author, in July 1989, Khalid al-Hasan repeated the story that a map in Israel's parliament claimed a Jewish state of the same dimensions. Incidentally, in the Jewish Bible the lands between the Nile and Euphrates are promised not to the Jews but to Abraham's descendants, who include the children of Ishmael, thus to both the Jews and the Arabs.

31. Khan Yunis area Fatah leaflet, responding to Hamas leaflet of January 21, 1992. On Hamas' view see, for example, *al-Ribat*, September 24, 1991 (*FBIS*, October 17, 1991, pp. 3–5).

32. Abu Iyad, Voice of the PLO (Baghdad), April 28, 1988 (*FBIS*, April 29, 1988, p. 43). On the Holocaust, Arafat said in 1989, "The Jews suffered, the Europeans suffered under that barbarism. But we Palestinians have been paying the price for the last 42 years." *Berlingske Tidende Sondag*, March 26, 1989 (*FBIS*, April 4, 1989). Abu Iyad complained in 1989, "The [German] position is being subjected to Zionist blackmail, given the guilt complex resulting from the Nazi era and the German attitude toward the Jews." *al-Yawm*, February 5, 1989 (*FBIS*, February 10, 1989, p. 7). For Arafat's statement on the camps, see *La Stampa*, February 16, 1988, p. 4.

33. *Al-Akhbar*, January 12, 1988 (*FBIS*, January 15, 1988, p. 8).

34. Amman Television, April 25, 1990 (*FBIS*, April 27, 1990, p. 7); Voice of the PLO (Baghdad), March 9, 1989 (*FBIS*, March 10, 1989, pp. 4–5.); Unified National Leadership of the Uprising, Call No. 21. Text, *FBIS*, July 8, 1988, pp. 5–6. See also Call No. 36, text, *FBIS*, March 16, 1989, p. 7.

35. *Al-Quds al-Arabi*, February 18, 1992 (*FBIS*, February 21, 1992, p. 8.)

36. Tape broadcast by CNN, February 11, 1992.

37. *Al-Qabas*, November 28, 1989. A number of activists from PLO groups, including Fatah, chose as a nom de guerre Hitler or Abu Hitler, including Fawzi Salim Ali Mahdi, a senior Force-17 official. A Force-17

member in Lebanon, Ian Michael Davison, was a British neo-Nazi who participated in the 1985 Force-17 murder of three Israelis in Cyprus. German neo-Nazi groups, most importantly that of Karl-Heinz Hoffman, were trained by Fatah in Lebanon. PLO officials in Europe were also involved in helping neo-Nazi groups some of which carried out anti-Israel terrorist acts. *Der Spiegel*, July 17, 1981; *Der Tag*, July 19, 1985; *The Observer*, February 5, 1989. These associations showed the PLO's insensitivity to their implications.

38. Salah Khalaf (Abu Iyad), "Lowering the Sword," *Foreign Policy*, Vol. 78 (Spring 1990), pp. 92–112.

39. *Los Angeles Times*, July 28, 1985.

40. U.S. Department of State, "Principles and Pragmatism: American Policy toward the Arab–Israeli Conflict," *Current Policy*, No. 1176.

41. Shamir, *al-Ahram*, October 8, 1988, p. 5 (*FBIS*, October 13, 1988, p. 34).

42. *Al-Akhbar*, September 22, 1989, pp. 3 and 8 (*FBIS*, September 25, 1989, pp. 1–5). *Al-Ra'y*, October 10, 1989, pp. 1 and 16 (*FBIS*, October 11, 1989, pp. 4–6).

43. *Jordan Times*, February 23, 1991; *New York Times*, January 21, 1991.

44. Al-Hallaj in Rubenberg, *The Palestinian Liberation Organization*.

10. Breaking the Mold, 1991–1993

1. Jordan television, October 31, 1991 (*FBIS*, November 1, 1991, pp. 1–4).

2. Ibid.

3. Notes of the May 17, 1939, meeting in Foreign Office file 371/6/31, Miles Lampson to Foreign Office, British Public Records Office.

4. Arafat, January 1973, *JPS*, Vol. 2, No. 3 (Spring 1973), p. 167.

5. Ironically, PLO leaders and supporters often denied themselves the argument that their policy had evolved over time by claiming that it remained the same as always, disavowing any intention of ever destroying Israel or using terrorism—at least after 1974. Aside from contradicting the massive weight of PLO documents and speeches, this contention could not explain why it took the organization until, at least, late 1988 to articulate such changes and until 1991 to do so clearly.

6. Speech on Fatah's anniversary, Voice of Palestine (Algiers), December 31, 1992 (*FBIS*, January 4, 1993, p. 1). According to a study by the Arab Monetary Fund, the 1990–91 Kuwait crisis cost Arab states an estimated $676 billion in losses or damages, threw hundreds of thou-

sands out of work, and retarded economic development. *New York Times*, April 25, 1993.

7. Monte Carlo Radio, January 12, 1992 (*FBIS*, January 13, 1992, p. 6).
8. *New York Times*, April 4, 1991.
9. Algerian Television, October 4, 1991 (*FBIS*, October 7, 1991, p. 5).
10. Speech of June 1, 1993, text in *Middle East Mirror*, June 2, 1993, p. 22.
11. *JPS*, Vol. 22, No. 1 (Autumn 1992), p. 39.
12. *Sawt al-Kuwait al-Duwali*, April 12, 1991 (*FBIS*, April 17, 1991).
13. Abd Rabbu on Jordanian television, September 26, 1991 (*FBIS*, September 27, 1991), p. 1.
14. Voice of Palestine, September 22, 1991 (*FBIS*, September 24, 1991, pp. 1–5)
15. *Al-Sharq al-Awsat*, October 27, 1991 (*FBIS*, October 28, 1991).
16. Political Communique, *al-Dustur*, September 29, 1991 (*FBIS*, September 30, 1991), pp. 1–5
17. *New York Times*, October 23, 1991.
18. Voice of Palestine (Algiers), September 29, 1991 (*FBIS*, September 30, 1991).
19. October 31, 1991 (*FBIS*, November 1, 1991, pp. 1–4).
20. Ibid.
21. *Al-Quds*, March 4, 1993 (*FBIS*, March 5, 1993), p. 5
22. For Husayni's view see, for example, his interview with Middle East Television, March 10, 1993 (*FBIS*, March 11, 1993).
23. Steinberg, "The Pragmatic Stream," p. 48; *Shu'un Filastiniyya*, February 22, 1990.
24. *Al-Shira'*, January 11, 1993 (*FBIS*, January 22, 1993, pp. 10–11).
25. *JPS*, Vol. 22, No. 1 (Autumn 1992), pp. 37–66.
26. Middle East News Agency, October 12, 1989 (*FBIS*, October 13, 1989, p. 2).
27. *Jerusalem Post*, August 25, 1993.
28. On Hamas's rejection of the PNC resolutions and decision to go to Madrid see, for example, *al-Ribat*, September 24, 1991 (*FBIS*, October 17, 1991, pp. 3–5); Ghawshah, *al-Sharq al-Awsat*, January 2, 1993 (*FBIS*, January 7, 1993, p. 5). Al-Rantisi, *Sawt al-Sha'b*, February 17, 1993 (*FBIS*, February 19, 1993); *al-Dustur*, January 25, 1993 (*FBIS*, January 26, 1993, p. 5). *Al-Sharq al-Awsat*, January 5, 1993 (*FBIS*, January 5, 1993, p. 4).
29. Videotape address to International Center for Peace in the Middle East symposium, February 22, 1989.
30. *Al-Anba*, April 5, 1989 (*FBIS*, April 7, 1989, p. 9); speech, December 11, 1989, text in *Middle East Mirror*, December 12, 1989.
31. *New York Times*, September 12, 1993.

32. *Mideast Mirror,* September 13, 1993, p. 27.
33. *International Herald Tribune,* August 25, 1993. Lt. Col. Munir Maqda, commander of Fatah's forces in Lebanon, called for Arafat's resignation. *Mideast Mirror,* September 13, 1993, p. 27.
34. Text of speech in *Jerusalem Post,* August 31, 1993.
35. Interviews; *Yediot Aharnot,* September 3, 1993; *New York Times,* September 5, 1993; *International Herald Tribune,* September 1 and 11–12, 1993; *Time,* September 13, 1993; *Jerusalem Report,* September 23, 1993.
36. Ibid.
37. Article in *al-Ahram* cited in *Mideast Mirror,* September 8, 1993, pp. 18–19.
38. Ibid.
39. *International Herald Tribune,* September 6, 1993.
40. Sarid cited in *Jerusalem Post,* August 30, 1993.
41. The text is presented in Government of Israel, *Declaration of Principles on Interim Self-Government Arrangements* (Jerusalem, September 1993), pp. 13–29. It was also published in *Yediot Aharnot,* August 31, 1993, and *Mideast Mirror,* September 1, 1993, with excerpts in *International Herald Tribune,* September 1, 1993.
42. *Jerusalem Post,* August 31, 1993.
43. Although no official tally was released, it seems that those in favor were: Arafat and Abu Mazin from Fatah; the delegates from the DFLP of Abd Rabbu, the PPSF, and the Communist party; and four independents—Surani, Ghusayn, Amr, and Nashashibi. Those opposed were the representatives of the ALF and PLF plus the independent Hourani. Two members—Shafiq al-Hut and Darwish—had already quit the Committee, the PFLP boycotted the meeting, and the DFLP-Hawatmah delegate walked out. Khuri, an independent member who supported Arafat, was ill, and Qaddumi abstained. Thus, if all 18 members had voted, the result would presumably have been a very close 10 to 8 in favor. For a discussion of the Executive Committee membership, see Chapter 8.
44. *Jerusalem Post,* September 10, 1993. For the text of the letters see *International Herald Tribune,* September 10, 1993, and Government of Israel, *Declaration of Principles.*
45. Among others, Arafat took with him Abd Rabbu, Abu Mazin, Yasir Amr, Jawad Ghusayn, Abu Ala, Hakim Bal'awi, Hasan Abu-Rahman, Nabil Sha'th, and Akram Haniyya.
46. It was Arafat's first trip to the United States since addressing the United Nations in 1974. In Washington, Arafat met with members of Congress, asking them to revoke laws barring U.S. aid or contacts with

PLO. He then flew to New York to be warmly received at UN headquarters.

47. *Jerusalem Post,* September 12, 1993.
48. Darwish and Hut had suspended their membership in the Executive Committee in August, and Hut resigned as PLO representative to Lebanon in September. See *Mideast Mirror,* August 23, 1993, pp. 9–12. For Darwish's critique of the agreement, see his article in *al-Hayat* translated in *Mideast Mirror,* September 1, 1993, pp. 16–17. For Hourani's view, see *Mideast Mirror,* September 9, 1993, pp. 10–11. Qaddumi's statement is in *Mideast Mirror,* September 10, 1993, p. 21.
49. *Mideast Mirror,* September 10, 1993, p. 22, and September 1, 1993, p. 21.
50. Interview with Judy Colp Rubin, September 12, 1993.
51. *Mideast Mirror,* September 2, 1993, p. 11.
52. *Mideast Mirror,* August 25, 1993, p. 13.
53. Interview by Judy Colp Rubin, September 12, 1993.
54. *The Economist,* "Return to an Unknown Namibia," September 23, 1989, p. 45. The Zionist model was the reverse: its inside forces, led by David Ben-Gurion, wrested power from the outside forces, led by Chaim Weizmann. Weizmann then became the country's revered, but powerless, president.
55. Speech, December 11, 1989, text, *Mideast Mirror,* December 12, 1989.
56. For optimistic assessments of how a Palestinian state could work, see, Walid Khalidi, "Thinking the Unthinkable," *Foreign Affairs,* Vol. 56, No. 4, (July 1978), pp. 695–713; Mark Heller, *A Palestinian State: The Implications for* Israel (Cambridge, Mass., 1983); Mark Heller and Sari Nusseibeh, *No Trumpets, No Drums* (New York, 1991).
57. For an analysis of governance in Third World nations, see Barry Rubin, *Modern Dictators.*
58. Abd al-Rahman Rashid wrote in the Saudi weekly *al-Majalla* about the potential parallel with Afghanistan where the fighters "ignored all potential differences because they felt these could divert their attention from their top priority: driving the Communists out." As a result, "More Afghans have been killed by Afghans since the liberation than were killed by Communists before it."
59. *International Herald Tribune,* September 8, 1993.
60. Interview, "Sixty Minutes" program, February 19, 1989.

> Selected Bibliography

In addition to those sources cited in the text, this book is based on many interviews with PLO leaders and activists conducted in Algeria, Jordan, Lebanon, Syria, Tunisia, and the West Bank.

Books

Adams, James. *The Financing of Terror.* New York, 1986.

Ajami, Fouad. *The Arab Predicament: Arab Political Thought and Practice since 1967.* Cambridge, Mass., 1981.

———— *The Vanished Imam: Musa al Sadr and the Shia of Lebanon.* Ithaca, N.Y., 1986.

Alexander, Yonah, and Joshua Sinai. *Terrorism: The PLO Connection.* Washington, D.C., 1989.

American Enterprise Institute. *A Conversation with the Exiled West Bank Mayors: A Palestinian Point of View.* Washington, D.C., 1981.

Amos, John. *Palestinian Resistance: Organization of a National Movement.* New York, 1980.

Arian, Asher, and Raphael Ventura. "Public Opinion in Israel and the Intifada: Changes in Security Attitudes 1987–88," *JCSS Memorandum No. 28*, August 1989.

Aruri, Naseer, ed. *The Palestinian Resistance to Israeli Occupation.* Wilmette, Ill., 1970.

Bailey, Clinton. *Jordan's Palestine Challenge, 1948–1983: A Political History.* Boulder, Co., 1984.

Barnea, Amalia and Aharon. *Mine Enemy.* New York, 1988.

Bechor, Guy. *Lexicon Ashaf.* Tel Aviv, 1991.

Becker, Jillian. *The PLO.* New York, 1984.

Ben-Dor, Gabriel, ed. *The Palestinians and the Middle East Conflict.* Ramat Gan, 1978.

Brand, Laurie A. *Palestinians in the Arab World: Institution Building and the Search for a State.* New York, 1988.

Buehrig, Edward Henry. *The U.N. and Palestinian Refugees: A Study in Non-Territorial Administration.* Bloomington, Ind., 1971.

Carre, Olivier. *L'Ideologie Palestinienne De Resistance.* Paris, 1972.

———— *Le Mouvement National Palestinien.* Paris, 1977.

Chaliand, Gerard. *The Palestinian Resistance.* Harmondsworth, 1972.

Cobban, Helena. *The Palestinian Liberation Organization: People, Power and Politics.* New York, 1984.

Committee for the Defense of Political Prisoners in Israeli Jails. *Israeli Political Prisoners.* Beirut, 1979.

Cooley, John K. *Green March, Black September.* London, 1973.

Dann, Uriel. *King Hussein and the Challenge of Arab Radicalism, Jordan, 1955–1967.* New York, 1969.

Dobson, Christopher. *Black September: Its Short, Violent History.* London, 1975.

Fallaci, Oriana. *Interview with History.* Boston, Mass., 1977.

Fath. *La Revolution Palestinienne et les Juifs.* Paris, 1970.

Frangi, Abdallah. *The PLO and Palestine.* London, 1983.

Gabriel, Richard A. *Operation Peace for Galilee: The Israeli–PLO War in Lebanon.* New York, 1985.

Golan, Galia. *The Soviet Union and the Palestine Liberation Organization.* New York, 1980.

Gowers, Andrew, and Tony Walker. *Behind the Myth: Yasir Arafat and the Palestinian Revolution.* London, 1992.

Gresh, Alain. *The PLO: The Struggle Within.* London, 1985.

Haddad, M.Y.S. *Arab Perspectives of Judaism.* The Hague, 1984.

abdel Hamid, Dina. *Duet for Freedom.* London, 1988.

Harkabi, Yehoshafat. *Fedayeen Action and Arab Strategy.* London, 1968.

—————— *Palestinians and Israel.* Jerusalem, 1974.

—————— *The Palestinian Covenant and Its Meaning.* London, 1979.

Hart, Alan. *Arafat, a Political Biography.* Bloomington, Ind., 1989.

Heller, Mark. *A Palestinian State: The Implications for Israel.* Cambridge, Mass., 1983.

—————— and Sari Nusseibah. *No Trumpets, No Drums.* New York, 1991.

Hirst, David. *The Gun and the Olive Branch.* London, 1977.

Hofstadter, Dan, ed. *Egypt and Nasser, Vol. 3: 1967–72.* New York, 1973.

Hourani, Albert. *Political Society in Lebanon: A Historical Introduction.* Cambridge, Mass., 1985.

Institute for Palestine Studies. *The Resistance of the Western Bank of Jordan to Israeli Occupation.* Beirut, 1967.

International Documents on Palestine, 1967–1982. Beirut, 1967-1982. (*IDOP*)

International Symposium on Palestine, *Palestine Discussion Papers.* 2 Vols. Kuwait, 1971.

Israeli, Raphael, ed. *PLO in Lebanon: Selected Documents.* London, 1983.

Jansen, Michael E. *The United States and the Palestinian People.* Beirut, 1970.

Joumblatt, Kamal, and Philippe Lapousterie. *I Speak for Lebanon.* London, 1982.

Jureidini, Paul, and William Hazen. *The Palestinian Movement in Politics.* Lexington, Ma., 1976.

Kadi, Leila S. *Arab Summit Conferences and the Palestinian Problem.* Beirut, 1966.

——— *Basic Political Documents of the Armed Palestinian Resistance Movement.* Beirut, 1969.

——— *The Arab–Israeli Conflict.* Beirut, 1973.

Kazziha, Walid. *Palestine in the Arab Dilemma.* Totowa, N.J.: 1979.

Kerr, Malcolm. *Arab Cold War, 1958–1970: Gamal Abd al-Nasir and His Rivals.* 2nd ed. London, 1971.

Khaled, Leila. *My People Shall Live.* London, 1973.

Khalidi, Rashid. *Under Siege.* New York, 1986.

Kiernan, Thomas. *Yasir Arafat: The Man and the Myth.* London, 1976.

Kirisci, Kemal. *The PLO and World Politics: A Study of the Mobilization and Support for the Palestinian Cause.* New York, 1986.

Laqueur, Walter. *The Age of Terrorism.* Boston, 1987.

——— *Confrontation: The Middle East and World Politics.* New York, 1974.

——— and Barry Rubin. *The Israel–Arab Reader.* New York, 1984.

Levran, Aharon, and Zeev Eytan. *The Middle East Military Balance, 1987–1988.* Boulder, Co., 1988.

Maoz, Moshe. *Palestinian Leadership on the West Bank: The Changing Role of the Mayors under Jordan and Israel.* London, 1984.

McLaurin, R. D., Mohammed Mughisuddin, and Abraham R. Wagner. *Foreign Policy Making in the Middle East.* New York, 1977.

Merari, Ariel, and Shlomo Elad. *The International Dimension of Palestinian Terrorism.* Boulder, Co., 1986.

Mickolus, Edward F. *Transnational Terrorism—A Chronology of Events, 1968–1979.* Westport, Ct., 1980.

Miller, Aaron David. *The Arab States and the Palestine Question: between Ideology and Self-Interest.* New York, 1986.

——— *The PLO and the Politics of Survival.* Washington, D.C., 1983.

Mishal, Shaul. *The PLO under Arafat.* New Haven, Ct., 1986.

——— *West Bank/East Bank: The Palestinians in Jordan, 1949–1967.* New Haven, Ct., 1978.

——— and Reuven Aharoni. *Avanim ze lo ha-Kol: Ha-intifada vay neshek ha-crozim.* Tel Aviv, 1989.

Moore, John Norton. *The Arab–Israeli Conflict.* 3 Vols. Princeton, N.J.

Muslih, Muhammad Y. *The Origins of Palestinian Nationalism.* New York, 1988.

Norton, Augustus Richard. *International Relations of the PLO.* Carbondale, Ill., 1989.

O'Ballance, Edgar. *Arab Guerrilla Power, 1967–1972.* Hamden, Ct., 1974.

O'Neill, Bard E. *Armed Struggle in Palestine: An Analysis of the Palestinian Guerrilla Movement.* Boulder, Co., 1978.

────── *Revolutionary Warfare in the Middle East: The Israelis vs. the Fedayeen.* Boulder, Co., 1974.

Palestine Liberation Organization Research Center. *Black September.* Beirut, 1971.

Peretz, Don. *A Palestine Entity.* Washington, D.C., 1970.

Porath, Y. *The Emergence of the Palestinian Arab National Movement, 1918–1929.* London, 1977.

────── *The Palestinian Arab National Movement, 1929–1939.* London, 1977.

Quandt, William B. *Camp David: Peacemaking and Politics.* Washington, D.C., 1986.

────── *Decade of Decisions: American Policy toward the Arab–Israeli Conflict, 1967–1976.* Berkekley, Cal., 1977.

────── *Palestinian Nationalism: Its Political and Military Dimensions.* Santa Monica, Cal., 1971.

────── *Peace Process.* Washington, D.C., 1993.

Quandt, William B., Fuad Jabber, and Ann Mosely Lesch. *The Politics of Palestinian Nationalism.* Berkeley, Cal., 1974.

Rabinovich, Itamar, and Hanna Zamir. *War and Crisis in Lebanon, 1975–1981.* New York, 1982.

Rayyis, Riyad Najib. *Guerrillas for Palestine.* New York, 1976.

Roth, Stephen J., ed. *The Impact of the Six-Day War.* New York, 1988.

Rubenberg, Cheryl. *The Palestine Liberation Organization, Its Institutional Infrastructure.* Belmont, Mass., 1983.

Rubin, Barry. *The Arab States and the Palestine Conflict.* Syracuse, N.Y., 1981.

────── *Cauldron of Turmoil: America in the Middle East.* New York, 1992.

────── *Inside the PLO: Officials, Notables, and Revolutionaries.* Policy Focus No. 12. Washington, D.C., 1989.

────── *Modern Dictators: Third World Coupmakers, Strongmen, and Populist Tyrants.* New York, 1987.

────── *The PLO's New Policy: Evolution until Victory?* Policy Paper No. 13. Washington, D.C., 1989.

────── *The PLO—A Declaration of Independence?* Policy Focus No. 8. Washington, D.C., 1988.

Sahliyeh, Emile F. *In Search of Leadership: West Bank Politics since 1967.* Washington, D.C., 1988.

────── *The PLO after the Lebanon War.* Boulder, Co., 1986.

Said, Edward. *The Question of Palestine.* New York, 1980.

────── *The Palestine Question and the American Context.* Beirut, 1979.

Sakhnini, Isam. *PLO, the Representative of the Palestinians.* Beirut, 1974.

Satloff, Robert. *Islam in the Palestinian Uprising.* Policy Focus No. 7. Washington, D.C., 1988.

———— *They Cannot Stop Our Tongues: Islamic Activism in Jordan.* Washington, D.C., 1986.

Schiff, Zeev. *Fedayeen: Guerrillas against Israel.* New York, 1972.

Scully, Eileen. *The PLO's Growing Latin American Base.* Washington, D.C., 1983.

Shadid, Mohammed. *The United States and the Palestinians.* London, 1981.

Shaked, Haim, and Daniel Dishon, eds., *Middle East Contemporary Survey, Vol. 8, 1983–84.* Boulder, Co., 1987.

———— and Itamar Rabinovich, eds. *Middle East Contemporary Survey, Vol. 9, 1984–85.* Boulder, Co., 1987.

————, Colin Legum, and Daniel Dishon, eds. *Middle East Contemporary Survey, Vol. 5, 1981–82.* New York, 1982.

———— *Middle East Contemporary Survey, Vol. 7, 1981–82.* New York, 1984.

———— *Middle East Contemporary Survey, Vol. 2, 1982–83.* New York, 1985.

Sharabi, Hisham. *Palestine Guerrillas, Their Credibility and Effectiveness.* Washington, D.C., 1970.

Shemesh, Moshe. *The Palestinian Entity, 1959–1974: Arab Politics and the PLO.* Totowa, N.J., 1989.

Shiff, Zeev, and Ehud Yaari. *Israel's Lebanon War.* New York, 1984.

Shuqayri, Ahmad. *Liberation, Not Negotiation.* Beirut, 1966.

Stephens, Robert. *Nasser: A Political Biography.* London, 1973.

Susser, Asher. *Double Jeopardy: PLO Strategy toward Jordan and Israel.* Washington, D.C., 1987.

Tessier, Arlette. *Gaza.* Beirut, 1971.

United Nations. *The Palestinian Refugees.* Beirut, 1970.

U.S. Department of Defense. *Terrorist Group Profiles.* Washington 1988.

U.S. Department of State. *Abu Nidal Organization.* Washington, D.C., 1988.

Wallach, John, and Janet Wallach. *In the Eyes of the Beholder.* New York, 1991.

Yaniv, Avner. *Dilemmas of Security: Politics, Strategy and the Israeli Experience in Lebanon.* New York, 1987.

Yodfat, Aryeh Y., and Yuval Arnon-Ohanna. *PLO Strategy and Politics.* New York, 1981.

Articles

Abu Khalil, As'ad. "Internal Contradictions in the PFLP: Decision Making and Policy Orientation." *Middle East Journal,* Vol. 41, No. 3 (Summer 1987), pp. 361–378.

Ajami, Fouad. "The Arab Road." *Foreign Policy,* No. 47 (Summer 1982).

———— "Stress in the Arab Triangle." *Foreign Policy,* No. 29 (Winter 1977–78).

———— "The Fate of Nonalignment." *Foreign Affairs,* Vol. 59, No. 2 (Winter 1980–81).

———— "The Struggle for Egypt's Soul." *Foreign Policy,* No. 35 (Summer 1979).

———— "Between Cairo and Damascus." *Foreign Affairs,* Vol. 54, No. 2 (April 1976), pp. 444–461.

———— "The End of the Affair: An American Tragedy in the Arab World." *Harper's Magazine,* Vol. 268 (June 1984), pp. 53–59.

———— "Lebanon and Its Inheritors." *Foreign Affairs,* Vol. 63 (Spring 1985), pp. 778–799.

———— "The Shadows of Hell." *Foreign Policy,* No. 48 (Fall 1982), pp. 94–110.

Altman, Israel. "The P.L.O." In Colin Legum, ed., *Arab Relations in the Middle East.* New York, 1979.

Amos, John. "The PLO: Millenium and Organization." In Peter Chelkowski and Robert Pranger, *Ideology and Power in the Middle East: Studies in Honor of George Lenczowski.* Durham, N.C., 1988.

Arafat, Yasir. "The Desirable, the Possible, the Acceptable." *Middle East,* No. 103 (May 1983), pp. 20–23.

———— "Playboy interview: Yasir Arafat." *Playboy,* Vol. 35 (September 1988), pp. 51–52, 56–59, 62–64, 66.

———— "The Way to Restoring the Violated Rights of the Palestinian People." *World Marxist Review* [Canada], Vol. 18, No. 2 (1975), pp. 123–132.

———— "Yasir Arafat: An interview." *Third World Quarterly,* Vol. 8 (April 1986), pp. 399–410.

Aruri, Naseer. "Palestinian Nationalism after Lebanon: The Current Impasse." *American Arab Affairs,* No. 8 (Spring 1984), pp. 54–65.

———— "The PLO and the Jordan Option." *Third World Quarterly,* Vol. 7 (October 1985), pp. 882–906.

Barakat, Halim. "Social Factors influencing Attitudes of University Students in Lebanon towards the Palestinian Resistance Movement." *Journal of Palestine Studies,* Vol. 1, No. 1 (Autumn 1971), pp. 87–112.

Bar-Haim, Sara. "The PLA: Stooge or Actor." In Gabriel Ben-Dor, ed., *The Palestinians and the Middle East Conflict.* Ramat Gan, 1978.

Beer, Eliezer. "The Emergence of Palestinian Arab Leadership: Husaini, Shuqairy, and Arafat." In Gabriel Ben-Dor, ed., *The Palestinians and the Middle East Conflict.* Ramat Gan, 1978.

Ben-Dor, Gabriel. "Nationalism without Sovereignty and Nationalism with Multiple Sovereignties: The Palestinians and intra-Arab Relations." In Gabriel Ben-Dor, ed., *The Palestinians and the Middle East Conflict.* Ramat Gan, 1978.

———— "The PLO and the Palestinians Following the Summer 1982 War in

Lebanon." In Israel Stockman Shomron, ed., *Israel, the Middle East, and the Great Powers.* Jerusalem, 1984.

Black, Ian. "Tunis Dilemma as PLO Lies Low." *The Guardian,* June 21, 1986.

Brand, Laurie A. "Palestinians in Syria: The Politics of integration." *Middle East Journal,* Vol. 42, No. 44 (Autumn 1988), pp. 621–637.

Browne, Donald R. "The Voices of Palestine: A Broadcasting House Divided." *Middle East Journal,* 29(2) (1975), pp. 133–150.

Cobban, Helena. "The PLO in the Mid-1980s: Between the Gun and the Olive Branch." *International Journal,* Vol. 38 (Autumn 1983), pp. 635–651.

Colvin, Marie. "The Ambiguous Yasir Arafat." *New York Times Magazine,* December 18, 1988, pp. 33–36, 60, 63, 66.

Cooley, John K. "China and the Palestinians." *Journal of Palestine Studies,* Vol. 1, No. 2 (Summer 1972), pp. 19–34.

―――― "Iran, the Palestinians, and the Gulf." *Foreign Affairs,* Vol. 57 (Summer 1979), pp. 1018–1034.

Cowell, Alan. "Through the Palestinian Labyrinth: A Key to the PLO and Its Rivals." *New York Times,* January 22, 1989 [Week in Review], p. 5.

Danziger, Raphael. "Algeria and the Palestinian Organizations." In Gabriel Ben-Dor, ed., *The Palestinians and the Middle East Conflict.* Ramat Gan, 1978.

Dawisha, Adeed. "Saudi Arabia and the Arab–Israeli Conflict: The Up and Downs of Pragmatic Moderation." *International Journal,* Vol. 38, No.4 (Autumn 1983), pp. 674–689.

Dhaher, Ahmad J. "Changing Cultural Perspectives of the Palestinians." *Journal of South Asian and Middle Eastern Studies,* Vol. 4 (Spring 1981), pp. 38–64.

Diskin, Abraham. "Trends in Intensity Variation of Palestinian Military Activity: 1967–1978." *Canadian Journal of Political Science,* Vol. 16 (June 1983), pp. 335–348.

Al-Fajr. Supplement on the PLO, May 30, 1986.

Franjieh, Samir. "How Revolutionary Is the Palestinian Resistance? A Marxist interpretation." *Journal of Palestine Studies,* Vol. 1, No. 2 (Summer 1972), pp. 52–60.

Freedman, Robert O. "A Talk with Arafat." *New York Review of Books,* Vol. 36 (April 13, 1989), pp. 8, 10.

Friedman, Thomas L. "West Bank Grows Critical of Arafat, But It's More from Love than Anger." *New York Times,* November 20, 1984, p. A8.

Garfinkle, Adam M. "Sources of the al-Fatah Mutiny." *Orbis,* Vol. 27 (Fall 1983), pp. 603–640.

Golan, Galia. "The Soviet Union and the PLO Since the War in Lebanon." *Middle East Journal,* Vol. 40 (Spring 1986), pp. 285–305.

Haddad, William. "Divided Lebanon." *Current History,* January 1982.

Hamid, Rashid. "What Is the PLO?" *Journal of Palestine Studies*, 4, No. 4. (Summer 1975), pp. 90–109.

Harkabi, Yehoshafat. "The Revised Palestine National Covenant (1968) and an Israeli Commentary Thereon." *New York University Journal of International Law and Politics*, Vol. 3, No. 1 (1970), pp. 209–243.

—— "The Palestinians in the Fifties and Their Awakening as Reflected in Their Literature." In Moshe Maoz, ed., *Palestinian Arab Politics*. Jerusalem, 1975.

Harris, Lillian Craig. "China's Relations with the PLO." *Journal of Palestine Studies*, Vol. 7 (Autumn 1977), pp. 123–154.

Hechiche, Abdelwahab. "Renaissance et Declin De La Resistance Palestinienne." *Politique Etrangere* [France], Vol. 38, No. 5 (1973), pp. 597–620.

Hoffman, Bruce. "The Plight of the Phoenix: The PLO Since Lebanon." *Conflict Quarterly*, Vol. 5 (Spring 1985), pp. 5–17.

Hudson, Michael C. "Developments and Setbacks in the Palestinian Resistance Movement, 1967–1971." *Journal of Palestine Studies*, Vol. 1, No. 3 (Spring 1972), pp. 64–84.

—— "The Palestinians after Lebanon." *Current History*, Vol. 84 (January 1985), pp. 16–20, 38–39.

—— "The Palestinians after Lebanon." *Current History*, Vol. 82 (January 1983), pp. 5–9, 34.

Ibrahim, Youssef M. "A Palestinian Revolution without the PLO." *New York Times*, February 14, 1988.

Ioannides, Christos P. "The PLO and the Iranian Revolution." *American–Arab Affairs*, No. 10 (Fall 1984), pp. 89–105.

Jenkins, Loren, and David B. Ottaway. "The Palestinians: Beyond Beirut." *Washington Post*, December 26, 1982, pp. A1, A36-A37; December 27, pp. A1, A16; December 28, p. A1, A8; December 29, pp. A1, A12.

Jiryis, Sabri. "On Political Settlement in the Middle East: The Palestinian Dimension." *Journal of Palestine Studies*, Vol. 7, No. 1 (Autumn 1977).

Kelman, Herbert C. "Talk with Arafat." *Foreign Policy*, No. 49 (Winter 1982–83), pp. 119–139.

Khalidi, Rashid. "The Resolutions of the 19th Palestine National Council." *Journal of Palestine Studies*, Winter 1990.

—— "Lebanon in the Context of Regional Politics: Palestinians and Syrian involvement in the Lebanese Crisis." *Third World Quarterly*, Vol. 7 (July 1985), pp. 495–514.

—— "Palestinian Politics after the Exodus from Beirut." In Robert O. Freedman, ed., *The Middle East after the Israeli invasion of Lebanon*, pp. 233–253. Syracuse, New York, 1986.

—— "The Palestinians in Lebanon: Social Repercussions of Israel's invasion." *Middle East Journal*, Vol. 38 (Spring 1984), pp. 255–266.

———— "The Asad Regime and the Palestinian Resistance." *Arab Studies Quarterly,* Vol. 6, No. 4 (Fall 1984).

Khalidi, Walid. "Regiopolitics: Toward a U.S. Policy on the Palestine Problem." *Foreign Affairs,* Vol. 59 (Summer 1981), pp. 1050–1063.

———— "Thinking the Unthinkable: A Sovereign Palestinian State." *Foreign Affairs,* Vol. 56 (July 1978), pp. 695–713.

el-Khazen, Farid. "The Rise and Fall of the PLO." *National Interest,* No. 10 (Win ter 1987–88), pp. 39–47.

Kifner, John. "For Arafat, Effort to Convene Palestinian Assembly Is a 'Matter of Survival,'" *New York Times,* November 9, 1984.

———— "For Arafat, Nothing Succeeds like Failure." *New York Times,* February 22, 1987.

———— "Hussein's Slap at the PLO." *New York Times,* August 2, 1988, pp. A1, A10.

———— "What Now for the PLO?" *New York Times,* August 3, 1988, pp. A1, A6.

Kuriyama, Yoshihiro. "Terrorism at Tel-Aviv Airport and a 'New Left' Group in Japan." *Asian Survey,* Vol. 13, No. 3 (1973), pp. 336–346.

Kurz, Anat. "Palestinian International Terrorism: Current Trends and Political Implications." In Anat Kurz, *Inter: International Terrorism in 1988.* Tel Aviv, 1989.

Kuttab, Daoud. "A Profile of the Stonethrowers." *Journal of Palestine Studies,* Vol. 17, No. 3 (Spring 1988).

Maoz, Moshe. "New Attitudes of the PLO Regarding Palestine and Israel?" In Gabriel Ben-Dor, ed., *The Palestinians and the Middle East Conflict.* Ramat Gan, 1978.

Markham, James M., et al. "The Palestinians." *New York Times,* February 19, 1978, pp. 1,16; February 20, pp. A1, A10; February 21, p. 14.

Miller, Aaron David. "Changing Arab Attitudes toward Israel." *Orbis,* Vol. 32 (Winter 1988), pp. 69–81.

———— "Lebanon: One Year After." *Washington Quarterly,* Vol. 6 (Summer 1983), pp. 129–141.

———— "The PLO: What Next?" *Washington Quarterly,* Vol. 6, No. 1 (Winter 1983), pp. 116–125.

———— "Palestinians in the 1980's." *Current History,* Vol. 83 (January 1984), pp. 17–20, 34–36.

———— "The Palestinians: The Past as Prologue." *Current History,* Vol. 87 (February 1988), pp. 73–76, 83–85.

———— "The PLO after Tripoli: The Arab Dimension." *American–Arab Affairs,* No. 8 (Spring 1984), pp. 66–73.

———— "The PLO and the Peace Process: The Organizational Imperative." *SAIS Review,* Vol. 7 (Winter-Spring 1987), pp. 647–675.

Miller, Judith. "Battle within the P.L.O. Threatens a Formal Split." *New York Times*, November 18, 1984, pp. 1, 12.

―――― "The PLO in Exile." *New York Times Magazine*, August 18, 1985, pp. 26–30, 63, 66, 71–72, 76.

Mishal, Shaul. "'Paper War'—Words Behind Stones: The intifada Leaflets." *Jerusalem Quarterly*, No. 51 (Autumn 1989).

Moughrabi, Fouad. "The Palestinians after Lebanon." *Arab Studies Quarterly*, Vol. 5, No. 3 (Summer 1983), pp. 211–219.

Muslih, Muhammad Y. "Moderates and Rejectionists within the Palestine Liberation Organization." *Middle East Journal*, Vol. 30 (Spring 1976), pp. 127–140.

Nafaa, Hassan. "Arab Nationalism: A Response to Ajami's Thesis on the 'End of Pan-Arabism.'" *Journal of Arab Affairs*, Vol. 2, No. 2 (Spring 1983), pp. 173–199.

New York Times. "Conflict in the PLO." November 18, 1985, pp. 1, 12; November 19, p. A10; November 20, p. A8.

Neumann, Robert. "The Search for Peace in the Middle East: A Role for U.S. Policy." *American–Arab Affairs*, Summer 1982.

Nosenko, Vladimir. "The Transformation of the Soviet Stand on the Palestinian Problem." Dayan Center Occasional Paper No. 109, January 1991.

Olmert, Yosef. "The Palestinians in Lebanon, 1948–82." In Israel Stockman Shomron, ed., *Israel, the Middle East, and the Great Powers*. Jerusalem, 1984.

O'Neill, Bard E. "Towards a Typology of Political Terrorism: The Palestinian Resistance Movement." *Journal of international Affairs*, 1978, Vol. 32, No. 1, pp. 17–42.

Peretz, Don. "Palestinian Social Stratification: The Policy Implications." In Gabriel Ben-Dor, ed., *The Palestinians and the Middle East Conflict*. Ramat Gan, 1978.

"Periodicals and Pamphlets Published by the Palestinian Commando Organizations." *Journal of Palestine Studies*, Vol. 1, No. 1 (Autumn 1971), pp. 136–151.

Prat, Tamar. "Palestinian Armed Struggle: Strategy and Tactics." In Anat Kurz, *Contemporary Trends in World Terrorism*. New York, 1987.

Qaddumi, Farouq. "Farouk Kaddoumi: An interview." *Third World Quarterly*, Vol. 8 (April 1986), pp. 411–424.

―――― "Qaddoumi: A West Bank State within Five Years." *Middle East*, No. 71 (September 1980), pp. 41–43.

Rekhess, Elie, and Dan Avidan. "The West Bank and Gaza Strip." In Colin Legum, ed., *Arab Relations in the Middle East*. New York, 1979.

——— "Arabs in a Jewish State: Images vs. Realities." *Middle East Insight,* January-February, 1990.

Rosen, Jane. "The PLO's influential Voice at the U.N." *New York Times Magazine,* September 16, 1984, pp. 59–60, 62, 70, 72, 74.

Rosensaft, Menachem. "Meeting the PLO." *Reform Judaism,* Spring 1989.

Rosewicz, Barbara, and Gerald F. Seib. "Aside from Being a Movement, the PLO Is a Financial Giant." *Wall Street Journal,* July 21, 1986.

Rouleau, Eric. "The Future of the PLO." *Foreign Affairs,* Vol. 62 (Fall 1983), pp. 138–156.

——— "The Palestinian Quest." *Foreign Affairs,* Vol. 53, No. 2 (1975), pp. 264–283.

Rubenberg, Cheryl. "The Civilian Infrastructure of the Palestine Liberation Organization." *Journal of Palestine Studies,* Vol. 12 (Spring 1983), pp. 54–78.

——— "The PLO Response to the Reagan initiative: The PNC at Algiers, February 1983." *American–Arab Affairs,* No. 4 (Spring 1983), pp. 53–69.

Sahliyeh, Emile F. "Jordan and the Palestinians." In William B. Quandt, ed., In the Middle East: Ten Years after Camp David, pp. 279–318. Washington: Brooking Institution, 1988.

Salem, Mohammed Anis. "Arab Schisms in the 1980s: Old Story or New Order?" *The World Today,* Vol. 38, No. 5 (May 1982), pp. 175–185.

Satloff, Robert. "Islam in the Palestinian Uprising." *Orbis,* Vol. 33, No. 3 (Summer 1989).

Saunders, Harold. "Arabs and Israelis: A Political Strategy." *Foreign Affairs,* Vol. 64 (Winter 1985).

Sayish, Yezid. "Palestinian Armed Struggle: Means and Ends." *Journal of Palestine Studies,* Vol. 16, No. 1. Autumn 1986.

Schiller, David Th. "A Battlegroup Divided: The Palestinian Fedayeen." *Strategic Studies,* Vol. 10 (December 1987), pp. 90–108.

Shadid, Mohammed, and Rick Seltzer. "Political Attitudes of Palestinians in the West Bank and Gaza Strip." *Middle East Journal,* Vol. 42 (Winter 1988), pp. 16–32.

Sharabi, Hisham. "Development of PLO Peace Policy." *New Outlook,* Vol. 23 (November–December 1980), pp. 16–19.

——— "Arab Policy and the Prospects for Peace." *American–Arab Affairs,* No. 1 (Summer 1982).

Shipler, David K. "Lebanese Tell of Anguish of Living under the P.L.O." *New York Times,* July 25, 1982, pp. 1, 12.

——— "Since Jordan: The Palestine Fedayeen." *Conflict Studies,* Vol. 38 (September 1973), p. 18.

Siniora, Hanna. "On the Palestinian Struggle." *World Policy,* Vol. 3 (Fall 1986), pp. 723–738.

Smothers, Ronald. "Palestinian Guerrilla [Muhammad Abbas]: Man of Many Factions." *New York Times,* October 13, 1985, p. 26.

Stanley, Bruce. "Fragmentation and National Liberation Movements: The PLO." *Orbis,* Vol. 22 (Winter 1979), pp. 1033–1055.

Steinberg, Matti. "The Pragmatic Stream of Thought within the PLO According to Khalid al-Hasan." *Jerusalem Journal of in ternational Relations,* Vol. 11, No. 1 (1989).

——— "The Radical Worldview of the Abu-Nidal Faction." *Jerusalem Quarterly,* No. 48 (Fall 1988), pp. 88–104.

——— "The Worldview of Habash's PFLP." *Jerusalem Quarterly,* No. 47 (Summer 1988).

——— "Arafat's PLO: The Concept of Self-Determination in Transition." *Jerusalem Journal of International Relations,* Vol. 9, No. 3 (1987).

Stockman-Shomron, Israel. "The Palestinian Arabs of Judea and Samaria under Jordanian Rule." In Israel Stockman Shomron, ed., *Israel, the Middle East, and the Great Powers.* Jerusalem, 1984.

Talhami, Ali. "How a Satirist Saw the PLO." *The Middle East,* No. 156 (October 1987), pp. 16–18.

Tarbush, Susannah. "Palestinian Groups: The Divided Front." *Middle East Economic Digest,* Vol. 22 (September 29, 1976), pp. 8–9.

Tully, Shawn. "The Big Moneymen of Palestine Inc." *Fortune,* July 31, 1989.

U.S. Department of State. *Abu Nidal Organization.* February 1989.

Yaari, Ehud. "[PLO] The Middle East: Runaway Revolution." *Atlantic,* 261, No. 6 (June 1988), pp. 24–33.

Periodicals

Federal Broadcast Information Service (FBIS)
Filastin al-Thawra
Joint Publications Research Service (JPRS)
Journal of Palestine Studies (JPS)
The Middle East
Middle East Mirror, 1989–90.
New York Times, 1965–1990
Shu'un Filastiniyya
Washington Post, 1965–1990

> Glossary

ALF: Arab Liberation Front, a pro-Iraq PLO member group formed in 1969.

Black September: A cover name for Fatah's international terrorist operations between 1971 and 1974.

DFLP: The Democratic Front for the Liberation of Palestine, led by Naif Hawatmah, a self-styled Marxist–Leninist group.

Fatah: The PLO's main member group, led by Yasir Arafat.

Fatah Revolutionary Council: Abu Nidal's group, supported at various times by Syria, Iraq, and Libya as a rival to the PLO.

Force-17: Fatah's internal police and special operations group, which also carried out terrorist attacks.

PCP: The pro-Moscow Palestine Communist Party, now called the Peoples Democratic Party.

PFLP: The Popular Front for the Liberation of Palestine, led by George Habash, a self-styled Marxist group with strong pan-Arab nationalist overtones.

PFLP-GC: The Popular Front for the Liberation of Palestine-General Command, a Syrian-backed group headed by Ahmad Jibril operating outside the PLO structure.

PLA: Palestine Liberation Army, the regular armed forces of the PLO, some of whose units have been controlled by Arab states.

PLF: Palestine Liberation Front, a set of splinter groups from the PFLP-GC which have enjoyed patronage from Iraq, Syria, and Libya. Factions, of which the most active was led by Abu al-Abbas, have been inside and outside the PLO.

PLO Executive Committee: In practice, the PLO's most powerful decisionmaking body, with members representing member groups or independents.

PNC: Palestine National Council, the PLO's parliament.

al-Sa'iqa: The Syrian-controlled Palestinian group which was once the second-largest PLO member but went into sharp eclipse following the Syria–PLO military showdown in Lebanon in 1976.

> Index